The Essential Elements of Karate

Karate develops a strong spirit, a calm mind, and an active body. Karate's basic techniques include:

Blocking techniques that are your first line of defense.

Striking techniques that give you 360-degree range.

Punching techniques that are the heart of your arsenal.

Kicking techniques—your advantage against bigger and stronger opponents.

Study well! Train hard! Have fun!

alpha
books

Karate's Most Famous Saying

"The ultimate aim of the art of karate lies not in victory or defeat, but in the perfection of the character of its participants."

—*Gichin Funakoshi*

The Five Principles of the Dojo (Dojo Kun)

The five principles of the dojo are often recited aloud at the beginning or end of a class. They are all numbered one because they are considered to be equally important.

One! To strive for the perfection of character!

One! To defend the paths of truth!

One! To foster the spirit of effort!

One! To honor the principles of etiquette!

One! To guard against impetuous courage!

Karate-Do Is the Art of the Empty Hand

Karate-do means "the way of the empty hand."

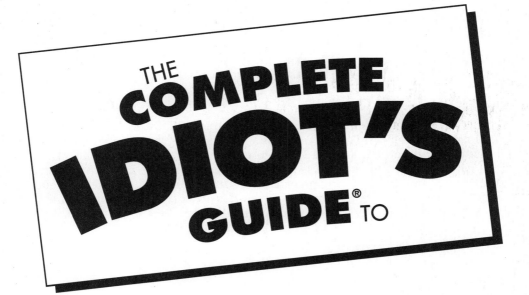

THE COMPLETE IDIOT'S GUIDE® TO

Karate

by Randall G. Hassell and Edmond Otis

alpha books

Macmillan USA, Inc.
201 West 103rd Street
Indianapolis, IN 46290

To the memory of A.R. "Dick" Allen, my friend, mentor, and true believer.
—Randall G. Hassell

To my instructor, Ray Dalke, who, after 30 years, continues to teach me karate. —Edmond Otis

Copyright © 2000 by Randall G. Hassell and Edmond Otis

International Standard Book Number: 0-02-863832-8
Library of Congress Catalog Card Number: Available upon request.

02   01   00   8   7   6   5   4   3   2

Interpretation of the printing code: The rightmost number of the first series of numbers is the year of the book's printing; the rightmost number of the second series of numbers is the number of the book's printing. For example, a printing code of 00-1 shows that the first printing occurred in 2000.

Printed in the United States of America

Publisher
Marie Butler-Knight

Product Manager
Phil Kitchel

Managing Editor
Cari Luna

Acquisitions Editor
Amy Zavatto

Development Editor
Alana J. Morgan

Production Editor
Christy Wagner

Copy Editor
Krista Hansing

Illustrator
Jody Schaeffer

Cover Designers
Mike Freeland
Kevin Spear

Book Designers
Scott Cook and Amy Adams of DesignLab

Indexer
Kelly Castell

Layout/Proofreading
Angela Calvert
Mary Hunt
Wendy Ott

Contents at a Glance

Contents

Appendixes

Foreword

Until quite recently, I thought I knew Randall Hassell pretty well. After all, we have both been practicing the art of the empty hand for the past 40 years. Over time, we have met, trained, traveled, and taught together. But above all, we have enjoyed sharing our experiences, aspirations, trials, and achievements.

Now Randall and fellow expert and co-author Edmond Otis have come up with a surprise package, *The Complete Idiot's Guide to Karate,* which I believe surpasses all of his other works.

Although this book has an underlying serious and authentic theme, the pages sparkle with spicy tidbits and thought-provoking touches of class. The authors' wry and charming sense of humor has an uplifting quality when they describe how to cope with the pressures of life that tend to push us down.

I have trained in Japan more than 25 times over the past 37 years, and I keep going back because it is there, in the disciplined and demanding training sessions, that my attitude is adjusted. Those of us who have trained in karate for a long time sometimes fall into the trap of growing arrogant about our karate skills. This has happened to me, too, but then I would return to Japan and within a single, sweaty training session with the deadly experts there, my vulnerability and sensitivity would be restored.

Reading *The Complete Idiot's Guide to Karate* was like a wake-up call for me. It was like working out in that Japanese class again and re-learning that the basics (techniques and concepts) are all-important, never to be forgotten—like breathing air, drinking water, eating, and sleeping. Yes, this book is not only for beginners; it is equally useful for advanced karate students.

This book makes karate available to every man. In fact, in my first three years of karate training, I did it all from books, in my own backyard, and I reached a reasonably competent level. If only *The Complete Idiot's Guide to Karate* had been available then I would have been able to bypass the many mistakes I made.

This book is a valuable book that deals with serious matters of life and death—matters concerning your physical and mental health; matters concerning nasty and sadistic people intent on hurting, maiming, or killing you, and what you can do about it; and it tells you where and why and how karate originated and how it expanded into the United States and worldwide.

The Complete Idiot's Guide to Karate is a witty, inspiring, and user-friendly book. It is a book for sensible people of all ages and all walks of life who desire to upgrade their health and self-defense skills to achieve peace of mind. It is a book for you if you want to step up to higher dan levels in your life, and the authors have made these important steps interesting and easy to follow.

Stan Schmidt

Karate Master of the Japan Karate Association (JKA)
Member of the JKA Shihankai (World Council of Masters)

Introduction

Traditional karate-do is probably the most widely practiced martial art in the world. Other popular martial arts, such as tae kwon do, judo, and aikido, are practiced in some countries and not in others. Karate, though, seems to be practiced everywhere.

The reasons are many. As a method of self-defense, karate is unparalleled. Its techniques and applications are precise, powerful, quick, and effective. On the other side of the karate coin is karate-do, the study of karate as a way of life. Everybody can benefit from this aspect of the art because each of us can become at least a little bit better of a person, with better character and increased sensitivity.

We believe, however, that one of the main reasons for karate's worldwide popularity is its intrinsic accessibility. It can be practiced by virtually anyone who enjoys average health, regardless of age or sex. Tae kwon do's high, spinning kicks, and judo's and aikido's hard, jarring falls eliminate many older members of society from practicing them. Karate, though, doesn't suffer any such limitations. You can practice karate fast or slow, hard or soft, intensely or gently. You can do it at your own pace, and you can practice effectively by yourself (provided, of course, that you are under the guidance of a qualified instructor).

We invite you to follow us along the path of karate-do. We promise you an interesting, exciting, challenging, and safe journey.

Acknowledgments

Our thanks to our instructors, training partners, and teammates throughout the years.

Our thanks to our students, who continue to teach us about karate on a daily basis.

Our sincere appreciation to our good friends, Paul and Luisa Godshaw, Del Saito, and Kevin Warner for providing support, encouragement and, more important, pictures of themselves and their dojos. All these contributed to making this book what it is. Also, thanks to David Gomez, chief instructor of the Georgia Karate Academy and director of Go-Fish Graphics for his time and skill in preparing the photos used in this book.

Randall Hassell offers special thanks to Marilyn, who continues to make it all seem worthwhile.

Edmond Otis offers special thanks to his wonderful sons, Nikos and Gabriel, and his breathtaking (smart, funny, beautiful, the whole deal) wife Roberta, for always providing unconditional love, support, and encouragement.

Special Thanks to the Technical Reviewer

The Complete Idiot's Guide to Karate was reviewed by an expert who double-checked the accuracy of what you'll learn here, to help us ensure that this book gives you everything you need to know about karate. Special thanks are extended to Rick L. Brewer.

Rick L. Brewer is a fifth-degree black belt with well over 30 years of training and teaching experience in traditional Japanese karate. He has a Master's degree in education from the University of Illinois and has been published in magazines and journals in both the United States and Europe.

Photo Credits

Cover photo: Edmond Otis.

The authors also wish to thank the following individuals and organizations for their contributions:

From the Traditional Karate Organization of Grants Pass, Oregon: Del Saito (8th Dan: Director of Shito-Ryu Karate)

From The Japan Karate-Do Federation of Mission Viejo, California: Paul Godshaw (7th Dan: director and chief instructor)

From The American JKA Karate Association of Riverside, California: Kevin Warner (4th Dan: senior instructor), Tai Cigar-Richards (2nd Dan), Stephanie Miner (2nd Dan), Lindy Rellias (1st Dan), Dean Patin (2nd Dan-ho), and Jamie Patin (2nd Dan-ho)

From the American JKA Karate Association of Carlsbad, California: Nikolos Otis (8th Kyu) and Aiden Wilson (8th Kyu)

From the American Shotokan Karate Alliance of St. Louis, Missouri: Carlos M. Yu II (3rd Dan) and Jeannie Byrnes (1st Dan).

For the line art: John Bergdahl.

For the photographs: Brett Perkins, William Fox, and Marilyn Hassell.

Trademarks

All terms mentioned in this book that are known to be or are suspected of being trademarks or service marks have been appropriately capitalized. Alpha Books and Macmillan USA, Inc., cannot attest to the accuracy of this information. Use of a term in this book should not be regarded as affecting the validity of any trademark or service mark.

Part 1
Let's Try Karate

Before you try karate, though, you should know what "karate" means—and it doesn't mean what you probably think it means. Thanks to movies and television shows, the word karate is frequently—and incorrectly—used as a catchall word for martial arts. Actually, kara *means "empty," and* te *means "hand." So in reality, karate means "empty hands" or "the art of empty-hand fighting." Karate originated in Okinawa as a system of self-defense, and it consists of techniques of punching, blocking, striking, and kicking. These techniques are combined into specific patterns called* kata *(forms) and are applied against opponents in* kumite *(controlled sparring). What follows is an introduction to an ancient art in its modern manifestations of self-defense, physical and mental development, and sport.*

Chapter 1

Why Try Karate?

In This Chapter

➤ Understanding karate and karate-do

➤ Deciding to try karate

➤ The physical benefits of karate

➤ The mental and emotional benefits of karate

➤ Learning karate based on your age and condition

Probably as many reasons exist for wanting to try karate as there are people wanting to try it. Maybe you want to learn self-defense, or maybe you just want an interesting way to get in shape. Maybe you are looking for new friends at the karate school, or maybe you are considering karate lessons for your child. Or, it may well be that you have just always been curious about karate and have decided that now is the time to give it a try.

Whatever your personal reasons for trying karate, you should know some important aspects of the art before you start.

Do: Connecting Mind and Body

As you will learn in the next chapter, karate originated around 1600 as a secret fighting art among the oppressed people of Okinawa, Japan. Its goal was simple: Kill the opponent before he kills you. While this served the needs of eighteenth- and nineteenth-century Okinawans, it was not something that was necessary in the more civilized twentieth century. So, when karate was introduced to the public around the

Talk the Talk

Do (pronounced as in "bread *dough*") means "way" or "path," and it is applied to many Japanese arts that are practiced with the goal of improving the lives of the practitioners. Karate-do is the way of karate; shodo is the way of calligraphy; kendo is the way of the sword.

turn of the twentieth century, it was introduced as a method of physical and mental development for people of all ages, as well as an incomparable method of self-defense.

Eventually, karate took on the form of a Japanese *do* (pronounced *dough*), which means that it became a method of developing the mind and the body together as one unit. Its strict discipline was codified to enhance concentration and mental sharpness, while its physical techniques were modified somewhat to provide an unparalleled method of physical development.

Today, the vast majority of Japanese and Okinawan-style *karate schools* emphasize this holistic development of the human being, and they teach an art that has the potential to unify the mind, the body, and the spirit into a fit and formidable unit.

Do literally means "way" or "path," so modern karate-do is a path to follow for a rewarding physical, mental, and emotional life.

Calligraphy for do, meaning "way" or "path."

Self-defense is the foundation of karate.

Jutsu—Learn That There Is a Time and a Place for Everything

When you check out a school, you should not only be sure that the instructors encourage the development and coordination of the body, mind, and spirit, but you also should ask about self-defense because effective self-defense is a hallmark of karate training. A few schools will advertise that they teach karate-*jutsu* (pronounced *jitsu,* but correctly spelled jutsu), or "combat" karate, or "street" karate, which means that they devote little or no time to character development. These schools' main—and perhaps only—goal is to teach you how to kick butt, and kick it hard!

Jutsu means "technique" or "art," so it implies that you will learn only the fighting techniques of karate. But if all you want to do is learn how to fight, why not just take up boxing? (Because boxing hurts, that's why!) Well, if a school advertises kicking butt as its main thing, it's probably going to hurt a lot there, too.

Certainly, a number of people just want to kick butt, but there are a lot more who would like to develop their concentration, improve their health, stabilize their emotions, and walk around secure in the knowledge that they can also kick butt when they have to. These are the people who study the way of karate—karate-do.

So, you ask, will I still be able to kick butt if I study karate-do? You bet! The main difference between the pure *techniques* of karate (karate-jutsu) and the *way* of karate (karate-do) is that karate-do develops the whole person—physically, mentally, and emotionally—and emphasizes both a code of ethics and a manner of conduct that avoids conflicts at all costs. The disciplined method of karate-do also teaches you how to recognize potentially dangerous situations before they develop, which gives you a major edge in deciding how to deal with them.

So, if you pursue the way of karate-do, you will have the weapons of your calm mind and stable emotions available to you in addition to your fists and feet, and you will have a big advantage in being able to recognize trouble before it starts.

You also will be able to kick butt confidently, but only when you have no other choice.

Talk the Talk

A **karate school** is called a **dojo.** *Do* means "way," and *jo* means "place," so a dojo is "the place where the way is taught."

Sensei Says

The ultimate victory is to win the fight using your brain instead of your fists.

Sporting tournaments are a popular part of modern karate.

The Sporting Life

Because karate originated as a deadly fighting art, it was practiced solely as a self-defense–based method of physical and mental development until the early 1950s. As it became more popular, and as more young people became involved in it, karate started to develop a sporting aspect. This happened partly as a natural outgrowth of the competitive nature of the youth involved and partly in recognition of the fact that the fastest way to spread karate to the rest of the world was as a sport. The young Japanese masters of the art, therefore, studied the rules of other sports and came up with rules and controls that enabled karate to be practiced as a sport as well as a self-defense art.

Karate Minute

Before the turn of the century, the only way to test one's technique against another person was to actually fight—sometimes to the death. Maybe that's why there weren't too many karate students before 1900!

Karate kata competition resembles gymnastic floor routine competition.

Today, many different associations and federations have sport rules for the karate they teach, and these rules vary from group to group. Generally speaking, though, karate is practiced as a sport in two main ways:

1. As a sparring (kumite) competition
2. As a formal exercise (kata) competition

Kumite contests require strict control of techniques, and contestants gain points by theoretically eliminating their opponents. That is, they stop their blows just short of contact, and the theoretical effectiveness of the blows is judged by a referee and a panel of judges. *Kata* competition, on the other hand, most closely resembles a gymnastics floor routine competition. Contestants vie for victory based upon points awarded by a panel of expert judges. Both kumite and kata competitions may include individual and team events.

Because of the strict regulations (you can't jab your fingers at your opponent's eyes, for example) and controls (you can't actually hit your opponent with force), almost anyone in average health can compete in karate tournaments. Divisions exist for men, women, children of almost all ages (from about four or five years old), and seniors (with no upper limits on age). For those who are less athletic, there often are divisions in which contestants compete against each other by having their most basic techniques judged by a panel of judges. This is similar to *kata* competition but consists of just a few selected techniques.

One of the most interesting things about modern karate is that it can be practiced effectively with or without a sporting aspect, so it truly is an art of value for a very broad cross-section of society.

Today, more than five million people around the world regularly compete in karate tournaments, from the local to the international level.

Karate Minute

The ring for karate sport sparring was originally conceived of as a circle, like the circular sumo ring. When the inventors tried it, however, they couldn't figure out how to define where the judges would be positioned, so they changed it to a square and put a judge on each corner.

A Thousand Good Reasons, but These Are the Main Ones

Because Karate can be practiced by young and old, male and female, and because it can be approached in so many different ways (for example, sport, physical education, and self-defense), there are probably as many reasons for taking karate as there are people who take it. In the following sections we will discuss some of the most common reasons people take karate.

Karate Is for Just About Everyone

Some physical conditions might limit your ability to participate, but your age surely won't. Naturally, the younger you are, the easier it probably will be for you to start practicing karate, but that's true for all physical activities, and no special skill or physical condition is necessary to try karate. If you can move your arms forward and backward, then you can learn how to punch, block, and strike; if you can lift your foot as high as your other knee, you can learn how to kick. If you can walk, you can learn how to get out of the way of a mugger. If you haven't guessed it by now, modern karate can be practiced safely by just about anybody whose health permits participation in regular, moderate exercise. Karate is especially beneficial to women because it is a great equalizer between the sexes. The effectiveness of karate techniques relies more on coordination, timing, and body momentum than it does on strength, and this gives the women the ability to deliver powerful—even devastating—blows.

Ouch!

Even though karate can be practiced safely by anyone in average or better health, it is important to consult your physician before beginning karate training or any other form of strenuous physical activity.

For children under age 12, karate is a wonderful way to develop concentration, coordination, and agility. Classes are rather rigidly structured, and the emphasis is on developing motor skills along with learning how to focus. The exercise component for kids is also usually very vigorous, which promotes healthy growth and peaceful sleep at night—and that's particularly important today, when more kids are getting less exercise.

In karate, all ages can practice together or separately. Adults and children often do the same techniques and practice the same skills.

For teenagers, karate is an excellent tool for the enhancement of social skills and confidence. Mastery of its complex body movements, and the confidence gained from facing and defeating opponents, both go a long way in minimizing the physical and emotional awkwardness that teens normally face.

For adults, karate's benefits really shine. Stress management, weight loss, strength, and confidence are among the most often cited benefits derived by adults in karate classes.

Sensei Says

In karate-do, it doesn't matter how strong or tough you are because the real purpose of karate training is the development of good character—and as long as you are alive, you can continue to become better at that.

In purely physical arts—take boxing, for example—you learn to defeat the opponent with your fists and feet, but as you get older, your body stiffens, your muscles shrink, and your fists and feet become less effective. In whole-life arts such as karate-do, you learn to defeat the opponent with timing, coordination, awareness, finesse, and experience. These things can continue to grow as you age, so combined with the great physical shape you will be in from practicing karate, you will also be able to kick butt for as long as you live. And you'll be able to kick it from your rocking chair, if necessary.

That's an important benefit of karate training: Purely physical arts such as boxing become less effective as you age, but whole-life arts such as karate-do become more effective as you age.

Kick Fast or Kick Slow

By now you're probably wondering how the heck a hot-blooded teenager and an old codger who hasn't exercised for 40 years could possibly be in the same karate class. You might be wondering if the karate class wouldn't be better for the young buck, and something gentle like Tai Chi wouldn't be better for the old dog. Well, allow us to reveal to you one of the secrets of karate-do: It can be practiced strongly, quickly, and vigorously, or it can be practiced softly, slowly, and gently.

In fact, the movements of an art such as Tai Chi can be practiced only slowly and gently, and an aerobic sport such as tennis can be practiced only rather vigorously. But in karate class, you can practice the movements in exactly the manner in which your physical condition will allow you to practice them. While the instructor will always encourage everybody in the class to move faster and sometimes harder, the older adult won't be left in the dust of the 18-year-old athlete because the adult is not competing with the teenager. When you start training in karate, you will be able to train at your own pace, and that pace will increase over time. In other words, you can find all the benefits of both Tai Chi and tennis in karate class.

Kick Those Pounds Away!

Granted, most of us who want to lose weight would much rather have a magic bullet than resign ourselves to a strict exercise routine. That's why the world spends billions of dollars on fad diets, creams, and pills that are supposed to melt our fat away. Sorry to break this to you, but the only sure-fire, 100 percent, foolproof way to lose and control body weight is through a combination of diet and exercise.

The problem with fad diets is that they get boring really fast, and usually they just don't work. Most people just gain the pounds they lost right back as soon as they go off the diet. The problem with exercise machines is that they are even more boring than the diets, and that's why the equipment usually becomes expensive dust collectors. You don't have to take our word for it: Just check the classified ads in your local newspaper next weekend, and see how many exercise machines are for sale.

As much as we all hate to admit it, regular exercise really is the best way to lose pounds and keep them off. The trick is to find some kind of exercise that doesn't bore you to death while it's supposed to be making you healthy. Our answer: karate!

Not only does karate training provide all the benefits of regular, moderate exercise, but it's also fun! In karate class, you get to meet new and interesting people, you get to punch and kick at them, and you get to scream and yell and get all your frustrations out. Most important of all, though, is that while you are kicking away those excess pounds, you also are learning how to take care of the mugger who might be lurking outside, waiting for you to go home. If you go to an aerobics class, all you are really learning how to do is dance.

Think about it: When you're walking down the street late at night and an ugly mugger suddenly jumps out at you, would you feel better knowing aerobics or karate? Yeah, we thought so.

Ouch!

While exercise does lead to weight loss, it also leads to increased appetite. So, it's important to satisfy that extra appetite with wholesome, nutritious foods instead of fast-food burgers and fries. Otherwise, you might exercise yourself into weight gain!

Kick Those Blues Away!

If you are like most people, you have days when you just feel blah. You don't feel particularly bad, but you sure don't feel particularly good. You want to eat, but nothing sounds good. You want to catch up on the chores you've been putting off, but you just feel too tired. So, you decide to take a nap, but your mind races and you can't sleep. Yep, no doubt about it—you're suffering from the blues.

The blues get to all of us from time to time, no matter what we do to avoid them. They usually are fleeting, but even for a short time, they can make us uncomfortable. When they hang around for weeks and months, they can turn into full-blown depression, and depression can even be deadly.

So, you want to keep the blues away, right? Then take our advice and *kick* those blues away! That's right, just stand up, start moving, and start thinking about your movements. You can't be blue when you're thinking about the timing of your punch. You can't be blue when you're thinking about getting your knee higher in that kick. In fact, you can't be blue at all when your mind is occupied with trying to remember the pattern of that kata you started learning last week.

The blues come and they go, but they always get worse when we let ourselves dwell on them. We should be able to just concentrate on something else and make the blues go away, but telling our minds to not think about being blue is akin to telling our minds not to envision a purple elephant on roller skates. Go ahead and tell yourself that right now. See, you can't do it, can you?

There are only two proven cures for the blues, and karate practice provides both of them. One way to get happy is to fully occupy your mind with something other than what is making you sad. The other way is to exercise your body until *endorphins*—the hormones that make the body feel happy—are released into your bloodstream and bathe your brain in happiness. The challenging and complex nature of karate techniques provides an abundance of the former, and the dynamic, full-body, multidirectional movements of the art provide the latter. The really great thing about karate, though, is that you don't have to go anywhere to do it. And unlike tennis, for example, you don't need a partner to practice karate. You don't have to go to a court, and you don't have to own a racket. All you have to do, in the privacy of your own living room, is stand up and punch and kick. In no time at all, you will find yourself feeling better, and your blues will fade right away.

So now you have found an adjunct method of curing the blues that—while perhaps not scientifically proven—seems to work very well. This method consists of going to the karate school, getting a partner, and knocking the bejabbers out of them—in a controlled manner, of course. It might not be science, but when you're feeling down, it sure can make you feel good.

The Least You Need to Know

➤ Karate-do is a way to a better life, not just a method of fighting.

➤ Karate-do is for all ages and both sexes.

➤ Karate-do is a great physical workout, no matter how young or old you are, and no matter what shape you are in when you start.

➤ Karate-do is great for the mind (concentration) and the spirit (emotional stability).

Chapter 2

The Roots and Branches of Karate-Do

The actual, precise origin of karate is not known, but many theories abound. Some believe that karate originated in China with the Buddhist monk Daruma, in the sixth century B.C.E. Others believe that it actually started in Greece much earlier, while still others are sure it originated in Okinawa in the eighteenth century. Because there are almost no written documents to support one theory over another, we have to look at karate's more recent history—the history that we can validate—to get an idea of why it is like it is today.

The Roots and Branches

Today more than 100 styles of Japanese and Okinawan karate are being practiced around the world, so it can be a bit tough to figure out which one is right for you.

The bad news is that new styles are being created all the time. The good news is that all modern styles of karate come from a couple common sources in Okinawa. If you can figure out the gist of those sources, you probably will be able to decide what kind of karate you want to learn.

When we say that karate is a tree with many roots and branches, we mean that the tree itself represents the fact that karate is a family with branches of different styles—both karate as a whole and its individual branches all have roots in common ancestors.

From Chinese Court to Rice Paddy

What we do know about modern karate is that it developed in Okinawa around the sixteenth century, that it was officially exported to mainland Japan in 1922, and that it has spread to the rest of the world since then.

Okay, you ask, so why Okinawa? As the largest island of the tiny Ryukyu Islands just south of mainland Japan, Okinawa was conveniently located between Japan, China, and Korea. Because of its location, Okinawa was a trade center, and the people there were able to learn fighting methods (and everything else) from all those sources.

Karate Minute

In 1477, Okinawa's king, Sho Shin, banned the possession of weapons to prevent his rivals from building up armies. In 1669, even the manufacture of ceremonial swords was banned, and the Okinawans literally were left empty-handed.

Sensei Says

Martial arts always spring up among oppressed people who need a way to defend themselves against their oppressors.

Second, the Okinawan people twice had all their weapons banned by their own kings, so it was natural that they would devise self-defense systems to take care of themselves and their families.

Because Okinawa was so small and sparsely populated, it never could mount an effective defense against the outside invaders who were forever trying to control it for its valuable trade location.

The third, and maybe most important, reason is that by 1350, when Okinawa was establishing formal relations with China, Chinese martial arts were highly developed, extremely intricate, courtly arts. The Okinawans—who considered themselves country bumpkins next to the wealthy, courtly

Chinese—jumped at the chance to learn and imitate anything Chinese. Because fighting techniques were so important to them given their situation, they started imitating and combining Chinese fighting methods with their own.

Of course, as Okinawa progressed into the nineteenth and twentieth centuries, there was less need for self-defense against aggressors, so the fighting methods became more ritualized and came more out into the open. When the Okinawans had been oppressed by foreign invaders, they had been forced to practice their art in secrecy, but as time went by, they were able to practice it more publicly.

History in a Name

As trade developed with more countries, foreigners took notice of Okinawan boxing and called it *Okinawa-te,* to distinguish it from other forms of fighting found in the South Seas.

By the mid-1800s, most Okinawans called their art *to-de. To* is an alternate pronunciation of *kara,* which means *Chinese* and refers specifically to things of Chinese origin in the T'ang Dynasty. By the time karate was opened up to the general public, it was generally known as *karate-jutsu.* The word *kara* was used to acknowledge its Chinese origins, and *jutsu* (meaning "technique" or "art") was a polite use of Japanese terminology (the Okinawans also held the Japanese in high social esteem).

So there you have it: the birth of modern karate!

Talk the Talk

Until the nineteenth century, the Okinawans called their empty-handed combat arts **te,** which simply means "hands."

Calligraphy for to-de, which means "Chinese hands."

Kick Hard or Kick Soft

When the Chinese introduced their boxing methods—called *chuan-fa*—to the Okinawans, their art was divided into two schools of thought: internal and external. Internal systems were characterized by soft, usually slow movements and were devoted to the development of what the Chinese called *internal power.*

15

This internal power was developed through meditation and special exercises that were supposed to stimulate the glandular and nervous systems. In combat, internal power was produced by a combination of will power, vital energy—*chi*—and muscular strength.

The external systems, on the other hand, were practiced in a hard and vigorous way, and they relied on external, physical power for their effectiveness.

The Okinawans got to see both kinds of systems and, in their ingenious way, managed to combine elements of both into their own art, karate. Of course, because the Okinawans were an oppressed people, they were naturally more attracted to the external systems because although they were not allowed to have weapons, they still had a need to kill their oppressors. The courtly Chinese could afford to practice the internal arts in a philosophical way and to commune with nature, but Okinawan farmers and fishermen had to bang their fists on boards and stones to make their hands strong enough to kill their opponents.

Over time, the need for karate as a survival technique has diminished, and many external systems have taken on some of the softer elements of the internal systems. Today, modern karate can be divided into two broad categories: *Shuri-te* (named after the city of Shuri, where it was developed), which represents the external systems; and *Naha-te* (named after the city of Naha, where it was developed), which represents a mix of both the internal and the external systems. Knowing the background for a particular style of karate will help you decide whether to join a particular school.

Throw Away Your Weapons and Fight!

As you will see in Chapter 18, "All the Colors of the Rainbow," Okinawan farmers and fishermen didn't rely solely on their hands and feet for self-defense, but they also turned many of the tools of their trade into weapons. When karate finally came completely out into the open at the turn of the century, however, its masters knew that it would not survive very long in modern society as a brutal, killing art.

Sensei Says

When karate was no longer needed for self-protection against oppressors, it was turned into an art of self-perfection for the public.

So, the people put away the weapons and concentrated on turning karate into a physical education activity emphasizing controlled punching, blocking, kicking, and striking.

In 1902, an Okinawan schoolteacher named Gichin Funakoshi performed the first formal, recorded demonstration of this controlled karate for a school commissioner from mainland Japan, and the stage was set for karate to move into the modern era.

Thanks to the efforts of Funakoshi, karate was introduced in 1905 into Okinawan schools as a method of physical and mental conditioning.

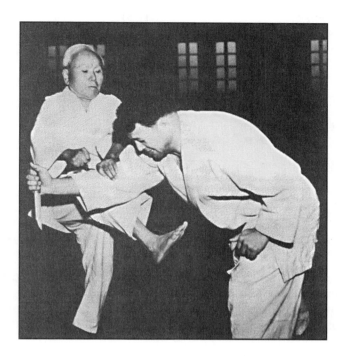

Gichin Funakoshi is known as the "Father of Modern Karate."

Going to Japan

In 1917, at the invitation of Japan's Ministry of Education, Funakoshi traveled to Kyoto to demonstrate the type of karate that was now a strong part of the physical education system in Okinawan schools. While his demonstration was well-attended, it didn't generate as much interest as he had hoped, so he went back to Okinawa thinking that karate would never be more than an Okinawan curiosity. All that changed, however, when the Crown Prince of Japan, who later became the Emperor Hirohito, visited Okinawa on March 6, 1921.

Hirohito stopped in Okinawa on his way to Europe, and on that day he saw a demonstration of karate by Funakoshi. What he saw excited him so much that he couldn't stop talking about it for the rest of his ocean voyage, all the way to Europe and back.

When he got back home, Hirohito announced that he would like to see karate again, so an invitation was issued to the Okinawan *Shobukai*—the Martial Spirit Promotion Society—to demonstrate karate at Japan's first National Athletic Exhibition in Tokyo in 1922. Because Funakoshi was the best-educated and most eloquent (in mainland Japanese language) member of the Shobukai—we should probably mention here that he also was its president—the Shobukai members selected him to conduct the demonstration.

Karate Minute

The Okinawan accent is very distinctive to any native-speaking Japanese. Because the Okinawan karate masters wanted to put their best foot forward in mainland Japan, they chose Gichin Funakoshi because he was one of the very few among them who could speak Japanese almost exactly as it was spoken in Tokyo.

Following Funakoshi's demonstration, karate took off like a skyrocket in Japan, and Funakoshi never returned to Okinawa. In 1922, he started teaching karate to groups of employees from various private companies, and by 1924, he had started the first collegiate karate club in Japan at Keio University. By 1930, clubs had been started at more than a dozen of Japan's top universities.

Of course, Funakoshi wasn't alone in Japan for very long. When it became obvious that the mainland Japanese wanted more karate, other Okinawan masters of many different styles made their way to the mainland and started teaching their own styles, too.

Talk the Talk

Budo is the formal name of Japanese martial arts. *Bu* is written as a combination of two characters, one meaning "fight" or "conflict," and the other meaning "stop." Combined with *do*, budo actually means, "the way to stop conflict."

By 1935, karate was so popular in Japan that Funakoshi changed its name to karate-do. By changing the name, he changed the characters that would be used to write it down. So now, the character for *kara* had changed from meaning "Chinese" to meaning "empty." From that point forward, karate-do would be known as "the way of the empty hand," an art that could be practiced safely by anyone. Another great milestone for Funakoshi was that karate-do became an accepted part of *budo*, Japan's formal martial arts. For an American, all this change might not make sense right away, but the important thing to remember is that this seemingly simple change in the name now meant that karate-do had become a pure Japanese art and that it should enjoy the same public status enjoyed by other Japanese martial arts such as judo and kendo.

Karate-do means "the way of the empty hand."

Coming to America

At the end of World War II, martial arts practice in Japan was banned for a time, except for the practice of karate. Karate escaped because the Americans thought that it was just a form of Chinese boxing and, therefore, harmless. So, in 1947, many of the masters who survived the war got together and started organizing among themselves. In 1949, they established a multistyle organization called the Japan Karate Association, and this organization ultimately got recognition from the Ministry of Education as an educational body.

The Americans were truly fascinated by karate, and the U.S. Air Force arranged for a series of demonstrations at several of their bases in Japan. These demonstrations went on twice a week from 1948 through 1951. In 1951, the Strategic Air Command (SAC) made karate a part of its regular training for long-range bomber crews in a program that lasted for 15 years.

Karate Minute

The Strategic Air Command (SAC) believed in 1951 that the United States' main bomber, the B-47, wouldn't be able to make long round-trip flights in a global conflict, and the pilots were likely to find themselves down in enemy territory. To prepare them for this, SAC helped them study martial arts to improve their mental and physical discipline and stamina.

Other martial arts were included in the program as well, and U.S. fascination with Japanese martial arts soon took off in a big way. Hundreds of American servicemen participated, many of them returning to Japan repeatedly to increase their skills in judo, aikido, and karate.

In June 1953, SAC sponsored a six-month tour of 20 of the most proficient judo, aikido, and karate experts to selected air bases all over the United States. The group visited each air base for approximately four days, and karate—along with judo and aikido—was given its greatest exposure ever.

A typical SAC training class in Japan.

Of course, Americans who had studied karate while in the service or privately did their part to spread the art, too. Robert Trias opened the first dojo in the United States in Phoenix, Arizona, in 1948, and taught his own style of karate. In 1954, Edward Kaloudis started teaching a style called *Koei-Kan* on the East Coast. In 1955, Edmund Parker opened the first West Coast *kempo* (a Chinese style of karate) karate studio in Pasadena, California. Tsutomu Ohshima, an exchange student from Waseda University, began teaching the *Shotokan* style (Gichin Funakoshi's) of karate in Los Angeles in 1956, and Jhoon Rhee began teaching a Korean version of karate, *Tae Kwon Do,* in San Marcos, Texas.

Talk the Talk

Ryu is a feudal term that means "school" and has also come to mean "style." Thus, **Goju–ryu** is the Goju style of karate. **Wado–ryu** is the Wado style, and so on.

Then 1957 saw the introduction of the *Wado-ryu* style of karate in Tennessee by Cecil Patterson, and the opening of the first commercial dojo in the Midwest, in St. Louis, Missouri, by *Goju-ryu* style practitioner Ed Cwiklowski. In the same year, *Isshin-ryu* (a modern Okinawan style) instructor Don Nagle began teaching his style of the art in Jacksonville, North Carolina.

1960 was a huge year for karate in the United States. In 1960, Yoshiaki Ajari introduced Wado-ryu karate in Hayward, California; Anthony Mirakian introduced Okinawan Goju-ryu in Watertown, Massachusetts; and S. Henry Cho opened the first Tae Kwon Do studio in New York. Also in that year, Steve Armstrong began teaching the Okinawan Isshin-ryu style of karate in Tacoma, Washington.

Indeed, the 1960s saw the introduction of virtually all the major styles of karate to the United States, the last two of these being the Shito-ryu style, introduced by Fumio Demura in Santa Ana, California, in 1965, and the Chito-ryu style, officially founded by William Dometrich in 1967 in Covington, Kentucky.

Meanwhile, back in Japan, the Japan Karate Association (JKA), which by 1956 had become a single-style organization representing only Funakoshi's Shotokan style of karate, had been very busy organizing, training, and preparing to dispatch instructors around the world. Except for Hirokazu Kanazawa, who taught locally in Hawaii starting in 1958, the first two of these in the United States were Hidetaka Nishiyama and Teruyuki Okazaki, both in 1961. Nishiyama set up base in Los Angeles and founded the All America Karate Federation (later called the American Amateur Karate Federation), while Okazaki set up first in New York and later in Philadelphia. Years later, he founded the International Shotokan Karate Federation.

All things considered, the 1960s were booming years for all kinds of karate in the United States.

Spread Throughout the World

Meanwhile, back in Japan, karate instructors were finding themselves in very heavy demand around the world, and many quickly took advantage of the chance to live and work in foreign countries teaching karate. The JKA which, by the mid-1960s, had become the world's largest single-style karate organization, had officially assigned 32 of its top instructors to foreign posts by 1970.

At the same time, the Wado-ryu and Goju-ryu styles grew very popular in Europe, and as Japanese exchange students familiar with karate started traveling abroad, karate dojos popped up in places as far from Japan as you can get, including Argentina, Australia, Brazil, Venezuela, and South Africa.

Today, millions of people in almost every country in the world practice some form of Japanese or Okinawan karate.

Styles, Styles, Styles!

So now you think that nothing on earth could possibly be more confusing than trying to figure out which style of karate is best for you. There are so many different styles and so many claims of mastery that it is difficult to figure out which one might be right for you—difficult, but not impossible.

First, keeping in mind that all styles have fairly similar Okinawan roots, let's take a look at the major Japanese styles and see if we can figure them out. First, there are only five major Japanese styles of karate, and only four participate in sanctioned international events.

Modern karate's major styles and founding masters.

> ## Japan's 5 Major Styles of Karate
>
> ### GOJU-RYU
> Gogen Yamaguchi, Founder
>
> ### KYOKUSHINKAI
> Masutatsu Oyama, Founder
>
> ### SHITO-RYU
> Kenwa Mabuni, Founder
>
> ### SHOTOKAN
> Gichin Funakoshi, Founder
>
> ### WADO-RYU
> Hironori Ohtsuka, Founder

Ouch!

Be wary of instructors who refer to themselves as "Grandmaster," "Soke," or "Shihan." A **Soke** is the founder or family inheritor of an established style. **Shihan** means a model for others and is legitimately applied sparingly. Also, in Japanese, it would be considered impolite, if not ridiculous, for someone to refer to himself using these terms. It might be okay in written documents, but not conversationally.

The bad news is that each of those styles has suffered internal splits into at least 20 different organizations, and each organization claims to teach the authentic style. It's really not as bad as it seems, though, because the vast majority of those suborganizations do still teach their authentic style. In fact, almost all the splits and divisions have arisen over administrative problems (everybody wants to be the boss), and almost never about the karate itself.

Sometimes, though, someone will take a year or two of lessons from a legitimate instructor and then fly off on his own, founding the Grand Intergalactic Universal style of karate and proclaiming himself Grand Poobah of the whole universe.

So, let's make that our first consideration: How long has the style been around, and how many times removed from the original is the current one? The biggest clue is to ask whether major changes in technique were made when the current organization split from the parent. If the answer is yes, you'd better look more closely because there is almost never a reason to make wholesale changes in techniques. Remember that the techniques of legitimate styles have been around for a very long time, and it's highly unlikely that some young whippersnapper has been training long enough to be qualified to change anything.

The second consideration should be to ask what the style emphasizes. If it emphasizes sport and you are primarily interested in self-defense, you probably need to look elsewhere.

Third, take a look at the people who are practicing the style. Ask yourself if what they are doing is what you want to do. Are they all heavy-set with crooked noses? That should tell you something. Or are they all huffing and puffing and seem out of breath all the time? That should tell you something else. Does their attitude and the attitude of the instructor seem like what you would like to imitate, or do the people and the instructor all seem like something from your worst nightmare?

Sensei Says

A good instructor will display the patience she has gained from her karate training when she answers your questions. A bad instructor will be curt and impatient. If she hasn't learned patience, how can she teach it to you?

A typical karate-do class in progress.

Finally, take a look at the overall picture. If the style is primarily external (physical), you will probably be looking at a lot of vigorous, controlled exercise. If the style is primarily internal, you probably will be looking at a lot of slow, heavy, breathing and strengthening exercises. You are the one who must decide what's right for you.

And don't forget: There are so many karate schools around today that you don't have to settle for one that doesn't do what you want. If you join and later decide that the school is not for you, quit! Join another one that fits you better. The days of blood oaths to a master are long gone!

The Least You Need to Know

➤ Karate started as self-defense for oppressed people.

➤ Both hard and soft versions of karate exist.

➤ Good karate can be found in every nook and cranny of the world.

➤ You are the final judge of which kind of karate is best for you.

Chapter 3

Karate Fitness Power: The Art of Contrast

In This Chapter

➤ Discover the importance of mind–body balance in fitness

➤ Understand how your emotions affect your fitness level

➤ Learn how to draw power from your center

➤ Learn how to breathe properly

➤ Discover how karate compares to other sports and activities

Probably everybody in the world has seen the yin-yang symbol, but very few people in the West have a clear idea of what it represents. According to Chinese tradition, the yin-yang is the ultimate and enduring symbol of the nature of the universe and all actions and forces. The darker side with the white dot is yin, and it represents negative, receptive, and passive. The corresponding white half with the black dot is yang, and it represents positive, active, and aggressive.

Let's talk about the yin-yang as a symbol of the unique contrasts found in karate training. In a single karate class, more contrasting kinds of physical things are happening than can be found almost anywhere else. Where karate is concerned, the most important contrasts represented by the yin-yang are …

Yin	Yang
Soft	Hard
Slow	Fast
Weak	Strong
Calm	Intense
Intuitive	Rational
Passive	Aggressive
Receptive	Active
Body surface	Internal body

The yin-yang symbol.

Get Ready: Is Your Body Off-Balance?

No matter what kind of exercise you have tried in the past, it most likely has not provided as much of a balanced workout as a karate class does. Physically, karate practice is all about contrasts and balancing them.

Be Soft and Be Hard

Various sports and games have a mixture of soft and hard movements, but most are predominantly one or the other. Soft movements are movements that require little or no muscle tension. Hard movements are movements that require sharp, hard contractions of muscles. Karate combines soft and hard movements in many techniques.

EEEE-YA!!!

Talk the Talk

In Japanese, the yin-yang symbol is called **in-yo.**

Some of the exercise activities that would be considered almost completely soft would be horseback riding, canoeing, social dancing, shuffleboard, and scuba diving. While all of these activities are good exercises and contribute to overall fitness, none requires sharp, hard contractions of large muscle groups.

On the other side of the coin are the almost completely "hard" activities, such as boxing, fencing, handball, and football. These activities require almost continuous hard, sharp contractions of large muscle groups. Also important to consider is that these exercises have almost no soft movement at all.

All these activities are unbalanced between hard and soft exercise. Karate, on the other hand, provides the best of both worlds. In every karate class, certain movements must be performed softly, and other movements must be performed in a hard fashion. In fact, you often have to perform the very same movements both ways. The instructor might tell you to try a blocking technique softly, without any tension at all, over and over again, to help you feel the correct course of the arm and to help your muscles learn what they have to do to execute the technique properly. She then might tell you to do the same movement sharply, with extremely hard tension of all the muscles at the end of the technique. This balance between soft and hard gives you a very keen awareness of the various muscles in your body, and it helps you isolate the specific muscles that you need to strengthen for each technique.

Be Slow and Be Fast

Okay, we admit that there are fast and slow parts to almost every physical activity, but we don't know of any activity that surpasses karate in requiring skilled performance of techniques in both a slow and a fast manner.

Cycling, for example, is a pretty fast activity interspersed with slow movements of the body while coasting or zipping downhill, but the slow part is pretty much incidental to the fast part. An almost completely slow activity such as snow shoeing stands in stark contrast to downhill skiing, which has nothing at all slow about it.

Very fast activities such as basketball and football have slow aspects, but those aspects also are incidental—like waiting for the other team to do something. Again, all these activities lack balance between slow and fast movements.

In karate, though, slow and fast are important parts of every class. Something you, as a beginner, can expect to hear from your instructor almost every time you see her is, "Okay, try this slowly. Go slow so that you can get the form right." Great emphasis is placed upon executing each technique

Sensei Says

A hand that is tightly clenched is called a fist. A hand that remains forever tightly clenched is called deformed. A balance between hard and soft determines usefulness.

Ouch!

When your sensei tells you to move slowly, it is for good reasons. If you move too fast or too soon, before your muscles figure out what it is that you want them to do, you can badly strain and even tear muscles.

slowly with proper muscle tension. Then, just as surely as the sun will come up to-morrow, you will hear your instructor say "Okay, speed up! Come on! Move faster!" This kind of training provides your body with a complete balance between slow and fast movements.

In a real self-defense situation, knowing when to move fast and when to move slow is extremely important. If a mugger has a knife in his hand, for example, you want to move very slowly and not startle him into using it. If he decides to use the knife, though, you have to move very fast to get out of the way. Slow and fast each have their important place in karate, and it is important to practice both ways.

Be Strong and Be Weak

Most people don't usually think of exercise activities in terms of weakness, but a number of activities require almost no strength at all. Fishing from a bank is one (at least until a big one bites), and croquet and shuffleboard are others. Contrasting activities that require pure strength and have no room for any kind of weakness include things such as mountain climbing, cross-country skiing, and backpacking.

In karate, though, both strength and weakness are highly valued. We don't usually call it weakness, of course. We usually refer to weakness as "lack of strength" or "take the power out." A technique without power or strength is a relaxed technique, and it is one of the most important factors in developing speed in techniques. The value of speed is pretty easy to understand: The faster you go, the harder you hit. Also, the faster you can get out of the way, the less likely you are to get hit. In karate training, you will learn that speed is not so much a factor of fast contraction of muscles as it is a factor of how completely relaxed (weak) you can make the muscles before moving. So, you learn how to take the power out in order to develop power on impact. This is a balance not found in very many other activities. Additionally, an important strategy in real self-defense and tournament competition is convincing your opponent that you are weak, thereby luring him into inattention and creating an opening to attack or counterattack.

EEEE-YA!!!

Talk the Talk

Zanshin means "remaining mind" and is likened to the ocean, softly rolling. **Isshin** means "one mind" and is likened to a tidal wave, destroying everything in its path.

Be Calm and Be Intense

Hiking and horseshoe pitching are popular activities that promote a calm mind and require almost no mental intensity. By contrast, boxing and fencing are activities that require virtually constant mental intensity. Yep, you guessed it: Karate requires both.

In karate, intensity and calmness are referred to as *isshin* and *zanshin*. *Isshin* literally means "one mind," and *zanshin* literally means "remaining mind." Zanshin may be thought of as the ocean—broad, slowly rolling, and calm. Isshin may be thought of as a sudden tidal wave, destroying everything in its path. In every karate class, virtually every time you return to your starting position after practicing a particular technique, you will be expected to maintain your mental alertness (zanshin) by standing very still and remaining calm until you are told to relax.

Also in almost every class, you will be told at various times to "go for it." Frequently, after you have performed a series of attacks slowly, softly, and then with more speed, you can expect the instructor to shout something like, "Okay, power now! Faster! Stronger! See an opponent in your mind's eye and overwhelm him! Drive him into the floor! Don't give him a chance!" This is isshin—focusing the mind completely on one task and overwhelming the opponent.

In another sense, zanshin is the calm, alert state of mind necessary for perceiving an attack and blocking it. Isshin is the piercing, intense state of mind necessary to execute a strong counterattack. Once the opponent has been defeated, the mind again returns to zanshin. One of the most important balances provided by karate training is the balance between calmness (zanshin) and intensity (isshin).

Sensei Says

Always be ready to release your mind from anger and fear. Releasing your mind will free it to do what is necessary.

Be Ready: Is Your Mind Off-Balance?

Karate-do is an art that requires a balanced use of the mind and body. Indeed, a famous karate saying is "shingi ittai," which means "mind and technique are one." This is particularly important in karate because your life might be at stake in a self-defense situation, and if your mind and body don't work together, you could be in real trouble. We have taken a look at some of the physical contrasts balanced by karate training, so let's take a look at some of the mental hurdles you can expect to face in your training.

EEEE-YA!!!

Talk the Talk

Shingi ittai means "mind and technique are one."

Control Your Anger

We all know that anger is a really nasty emotion, but in karate it can be a deadly emotion. Many dangerous situations develop simply because one person gets angry and can't seem to control his anger. Let's say that some jerk cuts you off in traffic and then calls you a bad name—although it irritates you, you hold your anger in and try to move on. But the jerk seems to be spoiling for a fight, so he shouts and calls your mother a really nasty name and then blasts you with a string of profanity so vile that your anger boils over. You just lose it. You both pull over to the side of the road and step out of your cars. You rush over toward him with an "Oh, yeah?" attitude, thinking, "I'll show this jerk!" Unfortunately for you, you are so angry that you don't even have time to realize that your last thought was, indeed, your last thought—the jerk has a gun in his hand and shoots you dead on the street. Ouch!

You know that this kind of thing happens almost every day, and it is 100 percent preventable. Of course, you could have avoided the whole thing by just driving on, but anger is such a powerful emotion that it often causes otherwise rational people to act in irrational ways. In karate, you are taught that anger is a blinding emotion that, uncontrolled, *always* leads to defeat.

Karate Minute

A student with a bad temper asked a master what he could do about it. The master replied, "Show it to me." The student said he couldn't right then because it just comes and goes. "Hmm," said the master, "You say you have something but can't show it to me. If it were a natural part of you, you could show it to me any time, so you must not have had it when you were born, and nobody gave it to you. Think about that."

So, how do you control your anger, and what does "control" mean, anyway? For starters, it doesn't mean that you won't get angry. Of course you'll get angry—it's only human. To control your anger is to "harness" it and to use it positively rather than be blinded by it. In the dojo, you will quickly learn that blinding anger will get you clobbered by your seniors, or it will get you hurt. If you're lucky, you'll have a good senior who will recognize your anger and attack you. If you continue to concentrate on your anger while under attack, you'll find that you'll be very quickly defeated because you can't concentrate on anger and technique at the same time. Gradually, you will learn to push your anger into the background so that you can concentrate on the situation at hand. By the time you finish with the situation, your anger will almost always lessen. In this way, karate teaches you to use your anger as a motivating force, but not to be blinded by it. If you survive the onslaught of your seniors in the dojo, it will help you remember to keep your anger in check and to use it to your advantage in your daily life.

When you get angry outside the dojo, a good remedy is to go to the dojo, train hard, scream your lungs out, and beat up the heavy bag. It always works, and it feels really good!

Control Your Fear

Now you know that control means to harness your emotions and use them to your own advantage. As powerful an emotion as anger is, it is overshadowed by the power of fear. Fear is a completely natural emotion, and it is worse than anger because it arises out of a sense of helplessness. Fear makes us want to run more than fight. Some universal signs of fear appear in almost everybody who is suddenly frightened or startled:

➤ Your eyes fly open, and your eyebrows shoot up.

➤ Your mouth flies open.

➤ You suck in air sharply.

➤ Your shoulders rise up.

➤ Your fingers open wide.

➤ You rise up on the balls of your feet.

Try all those things together in front of a mirror, and you'll see the face of fear.

In karate, you will be taught that, although you will still feel fear when you are startled, you can train your body to react differently to it. In karate, when you are suddenly frightened, you are taught to do this:

➤ Narrow your eyes and squint a little bit.

➤ Narrow and tighten your lips.

➤ Sharply exhale, preferably with a loud shout.

➤ Drop your shoulders.

➤ Close your hands into fists, and thrust them out in front of you.

➤ Bend your knees and drop your body down into a stance.

Look in the mirror while trying these things, and you'll see a fighter rather than a scared person. So will a mugger.

We're not saying that you won't still be afraid, but we can promise you that training your body to react to fear like we have suggested will give you confidence and enable you to use your fear as a positive, motivating force against your opponent, if necessary.

Fear and Anxiety: Control Yourself

The single most important factor in a self-defense situation, or when facing an opponent in sparring, is stable emotions. By stable emotions, we mean that although you might feel fear and anger, you will be able to use those emotions to your benefit. Controlling yourself really is about learning how to deal with stress and anxiety, which are two of the deadliest enemies of modern life. Just as strong emotions such as joy and sorrow always manifest themselves in some part of our lives, anxiety also manifests itself in one form or another in our bodies. Different people react differently to stress. Some develop ulcers, some get skin problems, and some experience heart trouble. The stress itself is the outer force that bears down on us and causes anxiety. Anxiety, in turn, can play a major role in causing pain, allergies, obesity, heart disease, learning disorders, speech disorders, sexual maladjustment, and mental illness.

Anxiety is an unpleasant state of tension or uneasiness that arises from the mind's perception of stress as a danger to the body. When we fight against anxiety, we often overreact and cause both the body and the mind to develop symptoms indicating that a severe conflict is taking place. This occurs because the body is pretty well-equipped to respond to fear because fear is a reaction to a short-lived, external threat or danger. But the body is ill-equipped to maintain the fear response over an extended period of time.

Fear occurs in response to a specific stimulus, while anxiety is like a drawn-out fear of something that you can't see or recognize or specifically define. When your brain perceives a threat, it "supercharges" your body's defense mechanisms and temporarily suspends a number of normal body functions. In fear, the heart beats faster, the blood pressure rises, and blood is redirected from the stomach and intestines to the heart. The spleen contracts and discharges its supply of red blood corpuscles to provide the increased oxygen necessary for the extra energy needed for fighting the danger. And the mind automatically decides to either escape from the danger or fight it. This is universally known as the "fight or flight" response. In a state of anxiety, these body functions continue to occur and produce extreme muscle tension, greatly increased energy expenditure, fatigue, a fast pulse, high blood pressure, nausea, heartburn, and many other nasty, ugly symptoms.

The basic karate method of achieving emotional stability and overcoming anxiety is to train the body and mind together, face stress and anxiety in the controlled atmosphere of the dojo, and find out firsthand what it's all about. A good instructor will place you in one stressful situation after another and teach you how to cope. Remember that, originally, the practice of karate was part of a life-and-death struggle. Of course, we don't think much about life and death in the dojo today, but that's where karate's roots are, and that's why the training needs to be strict and disciplined.

In the dojo you will learn the importance of placing your trust in the instructor because she will place you in stressful situations again and again. Basic sparring, for example, should be done in such earnest and with such intensity that you actually feel tense and stressed. When you learn to control your emotions enough to perform the correct block and counterattack, you'll feel a great relief and a sense of accomplishment. The more advanced you become, the more often you will be pushed by your instructor toward your physical limits. If you keep training, your limits will expand, and what you found impossible to face six months ago will seem like a piece of cake today. If you don't get discouraged and just keep training, you'll gain so much confidence and emotional control that the drunk at the end of the bar—the one who looks like he'd really like to hit somebody, and he's looking at you—won't seem like such a big deal.

The Ki to Success: The Force Is with You

Ki, pronounced *chi* in Chinese, is a Japanese word that means "vital force." That's not an exact, literal translation because there is no exact, literal translation. The concept of ki is very important in almost all Japanese arts, martial and otherwise. Ki is thought to be energy whose source is located in the lower abdomen, in the middle of a line between the tailbone and the navel. The vast majority of Asian arts tries to harness ki through deep, abdominal breathing. Some people believe that ki is a mystical and powerful force that can be intercepted and turned into power. We're not sure about that, but we can offer some ways that you can use your imagination and intuition to develop a sense of strength and mental energy from the idea of ki.

Talk the Talk

Ki (pronounced *kee*) means "vital force." In Chinese, it is **chi** (pronounced *chee*).

Strength from the Gut

Frankly, whether or not you want to believe that ki is some kind of special force you can harness doesn't really matter. What matters is that you understand that the largest muscles in your body are located in or near the center of your body, which is where ki is supposed to come from. By concentrating on keeping those big muscles in and around the gut toned and firm, you will have much more strength to bring to your arms and legs. To demonstrate this idea to yourself, bend down, tighten your stomach and buttocks, and pick up a heavy weight that makes you strain to lift it. Now put the weight down by the side of your bed, lie face down on the bed with your arms and head hanging off, and try to lift it again. See?

Talk the Talk

Kime means "focus." It is the pinpoint concentration of the mind and body together, for an instant, to deliver force to the target.

Can't do it, can you? In fact, the more you can involve the muscles around your hips, stomach, and upper legs in every karate technique, the stronger those techniques will be. Your gut is your major source of power.

In fact, every strong karate technique ends (at impact) with a conscious, strong contraction of all the muscles of the body, beginning in the center of the hips and moving outward to the arms and legs. This split-second contraction, coupled with total concentration of the mind, is called *kime*, which means "focus." All the power and energy of the mind and body are focused together, for an instant, to deliver force to the target.

Breathing Is Life, Not Breathing Is ...

Your brain controls your breathing, and your breathing controls your muscles. You can prove this to yourself very easily by picking up a heavy weight that makes you strain to lift it. If you breathe in deeply while trying to lift it, you'll feel your strength dissolving, and if you hold your breath while trying to lift it, you're likely to hurt yourself. No, the best way to get your muscles to contract to lift something heavy is to breathe out while you lift. Breathing out helps the muscles contract, so it is usually a good idea to learn to breathe out when executing karate techniques.

There are exceptions to this rule, just as there are exceptions to every rule, but generally, breathing in to prepare for a technique and breathing out slightly to execute the technique is a good idea. Also, breathing is the number-one source of life for human beings. We can survive incredible injuries and bodily disasters, as long as we can keep breathing. But cut off that breath, and it's all over. Here's a way to use your imagination to help develop your breathing and ki strength:

Sensei Says

Always move from the center of your body, where your major strength lies.

Ouch!

In karate, you almost never breathe out completely. The out-breath is more like sharply saying "Hut!" If you breathe out more than that, you will have to suck air back in, and before you know it, you'll pass out.

➤ Sit in a straight-backed chair with your feet apart, your back straight, your shoulders relaxed, and your palms resting on your thighs.

➤ Close your eyes, and forcefully breathe out all the air in your body through your lips. As you exhale, make a faint "ah" sound. When you feel that you have exhaled completely, try to exhale a little bit more. As you breathe out, let your body incline slightly forward.

➤ Start breathing in, very slowly, through your nose. Think only about controlling your breathing action. As you inhale, imagine that the air is going up, into the back of your head rather than to your lungs. As the air comes in, let it pull your body erect, stretching your neck and back upward in a straight line. When you can inhale no more, drop the air in your head down through your body to the lower abdomen. Drop the air slowly, like a large boulder rolling down a hill. Keep your buttocks and rectum taut, as if to prevent the air from escaping, but don't tense the stomach; remain relaxed.

➤ Hold the air in your abdomen and concentrate on nothing else. Holding the air for 10 seconds is good for a beginner, but each day you should try to hold it a little longer. After a few weeks, you should be able to hold the air and concentrate on it for about 30 seconds. The main thing to remember is to not let the air rise and cause your chest and shoulders to tense.

➤ Exhale the air through your mouth, very slowly, with a faint "ah" sound, and then repeat the exercise.

When you do this breathing exercise, use your imagination. When you inhale to the back of your head, imagine that the air is mixing with your thoughts and bad feelings. Then drop these feelings and thoughts down to the lower abdomen with the air, forcing the good parts into the bloodstream. When you exhale, imagine that you are sending your bad thoughts and feelings out to the ends of infinity, getting rid of them forever. This takes discipline, but it really pays big dividends—both physically and psychologically.

Talk the Talk

Keiko (pronounced *keh-ee-koh*) means "practice."

Focus on This: The "Secret" of Karate

Even with all the exercises and ideas we have described, it takes a long time to develop power—both physical power and mental power—with karate training. While it's true that you can learn a whole lot in even one day, it's also true that it takes practice, practice, and more practice to get the mind and body to work together smoothly and efficiently. Oops! We just gave away the most vital secret of success in karate: Practice. Or, as a wise old sage would say, "The more you practice, the better you get, grasshopper!"

In This Corner, Karate: How It Stacks Up

If you just take a look at people practicing karate, it should be obvious that they are working very hard physically. They are kicking and punching and striking and blocking, and usually they are breathing hard and sweating. So, karate must be pretty good for you physically. Exactly how good it can be for you, though, might surprise you.

Anaerobic Aerobics

Aerobic refers to an exercise done "with oxygen," and *anaerobic* refers to activity done "without oxygen." To be healthy and strong, you need both kinds of exercise, and karate provides both in abundance. For example, a good aerobic exercise is walking. To get a good aerobic workout, you need to walk increasingly faster until you reach the point that you are breathing heavy but still able to carry on a conversation. If you keep that pace for 15 to 30 minutes two or three times a week, you will help your cardiovascular system, improve your endurance, and increase your ability to burn fat. If you push yourself past the pace where you can still talk, you'll wear out a lot quicker, and you won't be doing yourself much good.

On the other hand, a good anaerobic exercise, such as weight lifting, can help you gain strength in specific muscles that you can't get from walking. So, if you want to be heart-healthy and strong, you need to vary your routine and do both kinds of exercises. This is where karate really shines because a good karate class provides the long duration movement you need for aerobic endurance, along with high-intensity snapping movements you need for anaerobic muscle building. When you move across the floor without power but with correct form, you get an aerobic workout that takes you to your limit. When you add snap and focus to those movements, you enter an anaerobic phase that really takes your muscles to exhaustion. Taking those muscles to exhaustion makes them much stronger.

Ouch!

Never start out karate practice—or any other exercise—at a very fast pace. It is hard on your heart, hard on your muscles, and hard on your breathing. Always start out slowly, and gradually build speed and power.

The best way to develop aerobic endurance is through interval training. A workload that can be carried out for only nine minutes continuously can be continued for an hour or more with interval training. Each period of exercise in interval training is known as a work bout. A work bout in karate might be a series of lunge punches across the floor and back, or a series of blocking techniques moving forward and back. It might be a series of kicks, or it might be combination techniques. No matter what technique is employed, there are four ways to increase aerobic capacity with interval training:

1. The number of work bouts can be increased.
2. The length of each bout can be increased.
3. The intensity of each work bout can be increased.
4. Rest periods between the work bouts can be decreased.

The most effective work bouts for developing aerobic conditioning are bouts of three to five minutes with rest and light movement in between. If you watch a karate class of intermediate or advanced students, this is exactly what you will see. The students move back and forth under all the conditions listed previously. In between each bout, they catch their breath and go at it again.

The best anaerobic workout is one in which successive, vigorous, intense movements are performed in about one minute. The muscles quickly become fatigued and dump lactic acid in the bloodstream, which your system has to learn how to handle. We can't imagine a better anaerobic workout than a kata—almost any kata—performed at full speed and with full power.

Karate training is virtually unsurpassed in providing a complete, well-balanced aerobic and anaerobic workout.

Throwin', Kickin', and Jumpin'

Since the 1970s, many sports medicine authorities have used a system of six fundamental categories of motion to analyze how good or bad a sport is in terms of total body exercise. The motions are …

➤ **Stance,** which controls the distribution of force during impact

➤ **Walking,** which includes forward, backward, uphill, downhill, side-step, and extreme rotation

➤ **Running,** which differs from walking in that both feet are off the ground at the same time

➤ **Jumping,** which is a ballistic motion of the legs that propels the body up or down and that includes pirouettes and sliding

➤ **Kicking,** which includes kicking against an object and kicking to propel the lower leg away from the body's center

➤ **Throwing,** which is the motion of transferring force from movements of the trunk to an object, such as a ball, a golf club, or a tennis racket

Each of these fundamental motions is assigned from 0 (no involvement) to 3 (heavy involvement) points, and then each type of sport or exercise is observed to see how much they utilize the motions. Because there are six motions, each worth 3 points, the maximum possible score is 18, but so far, no sport has gotten that score. The highest score, 15, has gone to basketball, football, and skiing. The lowest score, 3, has been assigned to camping and bridge. Anything over 12 points is considered maximum use of the whole body, but some of the sports getting that score might not be the best things for most of us to try because they include jai alai, rugby, rodeo, and circus acts! If you'd like to get a good workout without dangling from a trapeze or riding a buckin' bronco, karate might just be what you're looking for—it scores 12 points, which is as close as you can get to the maximum without risking life and limb. As a physical activity combining the most kinds of motions, karate compares favorably with diving, gymnastics, tennis, boxing, fencing, and handball. It just doesn't get much better than that.

Stretch, Stretch, Stretch!

In Chapter 8, "How to Practice Karate," you will find numerous stretching exercises to help you gain flexibility. Flexibility is defined as the range of motion of a given joint. Many people, though, think that flexibility is related only to muscular flexibility, which is a matter of how much motion is limited by muscles and tendons surrounding the joint. An often overlooked factor in flexibility is how much freedom of movement is allowed by the ligaments that hold the bones together at the joints. Karate really shines when it comes to strong muscles, tendons, and ligaments because almost all karate techniques involve very strong rotation of the joints in application; joint rotation exercises are one of the best ways to increase ligament strength and flexibility. In all the major flexibility tests—trunk flexion, trunk extension, hip flexion, and shoulder flexibility (these are the things they test if you go to the YMCA and ask for a fitness evaluation)—karate training has been shown repeatedly to improve all of them.

Lift, Push, and Hold

The actions of lifting, pushing, and holding are the primary actions for training against resistance. Resistance exercises such as weight lifting, of course, increase muscle density and strength. The more resistance you can work against, the stronger you will get. In karate, lifting and pushing are practiced against resistance in almost every class, and holding is practiced sometimes. Every time you block an opponent's arm with a rising block, you are lifting and pushing against resistance. Every time you execute a forearm block or a knife hand block, you are pushing against resistance. And every time you punch the makiwara (punching board) and hold your hand against it for a second, you are practicing pushing and holding. The harder your opponent attacks you, the more resistance you are working against, and that makes you stronger.

Karate Minute

Gichin Funakoshi, the man who introduced karate to Japan, was reputed to climb onto the roof of his house in the middle of a typhoon to help build his strength and determination. We're really glad that this particular strengthening exercise didn't make it into modern karate!

Karate training also helps you build endurance, which is resistance to fatigue and quick recovery after fatigue. Three types of endurance exist:

➤ Total body endurance

➤ Cardiovascular endurance, which is the ability of the circulatory system to deliver oxygen to the cells and to remove the waste products of metabolism

➤ Muscular endurance, which is gained from many repetitions and actions against progressively harder resistance

It is clear that karate is a highly effective form of exercise that improves both physical and mental fitness. It's also a lot more fun than calisthenics!

The Least You Need to Know

➤ Karate fitness comes from a balanced use of the mind and the body.

➤ The main source of power is in the center of the body.

➤ Proper breathing is an integral part of karate fitness.

➤ Karate is one of the most dynamic whole-body exercises you can do.

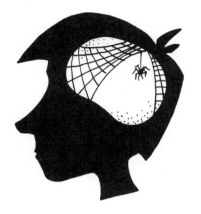

Chapter 4

Kick the Cobwebs Out of Your Head

> ### In This Chapter
>
> ➤ Clearing your mind with karate
>
> ➤ Understanding karate's code of ethics
>
> ➤ The value of karate for kids
>
> ➤ How karate lets everybody be a winner
>
> ➤ How karate improves academics

Ever have one of those days when it feels as if your head is full of cobwebs? Does it sometimes feel as if the world around you is spinning faster than you can keep up with? If you're a mom or dad, doesn't it sometimes feel as if you're going faster and faster without getting anywhere? Think about it! You're running the kids here and there at a frantic pace, trying to manage a household that demands more energy than you seem to have, and constantly trying to balance work with family responsibilities. If you're in business, does it seem like the stress of "just one more thing" is going to cause you to explode? And if you're a student, do you sometimes wonder whether your head even has enough room left for all the facts it needs for that big exam?

Well, if your head gets filled with stresses that seem to clog up the works like huge cobwebs, have we got a solution for you! You can literally kick those cobwebs out of your head with karate. That's right, the practice of modern karate-do is one of the greatest stress-busters of all time.

Karate works on the body, mind, and spirit all at once, and its goal is to create a centered, calm, aware person who can clearly see through all the cobwebs and get down to the heart of the matter, no matter what the matter is.

Karate's Code: The Citizen Warrior

In the old days, when a samurai wanted to test his sword, he might just grab an Okinawan peasant and slash away. It was legal, and it was easy because the peasant wasn't allowed to have any weapons. So, the essence of karate for peasants in those days was pretty straightforward: Kill your opponent before he kills you.

Sensei Says

Do not think that karate training is only in the dojo. Karate-do's code must be studied in the dojo and applied in everyday life.

Sensei Says

Human progress in karate-do is like climbing a series of steep steps. As the mind and body grow together, you move continuously onward and upward, one step at a time. Until the day you die, the process is endless because nobody is perfect, but you can always become a little better if you keep trying.

While we definitely still have a need for effective self-defense today, we have progressed, happily, to a point at which we don't have bands of samurai roaming the streets and hacking away at us. The techniques of almost any style of karate are more than adequate for our self-defense needs. They will take care of the nasty business of assault, robbery, rape, and the like, so we can feel very confident in that department.

Today, though, stress and anxiety are bigger enemies for most of us than muggers are. And it is in this department—the stress department—that karate really shines. The basic ways that karate helps control stress are through vigorous, regular exercise and greatly improved concentration. Beyond these basics, though, karate has a lot to offer that might not be readily apparent on first glance. Karate-do has a deeply embedded code that enables people to develop not only concentration, but control of their emotions as well.

While different schools of karate-do have different written codes, almost all of them can be summed up in five basic principles.

Character

So, you say, I have good character already. Do I need more? No, you don't need more or different character. What you need and can get from karate-do is *polished* character. Even if you are the nicest, most moral person in the world, you can still be better, but you have to work at it—and karate-do is a great tool for this. This idea in karate-do is usually expressed as "Seek perfection of character." That means that the premise of karate-do is as an art of virtuous people—people of high character—who continually strive to grow emotionally and mentally. In all physical activities—including karate—physical growth can increase only to the point that age starts causing it to decrease. When this happens, most people just accept the fact that they can't get any better. In karate-do, though, the emphasis is on developing the mind and the body together, so even when the body starts declining, we can still improve ourselves by concentrating on improving our character.

Karate-do's idea is that, using the techniques of karate, we can continually challenge ourselves physically and mentally until the day we die, no matter what our age or physical condition.

Improved character arises out of two types of discipline—self-discipline and imposed discipline—and karate-do provides both.

Talk the Talk

A famous karate expression is **"Do mu kyoku,"** which means that the path (do) of the karate-do student is endless and that there are no limitations.

Sincerity

In the original Japanese, sincerity is sometimes referred to as "Be faithful" or "Defend the paths of truth." It is a principle of karate-do that encourages us to be sincere and honest, both in the dojo and out. In the dojo, sincerity and honesty in dealing with classmates is essential to the smooth functioning of the class. Strong sanctions are imposed on people in the dojo who show a lack of sincerity in trying to learn and help their classmates learn, because a lack of sincerity often leads to injury.

Let's say, for example, that your opponent announces that she is going to step in and execute a punch to your face, but then she does it so lackadaisically that you don't feel any force or threat from it. She was insincere and dishonest with you, and she wasted both her time in the dojo and yours. She also created a situation in which she could be injured because, if you believe her to be sincere in her intent to attack your face, you will block strongly and seriously. If her arm was loose and insincere, she could be badly hurt by your blocking action. So, in karate-do, sincerity is honesty, and lack of sincerity or dishonesty with ourselves and others can lead to injury.

Effort

The principle of fostering the spirit of effort really is a warning that the practice of karate-do is not easy and that, to succeed, you will really have to sincerely try to do your best at all times. Gichin Funakoshi said "Karate is like hot water. If you do not give it heat constantly, it will again become cold water." If you've been paying attention, you'll see that all the core principles of karate-do are tied together in a neat bundle. Going back to your opponent who wasn't sincere in her intention to fire a punch at your nose, it's pretty easy to see that in addition to having the right intention, she would also have to try really hard to execute the technique properly.

Sincerity and effort are two sides of the same coin. For example, how many times have you said, sincerely and honestly, "I'd really like to try that!" but have not followed up with the effort necessary to actually try it? That's natural, but it's unacceptable in karate-do. What you honestly want to accomplish in the dojo can be accomplished only by exerting the effort necessary to accomplish it. People who have trained in karate-do for a long time believe that they can accomplish much more in their daily lives by exerting a sincere effort to get things done. They can also look at something and know that they honestly and sincerely would like to try it, but they make a conscious decision not to try it because they know that it will require effort that they are not willing to expend.

Practicing karate-do with a spirit of 100 percent effort also enables you to realize that anything you truly want to accomplish will require 100 percent of your effort to accomplish it. And the effort required to accomplish things in daily life is usually a lot less rigorous than the effort exerted to master karate-do.

Talk the Talk

Ikken means "one punch" and **hisatsu** means "death blow," so **ikken hisatsu** means "Each movement balances between life and death." There is never a second chance, so be sure to do it with all your might the first time.

Sensei Says

Karate-do begins with courtesy and ends with courtesy.

Etiquette

Etiquette is the form required for proper, formal behavior, and because the practice of karate-do involves strong, fast, physical fighting techniques, the rules of etiquette are strictly observed to be sure that nobody gets hurt. It's pretty easy to imagine how many injuries might occur in a karate class if people were allowed to just wander around the room, lobbing punches and kicks at each other at random. Ouch!

To avoid this, karate-do observes some strict rules of etiquette, the most obvious of which is bowing a lot. You will be required to bow when you enter the dojo and again when stepping onto the training floor. You will bow to your teacher and again to your seniors. You will bow to your partner before and after every encounter, and you'll repeat the whole process as you leave the dojo. Aside from the obvious fact that karate-do is a Japanese art and that the Japanese seem to bow a lot, why, you probably wonder, is so much formal bowing required?

Bowing is required because it forces you to take the first step in making your mind and body work together as one unit. If you think that your mind and body already function nicely as one unit, you're dead wrong in terms of self-defense. Some people are very strong mentally but are physically unprepared for a sudden attack. Others might be very strong physically but may have no idea how to cope with sudden violence. Most of us probably fall somewhere in between those extremes, but most of us probably are not prepared for a sudden, violent confrontation.

When a surprise attack is launched against you, you must be ready, both physically and psychologically, if you want to walk away in one piece. When you ask yourself "What would I do if somebody suddenly attacked me?" one of your answers might be "I'd have to think about it." Too bad— you lose. The last thing you want to do when you are attacked is to think about it.

Thinking takes too much time. While you are thinking, your attacker is wailing away at you, accomplishing his dirty deed. No, thinking won't work. The only thing that will work is for your mind and body to respond instantly as one unit.

Your body can respond with appropriate karate techniques while your mind remains calm and your emotions stable. This is the only way to win, and the formal rules of etiquette in the dojo are the foundation for training the mind and body to work together. In the dojo, where you have time to think, you are forced to do just that. You are given a formal code of conduct that is challenging both mentally and physically. Some schools require that people address each other in the formal Japanese manner of attaching "san" to names. So, good old Joe Smith would be addressed as "Smith-san" or "Joe-san." In another dojo, he might have to be addressed as "Mr. Smith." No matter what the requirement is, though, it is a method that forces you to think about your behavior and then apply both physical and mental effort to effect a formal behavior.

Talk the Talk

Rei means bow, and it is a command used frequently in karate classes. **Shomen ni rei** means "Bow to the front." **Sensei ni rei** means "Bow to the teacher." **Otagai ni rei** means "Bow to each other."

Talk the Talk

Mizu no kokoro means "a mind like water," and it means that the karate-do student should develop a mind like the water on the surface of clear, undisturbed pond. As the clear, calm surface reflects everything around it perfectly, so should your mind.

You will see in Chapter 6, "Welcome to the Dojo," that there are both written and unwritten rules in the dojo, and these rules help you to be more aware of your behavior both in the dojo and out. By learning and practicing careful rules of etiquette in the dojo, you become more aware of your behavior outside the dojo, and this helps you become more aware of potentially dangerous situations before they develop into trouble.

Also, as we said earlier, karate-do is an art of virtuous people, and virtuous people are expected to set the tone for the rest of society in terms of etiquette and proper behavior. Practicing karate-do is a big step in the right direction of kind and courteous behavior toward others.

Self-Control

Anybody who speaks a foreign language well knows that literal translation and meaningful translation are often two very different things. To exercise self-control seems pretty obvious at face value: Control yourself. But like the other parts of karate's code of ethics, that really doesn't do the idea justice.

Of course, self-control is a great virtue. If you have control over your emotions, you don't tend to get into arguments all the time, and you don't fly off the handle when somebody is rude or casts aspersions on your family heritage. But karate's idea of self-control goes way beyond that. Some translate the original Japanese principle to mean "Refrain from violent behavior," while others say that it means "To guard against impetuous courage." Refraining from violent behavior is pretty straightforward, and guarding against impetuous courage pretty much means, "Don't do something on the spur of the moment that you might regret later."

Our favorite translation, however, is farther away from the original as a literal translation but captures the idea beautifully. It comes from the late karate master Osamu Ozawa: "We shall be wary of foolishness." Ozawa's idea was that all violence is foolish, and that anybody who attacks another person is a fool. "Fools are easier to identify than normal people," he said, "so watch out for foolish behavior in others, and avoid it." Much more important, though, he said that the principle means that we must watch out for foolish behavior in ourselves, and we must do everything in our power to control our behavior in a way that will not invite trouble.

Sensei Says

Because karate's techniques are very powerful and potentially dangerous, it is extremely important to maintain your self-control while practicing. If you lose control, your opponent might also lose control, and that would not be a pretty sight!

In the dojo, self-control is learned by working with other people in a controlled, challenging environment. In karate-do, you will rather quickly learn that if you lose control of yourself in practice, you will be putting yourself in line for severe discipline.

You also learn that losing self-control outside the dojo can put you in harm's way. Controlling yourself is the first step toward controlling a confrontation.

What's All the Shouting About?

One of the first things you'll notice about a karate class is that the room is noisy. People are hollering, shouting, grunting, and sighing pretty much all the time. Why? Well, frankly, a lot of it is because they are physically struggling to make their techniques faster and stronger, and sometimes that hurts a little bit. The more advanced the people are, the more effort they exert, and the higher the level of grunting, groaning, and sighing becomes. Like any physical activity, karate requires effort, and in karate class that effort is often verbalized.

The most important noise you hear in a karate class, though, is the *kiai*. In the last chapter, we said that *ki* means vital, or mental, energy. *Ai* means "get together." So a *kiai* is a shout from the pit of the stomach that gets together your physical and mental energy and then focuses them for an instant on the target. It is a shout of spirit and a shout of concentration. The noise blots everything else out of your mind for a split second so that you can focus your mind on the target, and the tensing of the muscles needed to make the noise helps you focus your internal as well as external muscles on the target.

A kiai is a conscious extension of a natural phenomenon. That is, when you try to lift something heavy and struggle with it, you naturally grunt and groan a little, and you tense your stomach muscles and your diaphragm (the internal muscle that makes your lungs expand and contract). That causes you to put pressure on your breath and breathe some of it out. All this gives you extra strength for your task and really makes you concentrate harder on getting the thing lifted. A kiai is exactly like that, except that you make it faster, harder, and louder to bring extra strength and concentration together in an instant rather than slowly.

The benefit of the kiai is primarily for the person doing it, but there is also some chance that a sudden loud shout from the pit of the stomach might startle an opponent long enough to create an opening for a counterattack or an escape.

Talk the Talk

Kiai is a shout that unites mind and body for an instant and that adds strength to technique.

And not to be overlooked is the fact that executing a kiai just plain feels good. Every single one of us has faced a situation in which stress and anxiety have built up to the point that we could just scream. Well, in karate class, you can do just that: Scream! Let it out! Get rid of it! Scream and scream again! It feels good, and it's good for you.

An important fact about the kiai is that the sound you make probably won't sound anything like "Kiai!" or "Kiyah!" *Kiai* is a word that represents a particular set of sounds, just like the word "whistle" represents a particular set of sounds. So, if your karate teacher tells you to whistle, you wouldn't shout "Whistle!" No, you would form your lips into the appropriate arrangement and make the sound known as a whistle. It's exactly the same with a kiai. If your teacher tells you to kiai, don't shout "Kiai!" Instead, tense your muscles appropriately and make one of the sounds known as a kiai. There are several of these, including "eh-ee!" "yah!" "ha-ee" and others. Your instructor will guide you on which is appropriate at which times, but please don't shout out "Kiai!" It just doesn't make any sense.

Karate to the Rescue: Kids at Risk

Just as karate-do can help adults kick the cobwebs out of their heads, it also can be a great way to get troubled and confused kids on the right track and steer them away from danger.

Karate teaches children to work together.

Psychologists and criminologists tell us that many kids who are at increased risk of violent or criminal behavior are at risk largely because they are bored and have nothing to challenge them. Others are at risk because they have no group to identify with, so they turn to gangs for recognition. Still others are at risk because their economic or social position is so underprivileged that they feel inadequate and unable to gain significant self-esteem. Of course, there are many other risk factors, too, but underlying all of them seems to be a sense of negativity.

Teenagers and late preteen kids tend to want to see things in black and white, and when they start learning that the world is constructed on a graded color scale from black to white with every conceivable shade of gray in between, it can make them confused and angry. Without a way to channel their anger, they often become depressed and unwittingly tie themselves up in a negative state of mind. This negative state of mind can lead to real trouble when they start acting out their anger and confusion in socially unacceptable ways.

Karate-do to the rescue! While there is no sure-fire single method that will get all kids on the straight and narrow, we know that karate-do is one of the best ways to help a lot of them. For those who are bored, karate-do acts as a serious challenge because it forces them to think, and it forces them to exercise their minds and bodies together in a positive way. For those who lack group identity, karate-do puts them in an environment where everybody in the group is working toward the same goals, and everybody wears the same white uniform. For those who suffer from low self-esteem, karate-do provides a sense of accomplishment that is unsurpassed in providing positive reinforcement. Lack of ability in the karate dojo is never seen as a negative. Rather, the encouragement provided to those who learn more slowly is always positive and never-ending. The camaraderie among all the people in the dojo simply suspends any thoughts about social or economic status outside the dojo. All the people in the dojo are striving mightily toward the same goals of making better punches, better kicks, and better people, and these goals require the same training, regardless of whether the student is a doctor, a steelworker, a professor, a plumber, or an unemployed high school dropout. In karate-do, it simply doesn't matter. In the dojo, everybody is treated the same, regardless of race, color, creed, or gender.

In other words, training in karate-do for kids at particularly high risk can completely erase their negative mindset and turn it into a productive, positive mindset full of challenge, praise, and accomplishment.

No Teams, No Cuts, No Limits

One of the authors of this book was a nerdy little kid with good grades, big eyeglasses, and absolutely no depth perception. The lack of depth perception meant that he couldn't tell how far away most things were in relation to each other. If you held up two fingers in front of his face, one two inches farther away than the other, they looked exactly the same to him. He couldn't perceive 3D. This made for some interesting times when he tried to make the Little League baseball team. Sometimes he would swing at a pitch before it even got near the plate, and other times he would swing when the ball was already in the catcher's mitt. He could pitch the ball fairly well, but when the catcher threw it back to him, he often caught it with his lips instead of his glove because he just couldn't tell how far away it was. He tried hard, but the results were pretty much a foregone conclusion: Cut!

But a funny thing happened on his way to his teen years: He found karate. And what he found astonished him. Here was a physical activity that had teams, but it also had individual competition, and anybody could compete. Everybody participated at an individual level of skill, and everybody else admired that person for it. There were no cuts, and the teachers told him that he had no limits: He could go as far in this art as he decided to go. There also was no pressure to compete at all. If you wanted to just participate in the classes and enjoy the competitive spirit there, that was fine. Most amazing of all, though, was that after a few years of training, he was able to execute kicks, strikes, and punches with as much accuracy and control as his peers, in spite of his lack of depth perception!

Because of our own experience and the experiences of thousands of karate students over the years, we believe that karate-do and similar martial arts stand alone in their ability to engage people in challenging physical activity—and even in sport, if they choose to compete—without the humiliation of being cut from the team and without a hint of limits on the ability of the individual to participate.

Under the guidance of a good instructor, karate-do is a positive life experience that leads to confidence and a rational sense of self-worth.

Sensei Says

In karate-do, you compete only against yourself. Competing against others is up to you.

Oh, and our depth-challenged author? By the time he was 15, karate training had taught him how to judge distances well enough that he could actually throw, catch, and hit a baseball, and he became the quarterback on his high school football team. And today, 40 years later, he still practices karate-do, every single day.

Up the Academic Ladder

We'll just admit it up front: We can't promise that karate training will improve your kid's GPA, or yours either, for that matter. But we can promise that it will provide an ideal atmosphere to *encourage* those grades to go up.

First of all, many schools of karate-do have programs that directly encourage the attainment of good grades in school, and you should inquire about this before you join or enroll your child. Some organizations have semester honor rolls to encourage academic achievement among their members, and some even award good grades with ribbons or trophies.

Second, the karate-do dojo provides an excellent atmosphere in which to teach kids to focus on one task at a time. As you learned earlier in this chapter, there is a strong emphasis in karate-do on developing mind-body connections through concentration. In fact, learning and following the karate-do code of ethics is an outstanding educational experience in and of itself. Any good karate instructor will constantly emphasize to students that what they learn in the dojo will prepare them for real life outside the dojo.

Third, karate-do provides the vigorous regular exercise that is so important in maintaining energy levels, healthy circulation and breathing, and general good health. Combined with proper rest, these factors lay a foundation that enables the student to be clear-headed, alert, and energetic—an ideal foundation for learning.

For adult learners, an additional benefit of karate-do is the relief of stress, which is one of the main roadblocks in adult education. Adults have lots to worry about, and this often stands in the way of their own academic achievement. With karate-do, you can kick the cobwebs out of your head, scream your stress out, and clear the path for a great academic experience.

The Least You Need to Know

➤ Karate is an ideal way to conquer stress.

➤ Karate's code of ethics seeks to develop the whole person—physically, mentally, and emotionally.

➤ Karate changes negative thinking into positive thinking and can put troubled kids on the right path.

➤ Even if you're not good at other sports, you can participate in karate.

➤ Karate provides a great atmosphere for attaining higher grades for both kids and adults.

Part 2

Let's Get Started

Walking into a karate school for the first time can be like stepping into a different world because ritual and formality are a big part of karate training. Before you do that, it would be a good idea to find a school that is right for you and to know what might be expected of you when you enroll there. As you will see, even the uniform has ritual and formality associated with it.

Chapter 5

Find the Right School

In This Chapter

➤ What to look for in a karate school

➤ How to tell a good instructor from a bad one

➤ How much you should pay for classes

➤ The risks of karate training

➤ The difference between karate as an art and karate as a sport

---

When you have decided that you want to try karate, the most important decision you will make will be to find the right karate school for you.

We can't make the decision for you, but we have put together some practical advice and ideas in this chapter which we think should be very helpful.

More Than Just Kicks and Punches

When you start learning karate-do, you will be learning a lot more than just kicks and punches. Remember, we said that karate can be a lifetime art, and its code of ethics and conduct is designed to polish the character of the people who practice it.

The first thing you want to look for is a karate school advertising that it teaches more than just kicks and punches. Specifically, you should look for schools that advertise confidence, stress management, improved concentration, discipline, or a combination of these and similar qualities. Other keywords to look for might include respect, self-discipline, or traditional. Looking for these words won't guarantee that you are joining a good school, but at least you will be looking at schools that advertise some of the more positive aspects of karate-do training.

Is Karate an Art or a Sport?

This is an important question to ask before you join a school, because the answer to it will help you determine what the emphasis is in that particular school. The correct answer, of course, is that karate is *both* an art and a sport. If the instructor hedges on the answer, you'd better question further and ask what is emphasized in that school.

If you're interested in sport, and sport is what the school emphasizes, great! But if you have little or no interest in competition, you need to know up front whether members are required or "strongly encouraged" to participate in sport competitions. On the other hand, the instructor might say that the school doesn't participate in sport karate at all and bans members from competing. If that's the case, and if you think that you might want to explore karate's sport aspect, you probably need to look for another school.

Sensei Says

It will take your entire life to master karate. There *is* no limit.

The bottom line is to be sure that you feel comfortable with what the school says it emphasizes. Don't join thinking that you will be able to change the rules or avoid the requirements later. Trust us on this: It won't happen!

How Do I Know Which School Is Right for Me?

The very first thing you should do to find a school is to talk to somebody you know who currently is training in karate-do. Ask them all the questions suggested in this chapter, and then discuss with them any concerns or questions you still have. A friend who is already training can be a great asset to you, too, when you actually join the school because you will have somebody you know to show you around and to guide you through the enrollment process. But if you don't know anybody like that, your best bet is to let your fingers do the walking through the Yellow Pages.

In some areas, karate schools are listed under "Karate" in the Yellow Pages, but in most areas they are listed under "Martial Arts Instruction," which lumps them together with all types of martial arts and makes it even harder to find a good school. And it is simply amazing how many martial art schools there are in all the major metropolitan areas of the United States. The first thing you have to do is whittle the list down to a manageable number of schools.

It's All in the Name

The first thing to look for is the word "karate" or "karate-do" in a school's name. The second thing to look for is some form of the words "Japan" or "Okinawa." If you can find a place that advertises Japanese or Okinawan karate-do, you are really on the right track.

The second thing to look for is any school that advertise anything else—and eliminate those schools. Any school that has "Martial Arts" as the primary part of its name probably doesn't teach karate-do, and unless its ad says something to the contrary, you can eliminate such a school. Definitely eliminate from your search any ad that says "aikido," "judo," "jujutsu," "Tae Kwon Do," "Tang Soo Do," "kickboxing," "combat karate," "grappling," "Chinese," "Indonesian," "Filipino," "ninja," "ninjutsu," "Muay Thai," "Tai Chi," "yoga," "kung fu," "wushu," "Moo-do Kwan," "Kuk Sool Won," "submission," or any variation of the phrase "fear no man." These places might teach wonderful martial arts, but they definitely do not teach karate-do.

Karate Minute

Even though karate-do is practiced by millions of people all over the world, no single governing body defines karate-do, and there are no legal controls over use of the word *karate-do*. Anybody can claim to know it, and anybody can claim to teach it.

After these first two steps, you will find that you have a relatively small number of schools left, and it's time to start calling. The first schools to call are the ones closest to your location. If you decide to continue karate training for the long haul, the location of the school might be a big consideration. Also, some of the very best karate-do training can be found in small, part-time schools with very dedicated instructors. A large ad might indicate a more commercially successful school, but it does not indicate better karate training.

Size Really Doesn't Matter

As you investigate, you need to be aware of a very simple fact: The size of the dojo is not necessarily related to the quality of the school. You may very well find that the largest schools in the area are not necessarily the best. As a matter of fact, you may find a hidden gem in a small school where the instructor has been teaching steadily

Sensei Says

Remember, biggest does not necessarily mean best. It just means biggest.

Ouch!

Don't join a school just on the basis of a free introductory lesson—it might not reflect the regular training. Be sure to watch a regular class or two before joining.

Sensei Says

Never consider joining a dojo that won't let you watch a class. They are hiding something, and you should not stick around to find out what it might be.

for 20, 30, or even 40 years. But it's not all that simple—it could just be that the largest school might be the largest precisely because it has an instructor who has been teaching in the same location for 20, 30, or 40 years. The bottom line is that you have to call and visit the schools to decide which one is right for you.

Ask Questions First, Act Later

We recommend that you call before visiting, because that phone call might tell you all you need to know to decide that you don't want to visit that particular school. When you call, you should say that you have never taken karate and that you are looking for a school. Once you have established that, there is a very simple list of questions that you should ask.

➤ **What style does the school teach?** The first thing to ask is whether the school teaches karate-do and what style it is. If you don't recognize the style from this book, ask if it is a Japanese or Okinawan style. If it's not, thank the person, hang up, and call another place. Remember: All karate-do has Okinawan or Japanese roots, and the person answering the phone should definitely know this, too.

➤ **When are classes held?** Ask for the beginners' class schedule. If it seems that the class schedule would work for you, then it's time for the next, and possibly most important question.

➤ **Can I observe a class?** Any legitimate school will allow you to do this, although some might require an appointment so that they can give you their sales pitch when you come in.

Getting to the Heart of the School

Some schools may offer a free introductory lesson, but we suggest that you watch a regular class before trying a free lesson because introductory lessons can be conducted in a manner that is completely different from the regular classes. Let's face it: A free lesson is a sales pitch, and the school is not going to put you through something in a free lesson that might discourage you.

If any of the schools you call say that you cannot watch a regular class, don't walk away—run away! There is no legitimate reason for a school to hide what is done in classes from prospective students. Trust us on this point: If they won't let you observe a class, it's because they have something to hide, so get out of there as soon as possible.

One thing to remember, though, is that a school might insist that you observe a beginner class first rather than a more advanced class. This is okay because observing advanced training first really might give you the wrong impression of what your training might be like.

Advanced karate people can look awfully fearsome to a person with no experience, and because the classes are loud and vigorous, you might forget that those people have been training for years and have built themselves up gradually over a very long period of time. It's much better to observe beginners in action because the beginners' class is where you will be if you decide to join.

Ouch!

Don't base your decision to join or not to join on your impressions from watching just an advanced class. An advanced class can be scary, and it's hard to remember that advanced karate people have been training for years to develop their level of skill and fearsomeness.

Money Matters

If the style, class times, and visitation policy seem okay, then it is time to inquire about price. You don't need to get exact figures at this point, but you do need to have a ballpark idea so that if a school's price range is way beyond your budget, you won't waste your time by going further. Some schools won't give you an exact price over the phone—partly to conceal their prices from their competition and partly because price negotiation is often part of their in-person sales pitch—but they usually will give you a price range of some sort. Even if they won't, don't let that be the reason for dropping them from your list. Go in and listen to the sales pitch—it might be okay.

Sensei Says

When you are looking for karate instruction, don't forget to check out the local YMCA, YWCA, JCCA, and community education programs in local school districts. Often you can find excellent karate instruction in those places, too.

A dojo should be a clean, well-lighted, inviting place.

Watch and Decide

When you've made an appointment to visit the dojo, plan to arrive about 10 minutes early. This will give you a chance to observe the comings and goings of the students and might give you a chance meet a couple of them. The instructor may or may not be the one who talks to you about the school; frequently a staff member will be the one to give the sales pitch.

You might get the sales pitch before or after the class, or even 15 minutes into the class. No matter what, though, be sure to watch the class closely and observe the interaction between the students and the instructor. Ask yourself whether the students seem to be somewhat like you or the people you associate with. For example, if they all have long hair, headbands, and tattoos up and down their arms, and you don't, you might just want to politely excuse yourself and go somewhere else.

Another thing to watch for is whether children and adults are in the same class. School owners are pretty much divided down the middle on this issue, so there may or may not be a mix of adults and kids. Still, this might be a consideration for you. If there is a mix of adults and kids, it probably won't affect your training much, but if there are 20 little kids and no adults, that might not be the best situation for you. (If you are thinking about enrolling your child in the school, though, the situation might be ideal.) The main thing is to watch and decide whether you think you would be reasonably comfortable in the class.

One of the main things to watch for is whether the people in the class seem to be enjoying themselves. Remember that this isn't eighteenth-century Okinawa, and samurai aren't hacking peasants to death in the streets, so the training atmosphere doesn't have to be grim and dark. It might be (and should be) highly disciplined, but the people should be enjoying their experience there, and they should display motivation and interest. If they don't, run for the hills!

Is She a Good Instructor?

Because karate has such a history as a macho activity for men, it might not have occurred to you that the instructor might be a woman, but today that is a very distinct possibility. Not only have some women been training in karate for 30 years or more, but some of them have become renowned competitors, and some have become outstanding teachers. Our view is that it doesn't matter one bit whether the instructor is male or female. The only thing that matters is whether the instructor is a good instructor.

The two biggest criteria for you to use to decide whether the instructor is any good are these:

1. How does the instructor relate to and interact with the students in the class?
2. How does the instructor relate to you, directly, as a prospective student?

After all, karate-do is a very serious subject, and instructors usually take their role very seriously. Sometimes, in fact, even good instructors will carry an air of samurai dignity and even aloofness around the room with them while they are teaching. Sometimes this is necessary for the reinforcement of a particular lesson. This attitude might be okay if the instructors also seem to interact humanely and compassionately with their students. It is definitely okay if they switch off those airs when they leave the floor and come over to shake your hand. Once they are off the training floor, there is no real reason why they should continue to be aloof.

Indeed, one of the goals of karate training is to eliminate phony behavior and to achieve *heijo shin,* which means "everyday mind."

Off the training floor, they should be just like you—they should be friendly, approachable, interested, and able to smile. If they act any other way, you can be sure that it will be reflected in their students, because students always try to imitate their instructors. So watch the instructor closely, both on and off the training floor, if possible.

The other thing to watch for when you are trying to decide about the school is what the students are doing, how much trouble are they having doing it, and how much help are they getting from the instructor in trying to get it right. These things are really important to you because, if you join the school, you will be doing those same things within a couple weeks. When you watch what the students are doing, ask yourself whether that is the sort of thing you would like to be able to do. Don't ask yourself whether you would be able to do it. Of course you're not able to do it—you've

> EEEE-YA!!!

Talk the Talk

Heijo shin means "everyday mind," and it is the natural, unaffected state of mind that karate instructors strive for, both in the dojo and out.

never taken karate before! Under a good instructor, however, you can learn to do things that you never would have thought possible.

Sensei Says

Don't be discouraged by the skill of the advanced karate students. They are just like you, and if they can reach that level of skill, so can you.

If you would like to be able to do what they are doing, that goes in the plus column. If the students seem to be struggling mightily with the techniques and are not receiving much help from anybody, that goes in the minus column. On the other hand, if they are struggling but are being helped or at least encouraged by the instructor or the assistants, that goes in the plus column.

Remember that in the dojo, karate is an individual activity performed and perfected in a community atmosphere. That means that everybody in the dojo should be trying to help everybody else. Even if you don't see people physically helping, the atmosphere should be one of community effort.

How Long Are the Classes?

The length of classes should be geared to the attention span of the people in the class. Schools that offer classes for children under the age of six or seven usually have about 30-minute classes—it's almost impossible to hold the students' attention for much longer than that. Beginning classes for adults usually run about 45 minutes to an hour; sometimes they run as much as an hour and a half, but that's unusual. Intermediate and advanced classes might run as much as an hour and a half because the people in them have attained a physical condition that supports that length of time on the floor.

Karate Minute

When karate was still practiced in secret in Okinawa, there were no fixed classes or time limits on classes. A student might sneak to the master's house late at night and practice until dawn. Only when karate was introduced to the schools did classes and class times become an issue.

You should decide before you join whether the classes seem too long for you. Again, watch a whole class and see how the people do. That's really more important than the length of the class.

How Much Should It Cost?

Prices vary widely across the country, so much so that it is impossible to nail down even a ballpark figure. What we do know is that commercial schools, by and large, charge somewhere between $40 and $100 a month for full memberships. You might find something a little bit lower if you live in a small, Midwestern town, and you might find something a little higher if you live in a major city on the East Coast. But again, these are broad generalizations because we know of at least one school on the East Coast where training is free, but membership is selective, and we know of a chain of schools in the Midwest that charges $180 a month!

We suggest that you investigate the prices at several schools in your area and then decide whether you are happy with the value you are getting for your money. Ask yourself if it is worth it to you to pay $80 a month for something that gives you good health, confidence, and self-defense skills. On the other hand, if all the other schools in the area seem to be providing the same benefits for $40 a month, is it still worth it to you to pay $80? It very well might be, if you consider the location, convenience, instructor, and friendship with the other students.

While we don't have a solid answer on the cost issue, we do offer two cautions:

1. Be wary of schools that charge much less than $40 a month or much more than $100 a month, unless that is within the average price range of similar schools in your area. As in most areas of commerce, there's likely to be something wrong with a product sold too cheaply or too expensively.

2. Watch out for hidden costs. Some schools might offer you very attractive special packages with extremely low monthly rates, but before you sign, directly ask for a list of all additional costs over the course of your membership. That low monthly rate might not be so low if there are required rank examinations that go up in price as the rank goes up. If special seminars are required, be sure to ask exactly how much they will cost.

Sensei Says

The value you receive for your payment for lessons is more important than the total amount of your payment.

Ouch!

Beware of hidden costs before you join a school. The reasonable monthly rate might not reflect equipment or examination costs.

Also be sure to ask about the cost of required equipment, uniforms, patches, books, videotapes, and anything and everything else that you will be expected to buy. These can all be hidden costs that you don't know about when you join.

Should I Sign a Contract?

In today's world, it's getting harder to find a karate school that doesn't require some sort of commitment like a contract. In fact, there are many different payment systems ranging from paying by the lesson to paying for a fixed number of months in advance, to signing multiyear contracts. Each of these methods has good points and bad points for both the school owner and the student. A method of paying by the class might appeal to you if you can attend only a limited number of times or have a constantly changing schedule, but the downside is that such an arrangement usually requires a large down payment or a substantial annual maintenance fee.

Paying month to month with no contract sounds good on the surface, but being late with a payment often carries a whopping penalty fee. Almost all schools require some sort of enrollment fee, and some that operate on a month-to-month basis will require you to pay that fee again every time you are late with a payment. Schools that require payment in advance for a fixed period of time—usually three months at a time—make out pretty well if you decide to quit because they have your money up front, and you don't get it back.

Contracts range in length from about three months to about five years. The good points of a contract are that you can usually pay less per month by enrolling for a longer time, and a contract commitment can be a good incentive to keep you going when you reach a plateau and feel like you don't want to go on. If you know that you have to keep paying, you'll probably keep going. The bad side of a contract is that you have to pay, whether you keep going or not.

Almost all contracts are iron-clad and difficult—usually impossible—to break, and you should consider this before signing one. Here are a couple important questions to ask before you sign on the dotted line:

➤ "What happens to my contract if I move away from the area?"

➤ "What happens if the school goes out of business or moves to another area?"

➤ "What happens if I have an auto accident and can't train for a period of weeks or months?"

A reputable school will have ready answers to all these questions, but you owe it to yourself to check with your state attorney general's office to see how the law applies to contracts in your area. Be sure to do this before you sign. Once you sign, it may be too late!

Will I Get Hurt?

Believe it or not, statistics tell us that karate-do has a lower injury rate than golf. The emphasis in karate classes is on control, and the atmosphere is very serious, so serious injuries are rare. Will you get bumps and bruises? Yes, of course you will, but you will get fewer bumps and bruises than if you play basketball, baseball, or soccer. Is there a chance that you could get seriously injured or even killed? Yes, there is, but no more chance of it, frankly, than having it happen while you are out walking your dog.

The biggest risk of serious injury in karate occurs while you are traveling to and from the dojo in your car or on your bike, and that's a risk you already take every day. Don't be surprised, though, when the instructor demands that you sign a release and waiver of liability before beginning your training. She knows that any physical activity carries some risk of injury, and she is just wisely protecting herself. And if you think that karate's release and waiver is detailed, you should see what they want you to sign when you join a boxing club or take skydiving lessons!

Who Certifies Whom?

We're sorry to say that no single governing body for karate oversees rankings and certifications. There are numerous governing bodies, both technical and sport-oriented, in the United States and abroad (see Appendix A, "Associations and Federations"), but no single umbrella organization oversees everybody. You should ask the instructor whether the school is certified by a larger governing organization, but don't be surprised if the school is completely independent. There's a lot of that in karate, and it's not all bad.

Some very good training can be found in some independent schools. On the other hand, there is comfort in knowing that the school's standards are shared by other schools and that there is some consistency of rankings and certifications among schools. Such certifications can help keep standards high, and they almost always provide opportunities for personal growth through special training seminars with high-level instructors in the organization.

Special training seminars and camps are a great way to obtain advanced instruction.

If you travel around the country a lot, it might be beneficial to you to be part of a larger organization so that you can get consistent training when you are in another city. The main thing to remember, though, is that you are seeking to learn Okinawan/Japanese karate-do, so if the school doesn't seem to be tied to any larger group, concentrate your questions on its roots. If the school is legitimate, instructors will be able to tell you its karate lineage, and you will be able to use this book to see where it came from.

The Least You Need to Know

➤ Good karate-do schools teach more than just punching and kicking.

➤ Good karate-do schools will always let you watch a class before you join.

➤ Tuition rates vary widely, but $40 to $100 a month is about average.

➤ Karate-do is a safe activity with very low injury rates.

➤ Finding a good karate teacher is more important than finding one who belongs to a big organization.

Chapter 6

Welcome to the Dojo

In This Chapter

➤ What to expect

➤ The rules of the dojo

➤ Learning the pecking order

➤ The importance of trying your best

➤ How to apply the rules to your daily life

➤ Preparing for your first class

Now that you have done your homework and decided on a school or two to visit, you can use the information in this chapter to minimize the culture shock you will likely experience the first time you walk into a karate dojo. Remember that karate is an Asian art, and most karate dojos reflect at least some aspects of Asian culture.

The Stuff on the Walls

One of the first things you will notice upon entering a karate dojo is that there are a number of unusual things hanging on the walls. Almost all dojos have a picture of the founder of their style of karate or a picture of the teacher's teacher hanging on the wall in the center of the training area. The picture is there to remind the students of their roots, and students and teachers generally bow in the direction of the picture, both before and after class, to show respect for the person pictured.

By bowing, they acknowledge the great contribution of the person to their art, and they remind themselves that they are part of a continuing legacy of human development. Bear in mind that karate students take this very seriously, so it would be a very bad idea for you to ask "Hey, who's the old guy in the picture?"

In some dojos, you might see a shelf or table under the picture, and it might contain pieces of fruit, rice cakes, flowers, small bells, or hanging strips of paper. Such a shelf or table is called the *kamiza,* which means "deity seat." The kamiza is a tradition that comes from the Buddhist practice of keeping a small altar inside the home. While the altar itself is a religious symbol, the kamiza in the dojo has come to be a symbol of remembrance of the founders and great masters of karate. While the food and flowers originally were meant as offerings to the spirits, they have now become a token gesture to remind students that their art has a long and deep background and that those who have gone before should be remembered for their efforts.

In addition to the central picture, the things hanging on the walls vary widely from school to school. Some of the more common things you might encounter include these:

1. **Scrolls or framed calligraphy.** These might be calligraphy representing the name of the style of karate taught in the school, or they might be the special principles emphasized in training. Sometimes they are just a favorite saying of the teacher, but always they are important to the teacher and the students.

2. **Name plaques.** It is a very old Japanese tradition to place the names of members of the dojo on small plaques and display them on the dojo wall. Usually, these plaques are reserved for people who have attained ranking.

3. **Weapons.** If the school does not teach weaponry as part of its curriculum, you might see only a *bo* (a long staff), *shinai* (a bamboo sword), or *bokken* (a wooden sword). These are used by the instructor at various times in training to illustrate the meaning of certain movements. If the school regularly teaches the use of weaponry, you are likely to see rows of weapons hanging on the walls or neatly arranged in racks against the walls.

Talk the Talk

The front of the dojo, where the picture hangs, is called the **shomen.** So, when the teacher or seniors say, "Shomen ni, rei," they are saying "Bow" (rei) to (ni) the front (shomen)."

Ouch!

Karate students take their heritage very seriously and always show great respect to their teachers and seniors. If you aren't sure of the proper word to use when referring to a teacher or senior, use the term **Sensei,** which means "teacher." If you are wrong, the teacher will correct you, but if you use some other term, she won't like it at all, and you'll be in big trouble!

68

4. Mirrors. Many schools have mirrors on the walls so that the students can see their form as they practice. Typically, the instructor will not allow students to gaze in the mirrors as they move in class because of the danger of crashing into other people. But before and after class, it is common to see students standing in front of the mirrors, endlessly practicing individual movements and checking their form.

A kamiza set up to honor the deceased founder of a karate school.

Most dojos have a picture of the founder of their style—in this case, along with calligraphy and name plaques.

The one thing that you will notice in any dojo that teaches traditional karate-do is an uncluttered floor area. The training floor is the single most important piece of "equipment" needed for effective karate training.

The Written Rules

While every dojo is different, they all share some common rules, both written and unwritten. The written rules might vary slightly from dojo to dojo, depending on the emphasis of the individual instructor, but almost all traditional karate dojos issue students written rules similar to the following:

Talk the Talk

Osu is a contraction of **osae** (meaning "to press or keep") and **shinobu** (meaning "patience"). Karate students say "Osu" to greet each other, to say good-bye, and to answer affirmatively. What they are saying, in effect, is "I am keeping my patience and doing my best to understand, to train, and to work with you."

Ouch!

Jewelry, rings, and other ornaments on the body are very dangerous because they can cut and tear flesh—yours and your training partner's.

1. Endeavor to understand and follow the guiding principles of karate-do:

   ➤ Endeavor to develop commendable character.

   ➤ Adhere to a life of honesty, integrity, and dignity.

   ➤ Put forth the utmost effort and spirit in all undertakings.

   ➤ Practice courtesy and compassion.

   ➤ Maintain strict self-control over temper.

2. Upon entering and leaving the dojo, salute (bow to) those present by saying "Osu" (pronounced *ohss*). Those present will respond by saying "Osu," unless they are taking a lesson.

3. Upon entering and leaving the training floor, salute (bow) and say "Osu."

4. If you enter the dojo after class has started and while warm-up exercises are being performed, perform a standing bow, and join in the class. If the warm-up exercises are finished and training has started, kneel in a formal position at the edge of the floor, and wait for the instructor to invite you to join. When you are invited to join, perform a seated bow (don't rush) and join the class.

5. Senior members must be kind to junior members and help them in studying.

6. Junior members should always show the greatest respect for senior members and salute (bow) when meeting the senior member.

7. When addressing other members, use the polite form (Mr. or Ms.).

8. Members must use polite language and respect the character of each other.

9. Eating, drinking, smoking, and chewing gum are prohibited in the dojo.

10. The wearing of jewelry or other ornaments is prohibited during training.

11. Always address the instructor as "Sensei," and salute (bow) when addressing the instructor.

12. Members should respect the instructor, and the instructor must always maintain a respectable character.

13. Remember that the dojo is an important place where you gain important knowledge and abilities. Therefore, do your part to keep it clean and orderly.

14. No shoes are allowed on the dojo floor.

Sensei Says

Respect for your seniors is the foundation of respect for others. Respect others, and they will return the respect to you.

The Unwritten Rules

The unwritten rules of traditional karate dojos are the hardest rules for non-Japanese karate students to understand. It's important to understand that traditional karate dojos are structured according to the Japanese system of *tate shakai*, which means "vertical society." Tate shakai means that the entire Japanese system of personal relationships is based on a system called *oyabun-kobun*. *Oya* means "parent," and *ko* means "child." Everyone in Japan understands this system, and everyone adheres to it. It is a system that not only defines the parent-child relationship, but that also defines the boss-employee relationship and the master-follower (or master-retainer) relationship.

Within the overall system of oyabun-kobun is the *sempai-kohai* system, which is what you will encounter in the dojo. Sempai-kohai is the structure of seniors and juniors, and it is based upon education, economics, and time. In every relationship, every Japanese person knows who is *oyabun*, who is *kobun*, who is *sempai*, and who is *kohai*. In the dojo, sempai-kohai most often is based on who has been training in karate the longest, or, rather, who has the most experience. Regardless of physical skills, the person with the most experience is always regarded as sempai, and the person with lesser experience is regarded as kohai.

The *oyabun-kobun* relationship is more likely to be found in the Japanese workplace and take on the form of supervisor-employee. The sempai-kohai relationship in the dojo, though, is more of the helpful senior to the less experienced junior. Rather than acting as a boss, the sempai is expected to help the kohai succeed.

The unwritten rules say that the seniors will be attentive to the needs of the juniors and will do all they can to help guide the juniors along the correct path of training. They also say that juniors will show utmost respect for their seniors and will do everything they can to do their best and try their hardest at all times.

Say What, Sensei?

One of the most important things you must learn is the proper way to address the sensei. Karate-do is a very formal, serious art, and the way you address the teacher sets the tone for the way the teacher will treat you. If the sensei says something that you don't understand, the last thing in the world you want to do is say "Huh?" or "I don't get it!" or "Say what, Sensei?" Put it in your mind before you even go to visit a school that the teacher's name is Sensei. It is not Pat, or Mike, or Alice, or Mr. Smith, or Ms. Jones. It is Sensei—period. Sensei is a term of respect and must be thought of as such. Unless the teacher specifically tells you otherwise, you should address the teacher as Sensei both in and out of the dojo.

When to Talk, When to Listen

Karate is a complicated art, and it's not always easy to understand what the teacher is trying to get you to do. There is nothing wrong with asking questions, but knowing when to ask is really important. Because karate is a serious, formal, complicated art, it adheres to rather strict guidelines about conduct in the dojo. Although you eventually will learn when to talk and when to listen, we can give you some guidelines here that will make that learning process a little bit easier:

1. Do not ask questions while the teacher is talking. This might seem obvious, but in addition to being rude, it might lead to an irritated karate teacher, and you sure don't need that in your life!

2. Always show that you are listening carefully by not asking irrelevant or unrelated questions. For example, if the teacher is detailing the execution of a straight punch and asks if you have any questions, don't ask how high you should raise your knee when doing a front kick. That kind of question shows that you aren't paying attention—or worse, that you aren't interested in what the teacher is talking about.

3. Don't stand there with your hand up in the air while the teacher is talking. A karate class is not grammar school, so always listen until the teacher is finished talking, and then raise your hand. When the teacher acknowledges you, bow politely, address the teacher as Sensei, and then ask your question. When you have your answer, bow again, and say "Thank you, Sensei."

You'll do okay if you keep in mind that karate is a formal art with a formal code of conduct. Conduct yourself formally and with dignity.

Try Your Best

A famous karate-do saying is "There is no dishonor in mistakes; there is no honor in not trying your best." We know that by now it must sound to you like there are an awful lot of rules, details, and formalities to learn in the dojo, and there are. But don't let this bum you out. Even if you can't remember all the rules and details right away (nobody expects you to, anyway), you can still get by just fine by making it clear that you are doing the very best you can do at all times. Remember the important principles of the dojo? Over and over again you see words such as *effort, sincerity,* and *spirit*. All these together tell you that if you try your best and give your training all the effort you can muster, your little mistakes will be overlooked. In karate-do, it's not how well you do it that counts, but how hard you try to do it.

Sensei Says

Karate *is* like hot water. If you do not give it heat constantly, it will again become cold water.

—Gichin Funakoshi

From the Dojo to the Street—Follow the Rules

We know that the seniority system and a lot of the formality of the dojo probably seem foreign to you, but we want you to know that just about everything you do in the dojo can be reflected in your everyday life and can make you a happy person. For starters, the health benefits of regular training carry over directly into your everyday life, without you having to even think about it.

Beyond that most obvious benefit, though, many other benefits can be yours, if you think about them and want them to be.

Be Aware

Let's start with awareness. If you think about it, you can probably see that a lot of the formality of how you act in class, such as waiting for the teacher to finish before asking a question, is actually designed to increase your awareness of what is going on around you. That kind of formality forces you to focus on the other person—in this case, the teacher—rather than on yourself. It teaches you to listen and to have patience while you're listening.

If you think about it, you can apply that same focus and patience in your daily life. When you are discussing something important with somebody, you can (if you take the time to think about

Ouch!

Losing your awareness in the dojo can get you hurt when people crash into you. Losing your awareness on the street can get you mugged—or worse!

it) apply your focus and patience to them. You can tell yourself to listen completely, just as you do with the sensei, and then offer your questions and comments. This not only helps you more clearly understand what the other person is saying, but it also goes a long way in avoiding arguments, which often are triggered or aggravated by interruptions. Likewise, tuning your senses to what is going on around you in the dojo can be applied when you are walking down the street. Be as aware of your position on the street as you are in the dojo, and you will make yourself far less vulnerable to danger.

For the most part, you will be able to see a bad situation coming and not be surprised.

Sensei Says

Always think and devise ways to live the precepts of karate-do every day.

Giving It Your All

Where trying your best and putting forth your best effort are concerned, just imagine how much better you could be in school or on the job by always applying yourself the same way you do in the dojo.

In fact, if you consciously try to behave according to the dojo rules of conduct in your everyday life, you'll find that they work just as well on the street as they do in karate class. When you treat people with respect and deference, they will tend to treat you the same way.

Karate Do's

While life with karate may seem very complicated right now, there is actually a very simple way to keep things on the right foot. Here's a list to help you out:

1. Always come to the dojo with a clean body and a clean uniform.
2. When you go to the dojo, be prepared to train. If you are too sick to train, you are too sick to watch, unless the instructor specifically gives you permission to do so.
3. Take off your shoes when you enter the dojo.
4. Try your best to learn the Japanese terms that the teacher and seniors use.
5. Get to class a little bit early; it will show that you are eager to learn.

Karate Don'ts

Just as there are some simple rules of thumb for which things you should do, there are also a few simple things you should not do. Here's a list:

1. Never, ever talk in class, unless you are instructed to do so.
2. Once you walk onto the training floor, do not attempt to leave without permission.
3. Don't use profanity of any kind in the dojo.
4. Don't ask to use the bathroom during class. Take care of that beforehand.

Now that you are somewhat familiar with what's going on around you in the dojo, you're ready to try your first class.

Karate Minute

Japanese is the universal language of karate-do. This makes it possible for people from many different countries to get together and practice karate or compete in tournaments.

Scared Stiff: Your First Class

Even armed with all the wonderful information you have found in this book, you're still going to be scared (at least really nervous) when you actually go to the dojo for your first class. The class might be a one-on-one session with you and the sensei or one of the sensei's assistants, or it might be with a group, varying in size from 2 or 3 people to 12 or more.

Whatever the size, though, the first thing you have to do is conquer the feeling that you are being watched by everybody else in the room and that they think you are awkward and silly looking. Believe us when we tell you that everybody else in the room is so focused on his or her own awkwardness that the others have no time at all to think about you.

So, take a few deep breaths, relax your tense neck and shoulders, and try to just concentrate on what the teacher is saying to you. You've got nothing to lose and everything to gain, so you really need to relax and just go with the flow.

Ouch!

As a beginner, tension is your worst enemy because it can lead to injury. If you are too tense, your muscles can go into spasms, cause cramps, and even become bruised. Relaxation is essential.

Karate Minute

Years ago, when Japanese martial arts were used primarily on the battlefield and for killing enemies, a master usually had only one student at a time. The student was called **uchi-deshi,** which means "inside student" and was derived from the fact that the student lived in the master's house and studied his art full-time. He also took care of all the master's needs, including cooking and cleaning.

What Happens in Class?

Typically, a first class will begin with some light warm-up and stretching exercises, to get the body ready for karate techniques. Usually right after that, the teacher will give you some information about the type of karate you are studying and perhaps will explain a little bit about its history. Next you will be introduced to the protocols for bowing that are used in that dojo, and you'll be introduced to your first few words of Japanese. Don't panic! Nobody expects you to remember them on your first night.

The instructor will then introduce you to the most basic body positions and stance, and most likely will start you out with a basic punching, blocking, or kicking technique. Some instructors like to take new students through a variety of techniques and stance, while others might show you only one or two things while emphasizing the philosophy or body mechanics of the art. Either way, your job is to try to relax and concentrate on what the instructor is saying.

It is highly unlikely that the instructor will push you to do anything too vigorous the first time around, but still the exercises might make some of your muscles sore, and you should expect that.

As we said before, your biggest challenge will be to forget about how awkward you feel. Everybody feels awkward when they first try karate techniques, so you're in good company.

Don't Be Late!

With the exception of blurting out "Who's the old guy in the picture?" probably the worst mistake you can make at your first lesson is being late. Showing up late irritates the instructors because they probably have prepared for a first-time class, and your late arrival screws up their class plan. If your first lesson is a group lesson and you arrive late, it puts you behind the eight ball, trying to figure out what you missed (forget it, you can't figure it out) and trying to catch up with the others. If your lesson was set for one-on-one, your tardiness has caused the instructor to stand around, cooling her heels, and probably has left her seething. Being late is just not a good idea—don't do it.

It is better to reschedule a first lesson at another time rather than be late for it.

Sensei Says

Always arrive early for class to show respect for your training and courtesy to your sensei.

When to Bow

The simple answer to the question of when to bow during your first lesson is simple: Bow all the time—really. You have this book, so you already know that you're supposed to bow when you enter the dojo, bow when you meet the instructor and seniors, bow when you enter and leave the dojo floor, and bow when you leave the dojo. In between, if you have any doubts about what you are supposed to be doing, bow again. It will reflect positively on your sincere attitude, and if you are bowing too much, the instructor will let you know about it. Bowing shows both respect and humility, and you really can't have too much of either when you first enter a karate dojo.

Hold That Pose!

Okay, we've made the first lesson sound pretty easy, except for the awkwardness thing, but there is one thing that might not be quite so easy. Karate instructors have a habit of positioning students in a particular stance with tension pushing against deeply bent knees, and then seeming to forget that they put the students in that position. As the forgetful instructor continues to talk, the leg muscles start to burn a little bit, then ache a little more, and then twitch and shake. You would think that the instructor would notice this and ask the students to stand up and rub their legs, but karate instructors frequently seem oblivious to the problem. Indeed, they have even been known to firmly push a student's leg back into a bent position upon discovering that she has straightened it. The purpose of this activity is threefold:

1. It starts the leg-strengthening process needed for karate techniques.

2. It gives you your first firsthand hint that karate training is not all as easy as the first lesson makes it seem.

3. It starts you on the road to discovering the difference between pain that is annoying (which this is) and pain that is the result of an injury that might be incapacitating (which this is not).

We've warned you, so be prepared—and whatever you do, hold that pose!

Huh?

Especially during your first class, it is very important that you listen closely to what the instructor has to say and to ask questions when you don't understand. The most important thing to remember, though, is to ask questions at the appropriate time and in the appropriate way. When the instructor says something you don't understand, don't say "Huh?" If the instructor asks if you understand, don't say "Yeah." This kind of behavior indicates a lack of respect for the instructor, and mutual respect between instructor and student is one of the cornerstones of karate-do. Remember to wait until the instructor has finished speaking to raise your hand. When you are acknowledged, bow and ask your question politely. When you get an answer, bow and say "Thank you, Sensei."

Mental Notes and Written Quotes

The dojo you join will almost always give you some kind of written materials or will direct you to books and videos that might be helpful to your training. The most important thing, though, is for you to decide right from the first lesson to make as many mental notes as possible while the lesson is going on and to then make written notes as soon as possible after class has ended. We have found that, over time, the unusual quotes a sensei gives during class or the sensei's unique phrasing of a particular concept come back with enhanced meaning—often years later. Your written notes don't have to be copious, but you should make them meaningful to you so that you can use them as a training guide in the future. A typical note in your karate diary might just say "Learned rising block-reverse punch combination. Main point is rotate the body fully for both techniques. Easy alone. Hard with partner." Not only will your diary prove to be a valuable tool for practicing by yourself, but it also will show you just how far you have progressed in a short time.

Talk the Talk

Soji means "chores," and it is the word used to describe the chore of cleaning the dojo floor by hand with wet rags after a class.

The End

Different dojos have different routines for ending class sessions. Some have people perform a standing bow to the front and then to the sensei. Some require a kneeling bow to the front, to the sensei, and to the seniors.

Some dojos include a recitation of the principles of the dojo in combination with some of the previous routines, while others provide students with rags and a bucket to clean the dojo floor.

No matter what is required in the dojo you join, the one thing you should be sure to do is to thank the sensei verbally for the training you received. When this is done as a formal part of the ending routine, the students all at once, following the bow to the sensei, say "Thank you, Sensei!" The sensei acknowledges this either with a slight bow or a thank you. If it is not a part of the formal routine, you should try to stop by the sensei on your way out and say "Thank you for the class, Sensei." A thank you to the sensei after class lets her know how much you appreciate her willingness to share her knowledge with you. Her thanks comes back to you for being a good student and trying your best. Thanks to the sempai are also a good idea, for the same reasons. Honest thanks help everybody feel that what they are doing is truly worthwhile and appreciated.

A formal bow to the sensei at the end of class.

Soji in action.

The Least You Need to Know

➤ Karate dojo decorations have more meaning than mere ornamentation.

➤ Both written and unwritten rules are important in the dojo.

➤ Dojo rules are valuable both in and out of the dojo.

➤ Trying your best is more important than doing the technique well.

➤ Fear and nervousness are the worst parts of your first lesson.

Dressed to Kill: The Uniform

Have you ever noticed how in every sport and almost every art, the clothing worn by the participants sets the tone for the activity? Aside from the colors and numbers that separate sport teams, think about how what they wear affects the way they play. Baseball players obviously are dressed for play in the sun. Their collarless uniforms permit maximum freedom of movement for their necks when they are looking skyward for a fly ball, and their hats provide shade for their faces. Football players' uniforms are heavier and much larger to accommodate all the padding they must wear. A baseball cap visor on their headgear wouldn't last five seconds in a scrimmage; it would be crushed and torn to ribbons. Instead, their headgear is very hard and shock-absorbent to help protect their heads in collisions.

The point is that sport uniforms are utilitarian in their design—they are designed to fit the movements of the sport. As you'll see in a minute, karate uniforms are designed with karate movements in mind, too.

Looking the Part

Can you imagine a baseball player trying to play while wearing a football uniform? Of course not. With all that padding, he wouldn't even be able to swing the bat—and running down a fly ball in the outfield would be impossible. Likewise, a football player wearing a baseball uniform and cap would be squashed the first time he made contact with another player. Even worse, think about throwing a basketball uniform into that mix—ouch! Basketball uniforms don't have legs, arms, or necks because the players don't need them. Think about wearing a basketball uniform in a baseball game! Your skin would burn before the first inning was over, and you don't even want to think about what would happen to you if you tried to slide into a base! It's probably best also not to try to think about what would happen if you tried wearing a basketball uniform in a football game—it wouldn't be a pretty sight.

A proper uniform not only is designed to permit maximum freedom of movement when you train, but it also contributes to the tone of seriousness in karate classes.

But because karate is also an art, the uniform serves more than just a practical function. Think about other arts and how the performers dress, and you'll see that their clothing meets more functions than just the practical. Let's say that you're getting ready to go to a classical piano recital. Would you expect the pianist to be wearing jeans and a torn sweatshirt? Of course not! You would expect to see a tuxedo or a formal gown. Jeans and a sweatshirt just wouldn't contribute properly to the atmosphere. On the other hand, you probably would laugh out loud if you saw a performer in a tux or a formal gown at a country music jamboree. Again, the uniform just wouldn't fit the tone of the concert. There, the jeans and sweatshirt might be just fine.

It's not that the pianist couldn't play just as well in jeans and a sweatshirt. It's that the tone of the performance would be ruined because of such outlandish attire. The pianist wouldn't look the part, just as the country music performer wouldn't look the part in a tuxedo.

In traditional karate-do, the uniform (*gi*, pronounced *ghee*) is designed for both practical and esthetic reasons, so wearing the proper uniform in the proper way is of utmost importance. From a practical point of view, the karate gi is designed to permit maximum freedom of movement in all directions, to accommodate karate's widely varied techniques.

The jacket fits the torso loosely, and the armpits are cut extra wide. The sleeves do not cling to the arms, and

Talk the Talk

A karate uniform is called a **gi** (pronounced *ghee*).

Talk the Talk

Wabi is a Japanese esthetic term meaning "intentional understatement."

82

they extend about to the middle of the forearm, which permits free use of the hands and wrists without danger of getting the fingers tangled in long sleeves. Jacket lengths vary, but they always extend down at least to the middle of the buttocks, and never lower than the bottom of the hips. If they were any longer, they could restrict leg movement.

The pants have a waist that is much larger than regular pants, and they are secured with either drawstrings, elastic, or both. This permits you to keep your pants up without the help of a belt or suspenders. The hips and legs of the pants also are cut extra wide to permit freedom of movement, and they should never cling to your body. A large gusset is sewn into the crotch of the pants, which enables you to stretch your legs farther and kick higher without embarrassing yourself by ripping your britches. The pant legs extend down to only about the middle of your shins, which ensures that you won't get your feet tangled in them when you step, kick, or jump.

In traditional karate-do, as opposed to newer, eclectic martial arts, the esthetic emphasis in the gi is on simplicity. Because karate-do is a Japanese art, this emphasis on simplicity is not surprising. Simplicity is an integral part of Japanese art and architecture that comes from the Zen tradition. The Japanese word for this simplicity is *wabi*, which can best be described as "intentional understatement." Wabi is seen in Japanese art, architecture, flower arranging, tea ceremonies, and even karate-do. Arts and crafts that spring from the Zen tradition are not explicit, in that the artist rarely draws a complete, detailed picture of the subject. What is drawn, painted, or sculpted is usually incomplete or unbalanced and serves as a suggestion of the subject.

The suggestion is that there is something missing, and that to find it, we have to consciously try. It requires disciplined restraint to create paintings or pottery or flower arrangements that are simple and elegant, and this disciplined restraint is the simple and elegant nature of wabi.

Karate Minute

The complete, formal name of the karate **gi** is **do-gi** (pronounced *doh-ghee*), meaning, "the uniform in which the way (do) is practiced." Early on, Japanese instructors abandoned this phrase because every time they said it, English-speaking people would fall down laughing, thinking they were saying "doggie!"

Color Matters

The white (or sometimes black), unadorned karate gi is a perfect example of wabi. It tells us nothing about the skill or nature of the person wearing it. It gives no indication of his or her ability, and it does not confuse us with elaborate designs, flowing lettering, or informative patches.

Sensei Says

It is not the decorations on the outside of the gi that matter; it is the character of the person inside the gi that matters.

When the gi is white, it symbolizes purity—the purity of motives of the person wearing it. Such people do not set themselves apart from others with memorable costuming. Rather, they acknowledge with their simple gi that they are fundamentally the same as everybody else, and that their performance will have to speak for itself. In this sense, others are left to fill in the gaps—and, just as when we view a simple character drawn by a Zen master, we must see for ourselves if there is more to this person.

Wrapped and Tied

Okay, it's time to try on that new gi. Here's how to do it:

The first thing to do, after you take the gi out of the package and take off your street clothes, is to hold up the pants in front of you. If your gi is the drawstring type, there will be one or more loops of fabric sewn into the front of it. That's your first clue on a drawstring gi: The loops go in the front. If your gi has an elasticized waist, it also will have a string sewn into the elastic waistband. That's your clue on an elastic-waist gi: The adjustment string goes in the front.

1. Put the pants on, and adjust the waistband to fit your waist snugly.

   If the waist is elasticized, pull the adjustment strings until the waist is snug, tie the strings in a bow, and tuck them inside the pants.

   If your gi is a drawstring type, the long drawstrings will be hanging out on each side. Grasp one in each hand, and slowly pull them equally until the pants feel snug against your waist. It's a good idea to then pull them just a bit tighter, because they tend to loosen a little bit during training.

2. When you have adjusted the waist, run the drawstrings through the one or more loops on the front of the pants, and tie them in a bow or a half-bow at the center of your abdomen.

3. Wrap each side of the hanging end of the bow around the strings on your stomach. This reinforces the bow you have just tied, and it prevents the loose ends from hanging down under your jacket.

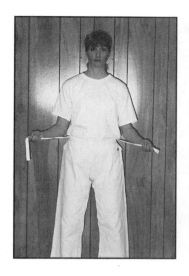  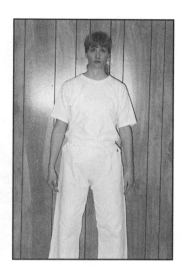

Now it's time for the jacket.

1. Put the jacket on as you would any jacket or shirt. You'll notice that there are four strings attached to the jacket, two on each side. You will use these to secure your jacket and keep it from flopping open during training.

2. Place the right side of the jacket against your chest and abdomen, and cross the left side over on top of the right. It's important to do it this way because doing it the other way (right over left) is how they wrap bodies in Japan to prepare them for cremation, and nobody wants to be mistaken for dead!

3. Now, to make your jacket even on both sides, even up the bottom edge of the right and left sides and tie a bow or a half-bow in the two strings on the right side.

4. Lift up the bottom of the left side, and tie a bow or a half-bow in the two strings on the left side. This will secure your jacket and get you ready to put on your belt.

Ouch!

Never secure any part of your karate gi with clips or safety pins. These can become dislodged during training and can pierce your skin.

As a general rule, men do not wear undershirts under their gi jackets, but it's not unheard of. If you would like to wear an undershirt under your gi, you should ask your sensei or one of the senior members whether that is acceptable. If they say it's okay, go ahead. If they say no, just grin and bear it for a couple of classes—you'll get used to it in no time.

Women always wear some kind of garment under their gi jacket. The most popular gi undergarments for women include sport bras, body stockings, T-shirts, or some combination of these. If you are in doubt about what to wear, just ask some of the other women in the dojo what they wear. They will be glad to help you.

Karate Minute

Several gi manufacturers in Japan manufacture gis especially for women. These gis have another set of tie strings sewn into the lapels of the gi at the top of the chest, and you might want to ask your instructor about this. Some women also attach Velcro strips to the lapels of their gi to help keep the jacket closed.

Tie It Square

Now that you have your gi wrapped and tied properly, it's time to tackle the belt. Tying a karate belt is a bit more complicated than putting on the gi, but it might be easier if you remember that your basic objective is to tie it in a square knot in the center of your body. Still, almost nobody gets it tied right the first time, or the second time, or lots of times. If you have trouble with it, don't hesitate to ask another member who knows how to do it.

The most common mistake in tying the karate belt is tying it in a half-knot so that one end hangs straight down and the other stays on top. In Japan, karate students of the Shinto religion see this as a symbol of death.

The instructions we give here are of a general nature, but be aware that some schools have very specific rules about how the belt must be tied, so be sure to ask before you put it on the first time.

1. Place the exact center of the belt against your abdomen.

2. Wrap the belt around your waist, crossing it in back (it doesn't matter which side crosses over), and bring the ends out evenly in front of you.

Talk the Talk

The Japanese word for belt is **obi** (pronounced *oh-bee*).

Ouch!

Never, ever wash a colored belt! Washing it will cause it to fade and change color, and as hard as you worked for that colored belt, you sure don't want it to change until your next promotion.

87

3. Bring the right end across your body, and press it against your abdomen.

4. Cross the left end over the top of the right, and wrap it all the way around both layers of the belt you have against your stomach.

5. Turn the bottom end over.

6. Wrap the top end around the bottom end.

7. Pull both ends firmly until they are secure.

The belt should be worn loosely around the hips and should hang a little lower on the abdomen than it does in back. In other words, don't wear it up high on your waist, like you would a regular belt. A very good reason for this is that when a training partner aims a kick or punch at your stomach, they will aim it above your belt. If there is any contact, the higher your belt is, the more the blow will hurt. When the belt is worn low, the strong lower and middle abdominal muscles will be able to take the shock better than would your solar plexus, which is where the shock from the blow will go if your belt is worn high. Wearing the belt low on the abdomen also will help you be more aware of your body center because the belt will press against your lower abdomen when you tense your muscles.

Going to and From

Now you know how to put your gi on and tie the belt, but after that first class, you're also going to have to know how to transport it. That's right, in karate-do there's a right way and a wrong way to do everything—including transporting your gi to and from class. The easiest way, which is almost always acceptable, is to carry your gi and belt in a gym bag. In the dojo, a gym bag is called a "gi bag." (That's not a rule; it's just the way it seems to work out.)

If you do not carry your gi in a bag, then you need to know how to fold it and carry it properly. Remember that karate-do teaches you to be orderly in your thinking and prepared for any possible surprise attack. If you have your karate gi slung haphazardly over your arm with pieces dangling, it's likely that you'd get tangled up in it if you had to deal with a mugger. So, for your protection and mental exercise, here's the right way to do it:

1. Fold the jacket in half, evenly.
2. Fold the jacket sleeves over the jacket.
3. Fold the pants in half, evenly.
4. Place the folded pants on top of the jacket.
5. Starting at the jacket collar, roll the pants and jacket together, tightly.

   Note: At this point schools and philosophies differ. Some instructors will tell you to tie your belt around your folded gi, while others will insist (strongly) that you fold your belt inside your gi. Make sure to ask your instructor the method your school uses.

Ouch!

If you get to class and realize that you have forgotten your belt, it is impolite to put on gym clothes or shorts to take the class. Just confess your error to your instructor, and ask to borrow or buy another belt.

Sensei Says

As a matter of courtesy and support for your school, always ask your sensei about buying a new gi before going to a martial art supply company to buy it.

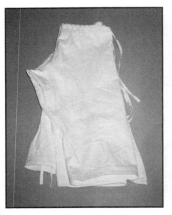
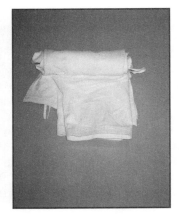

Ouch!

Wearing a gi that is too small for you can actually restrict your movement so much that you might strain or tear muscles, especially in your legs. It is better to wear a gi that is a little too big than one that is too small.

What About Size and Style?

Unfortunately, karate uniforms do not come in sizes that match any normal sizing standard. To make matters worse, sizes vary considerably among manufacturers, and lighter-weight gis generally are cut smaller than heavier-weight gis. Gi sizes range from 000 (for really tiny kids) to 7 or 8 (for a NFL linebacker). On average, though, a 6- to 8-year-old child will wear a size 1 or 2 if they are of average height and weight, and a size 3 if they weigh closer to 100 pounds. A size 4 is for a person about 5 feet, 6 inches tall, and a size 5 is for a person 5 feet, 9 or 10 inches. Uniforms usually come with a white belt, and some manufacturers will allow you to mix and match pant and jacket sizes to obtain a more comfortable fit.

Uniforms are manufactured in two basic styles: 100 percent cotton or cotton/polyester blends. There are positive and negative sides to each style. For 100 percent cotton, the main benefit is that cotton "breathes" as you perspire and allows more air flow around your body.

Karate Minute

Years ago in Okinawa, before karate became a do art form, men practiced karate in their underwear or in a loincloth similar to the ones worn by sumo wrestlers. This kept them cool in the hot, humid air of Okinawa, but, then again, there were no women training in karate at that time.

Cotton is also more absorbent, which has a cooling effect on the body when things get hot. Cotton absorbs perspiration, and air flowing through that perspiration and through the cotton helps cool your body. The biggest negative for cotton, however, is that it shrinks. Don't believe what manufacturers tell you about pre-shrunk cotton: Cotton always shrinks, no matter what you do to it. Over time, this can be distressing, because a really nice-fitting cotton gi will gradually get smaller. (If you put a cotton gi in a heated dryer, by the way, it will shrink overnight—you won't have to wait for it to change size.) Another negative to consider is that cotton gis are, on average, significantly more expensive than their cotton and polyester blend counterparts.

The big advantages of cotton and polyester blend gis are that they last longer than cotton gis, they tend to look less wrinkled when you put them on, and generally you can throw them in a heated dryer without fear that they will change size on you. They also tend to be cheaper than pure cotton gis. Still, cotton and polyester blend gis are by far the least popular type of gi among karate students, and for good reasons. They are hot because they don't "breathe" like cotton, and they go limp and tend to cling to the body when you perspire. Not only does this not look good, but it also feels awful and can actually restrict your body movements.

Ouch!

Never put a cotton gi in a heated dryer because it will shrink too much, and you will have to buy a new one.

Some instructors suggest polyester blend gis for beginning children because of their economy. Kids grow fast, and the gi will have to be replaced as they grow, so a cheaper gi makes sense.

At intermediate and advanced levels, though, instructors almost universally recommend (and, in some case, require) a heavyweight canvas karate gi. Its positives far outweigh its negatives. Besides, it makes a louder snapping sound when you punch and kick, which makes everybody feel good.

What, No Colors?

As we explained earlier in this chapter, simplicity is a key element of karate-do's esthetics, so it is unlikely that you will see very many colored gis in a karate dojo, with the exception of black. In some dojos, black gis are favored over white gis as a matter of the traditions of a particular style of karate. There are many theories about why some schools choose to wear black. Some say it is because the founder of the style wore black, so everybody in the style does, too. Some say that a black gi is to be worn only by black belts. Others say that only a black gi top should be worn over white pants. Some say that they wear a black gi like an arm band—as a token of grief for the passing of the founder of their style. Still others use a black gi or a black gi top to indicate those in the dojo who have ranking in weaponry. In fact, there are probably dozens of valid reasons to wear a black gi instead of a white one, but it doesn't really matter. The color is not as important as the simplicity and orderliness of the gi.

Worldwide, the white karate gi is by far the most prevalent and is, in fact, the only color permitted by the largest organizations in international competition.

Pins and Patches

Where pins on the karate gi are concerned, we have one word: No! They are dangerous to both you and your training partners, and, like all other metallic objects, they have no place in the karate dojo. Some people who like to collect pins issued in commemoration of special events or organizational logo pins often will attach them to their gym bag or to a towel. That's fine for display—they just shouldn't make it onto your karate gi.

Patches are another matter. Some organizations and some schools actually require their members to wear the organizational or school patch on their gis. This has been a common practice in Japan and around the world for many years. Wearing the organizational patch can be a matter of pride, and it can create team spirit among competitors. It also can be a valuable way of identifying who comes from where at a large seminar or tournament, and it can be a tasteful and profitable fund-raiser for organizations and schools.

As a general rule, when patches are permitted, a single patch is worn on the left breast of the karate gi. Sometimes, although rarely, a second patch is permitted on the sleeve of the gi. Although there are exceptions to every rule, almost never do traditional karate-do schools allow the wearing of more than two patches on the gi. Patches are much more common on streetwear jackets and gym bags.

A couple noteworthy exceptions to the two-patch rule are small patches worn to indicate additional ranking (usually in weaponry) and small patches issued to children like Scouting merit badges. The latter are becoming more popular as karate students are entering the dojo at younger ages. To keep children's interest level high, some instructors will divide a ranking level into numerous small pieces and then issue the child a cloth badge or patch for each piece mastered. When a child has accumulated the appropriate number of badges, he then becomes qualified to take the regular ranking examination. Children would not be permitted, however, to wear their patches or badges in most national and international competitions.

Cleanliness Is Next to Enlightenment

Karate training is a vigorous activity, so it makes you sweat a lot. Of course, this means that your gi gets pretty much soaked every time you practice. On behalf of your classmates, we ask that you wash your gi every time you wear it. You might get away with wearing it once, airing it out, and wearing it again, but don't try to wear it a third time! A smelly karate gi is obnoxious, offensive, and distracting.

Keeping your gi clean is really not much of a chore if you train two or three times a week. But if you train more than that, we strongly recommend that you buy two or three gis and alternate their use. Your classmates will smile upon you.

The Least You Need to Know

➤ Choosing the proper uniform sets the tone for your training.

➤ A karate uniform is specially designed to allow maximum freedom of movement without tearing.

➤ White and black uniforms are usually the only colors allowed in karate-do schools.

➤ Karate-do schools almost always limit the number of patches you can wear on your uniform.

➤ Keeping your uniform clean and neat is a must.

Part 3

Let's Get Moving

You're ready to get started! But remember, actually doing karate is much different than talking about karate, watching karate movies, and playing karate video games. First and foremost, karate is a physical art, and your body learns at its own pace. Part 3 is your comprehensive guide to learning karate principles and techniques—the "how to" of karate training. We start by building our foundation in Chapter 8. Here, you'll learn how to learn—by letting go of expectations and preconceptions (as the Zen saying goes, by "getting out of your own way"). You'll see how standing and bowing clearly express your character and your intent. You'll learn to strengthen, loosen, and use your body so that your karate becomes as smooth, powerful, fast, and effective as possible.

Chapters 9 through 13 take you step by step through the basics: stances, the foundation of your techniques; blocking, your first line of defense; punching, the heart of your arsenal; striking, 360 degrees of effectiveness; and kicking, your advantage against bigger and stronger opponents. Study well! Train hard! Have fun!

Chapter 8

How to Practice Karate

> **In This Chapter**
>
> ➤ What to concentrate on when learning karate
>
> ➤ How, when, and why to bow in karate
>
> ➤ Getting your body ready to train
>
> ➤ Why your breathing and eye position are so important
>
> ➤ Different ways to use your body to make more speed and more power

Okay, you're ready to start learning and mastering karate's techniques and principles. Keep in mind that, as a karate-ka your goal is not to simply learn these techniques intellectually, but also to learn them physically so that you can actually use them. Karate training is designed to teach your body what to do in situations that don't give you time to think and plan. After all, there's a big difference between knowing what you *should* do in an emergency—say, when you're grabbed from nowhere by someone in a dark parking lot—and actually being able to do it. This is the place where your mind, body, and attitude will all meet together to form a powerful whole.

Karate works best when it is learned as a combination of traditions and actions that are based on well-understood principles. This chapter introduces you to traditional karate's most common and important ritual—bowing. Additionally, you will learn the essentials of loosening and strengthening your body as you prepare to train. And finally, you will see how karate's basic concepts and the most fundamental principles of human movement, momentum and leverage, apply to each and every technique you use.

Open Eyes and Open Mind

At some point in your karate career, you will undoubtedly hear a version of the following story. An energetic young martial artist goes to the dojo of a famous teacher and asks to be accepted as a student. The teacher invites the student in, and as they sit waiting for a pot of tea to steep, the student begins to tell the teacher about all the battles he has won, the techniques he has mastered, and most importantly, what he wants this teacher to teach him. The teacher smiles politely. He listens. He waits. Finally the tea is ready and the teacher begins pouring a cup for his visitor. The cup fills to the brim and the teacher, still looking at the student, continues to pour more tea. The cup overflows until tea spills across the table and onto the floor. Quickly, the student jumps up and yells "Stop, master, stop. The cup is full. You can't put any more in." The master, still smiling and looking at the student says "Yes. The cup is just like you. Already full. I will not be able to teach you anything until you come to me with a cup that is empty."

Talk the Talk

"Rei!" *is the verbal command given to bow. A* **karate-ka** *is a person who practices the way of karate.*

Ouch!

Watch your distance when you bow to an opponent before sparring. The usual distance to stand is six to eight feet from each other. You don't want to be so close that if your opponent makes a mistake and attacks before he should, you are too close to respond. Always be on your guard!

As a karate student, you are entering a learning environment that may be very different from what you are used to. Be open to the experience. Aside from the techniques, you will learn new ways to act, new ways to carry yourself, and new things to be aware of. Be alert and pay attention to what goes on around you, but relax enough to let yourself learn. Immerse yourself totally in the lessons you learn without setting unreasonable limitations and expectations on yourself or others.

For example, one of the most fundamental things about karate that usually seems the strangest to Westerners (aside from all the yelling, bare feet, and wearing your pajamas out in public) is the focus on etiquette, formality, and ritual. These, however, are all essential parts of karate training and contribute directly to its overall effectiveness.

Bowing 101

Although karate is an international art and is practiced worldwide, it maintains many of the traditions and customs of its countries of origin, Okinawa and Japan. One of these traditions is bowing.

There are many reasons you will bow in karate, but basically, as a *karate-ka* you bow to indicate humility, demonstrate your emotional control, and to show your respect and acknowledgment of others. Think of it like shaking hands, standing to greet somebody you respect, and removing your hat in somebody's house or before sitting down to dinner. The bow you use in karate is about your relationship to the dojo, your instructor, and the people you train with. It has no religious connotations.

Although customs vary slightly among dojos and styles (for example, bowing from either a standing or sitting position at the beginning and end of a training session), you will generally bow in the following situations:

1. At the entrance of the dojo, when you enter and leave.

2. When you step on and off the training area.

3. When you first see your instructor at the dojo.

4. At the verbal command "Rei!" given by a senior student or instructor at the beginning and end of class, often from a formal seated position in a brief group ceremony.

5. To your opponent, before and after sparring (either in training or in competition)

6. Before and after performing your kata, either in training or in competition.

7. Before and after approaching your instructor with a question.

8. When you receive an award, trophy, promotion, or other indication of merit.

Standing Bow

Nobody likes to shake hands with someone who tries to crush the fingers, or who gives you a limp hand to wiggle around for a few seconds. Bowing is much the same way. Bowing should project humility but not subservience; respect but not arrogance; and spirit but not fanaticism. You will usually bow from a standing position.

1. Stand with your heels together, your back straight, and your head up. Your arms should rest at your sides, with your hands by your hips and your palms against the sides of your body.

2. Bow from the waist, keeping your back and neck straight. Allow your line of vision to align with your head angle, so as you bow you will be looking at your opponent's legs and the ground.

3. Bow to a 25- to 45-degree angle, and hold the bow for about half a second.

Proper bowing form.

Sitting Bow

Formal classes usually begin and end with a short period of preparation or meditation. As the class is called to order, you and everyone else will quickly fall into place facing the front of the dojo. Don't worry about where to go; your place is based on your rank and experience. If you are the instructor, you stand in front of the class. If you are one of the seniors of the club, usually of black belt level, you form a line to the side of the instructor. If you are one of the general students in the class, you are in a line behind the instructor in order of seniority. If you are a beginner, you are at the end of that line.

Karate classes meditate before and after class. Note the position of the instructor in front, the senior students to the side, and the general class, lined up by rank behind.

Again, dojos and styles vary somewhat in how they start class, but generally this is what will happen. At the command of the senior student, everyone kneels into *seiza*, a formal sitting position (see the following figure). At the command *"Mokusoh,"* the class begins a brief period of formal meditation. During this period, keep your eyes so lightly closed that you can see a little light where your eyelids meet (this will take some practice). Concentrate on relaxing your breathing and clearing your mind of thoughts that could interfere with your concentration during practice. After all, it's tough to think about perfecting your *kata* or sparring with that tough new brown belt if you are worried about bills, work, or whether you can get a date on Friday night. At the command *"Yame,"* open your eyes. At the command *"Rei!"* bow, along with the class, to the front (shomen), to the instructor (sensei), and to the senior students (sempai).

EEEE-YA!!!

Talk the Talk

Seiza is a formal sitting position.

1. Stand with your heels together, your back straight, and your head up. Your arms should rest at your sides, with your hands by your hips and your palms against the sides of your body.

2. Keeping your back as straight as possible (don't touch the floor with your hands), sit, first left

knee, then right knee, finally resting your weight on your crossed feet. Yes, this will be uncomfortable (well, really it's painful) at first.

3. Bow by leaning forward at your waist (don't move your hips off your feet) and placing your hands lightly on the floor in front of you to hold your weight. Your hands should be open, with your fingers together. Your left hand should touch the ground just slightly ahead of your right. Hold for about a half a second, and then return to a sitting position.

Kneeling in the seiza position and bowing.

Karate Minute

Bowing isn't just used in karate, it is an important and useful social custom in many Eastern, and to a lesser extent, Western cultures. Although the gesture is basic and has been with us throughout human history (lowering the head and upper part of the body as a gesture of respect, recognition, and acknowledgment), its uses are varied and subtle. While Western cultures now seem to use bowing solely to distinguish the relationship between classes (think of what most people do when they meet the Queen of England), many Eastern cultures (Japan for example) use bowing to define a multitude of relationships between family members, friends, co-workers, acquaintances, as well as opponents.

Up, Down, and Straight Across

So as not to step on any toes, hurt any feelings, and unintentionally insult anyone, you will have to pay some attention to how you bow to the people you bow to. Let's face it, a setting where the major activity is kicking and punching, and the most important value is respect, is not the place to go around making enemies or demonstrating bad manners.

First of all, when bowing from a standing position, don't rush. As much as anything else, bowing allows you the opportunity to demonstrate poise and to control your emotions. Second, it is traditional for the junior student to bow a little lower then the senior when the two face each other. And so on up the line.

This problem of timing is handled for you when bowing from seiza (sitting). Generally, at the verbal command of the senior student, you will bow as a group. Take their lead. You will notice that junior students allow the seniors and instructor to come up slightly sooner than they do.

My Body Won't Do That!

Face it, one of the things that first attracted you to karate is that you want to do things with your body that other people can't do. Yet, when you start, you may become frustrated or intimidated by what you see the advanced students doing. They're fast. They're graceful. They're strong. They have great reactions. They can kick each other in the head. It may occur to you "I'll never be able to do that." Get rid of that thought, ASAP! Look closely, and you'll see that the only difference between them and you is time, experience, and practice. This, in fact, is the essence of one of those mystical "secrets of karate" that you hear people talk about. Ready? Practice! Everyone climbs a ladder the same way—one rung at a time. In order to be able to attain your personal best performance in karate (and we do mean *personal* best)—don't evaluate yourself against others in your class.

If Your Body Is a Temple Build a Good One!

All sports and exercise experts describe five aspects of fitness that contribute to your overall health and ability to function in a physical world. As you will see, karate develops, and uses, each and every one of them:

1. **Flexibility.** The ability of your body to move through a wide range of motion.

2. **Cardiorespiratory endurance.** The ability of your heart and lungs to supply oxygen to your muscles during a physical activity.

3. **Strength.** The ability of your body to do work (lift, carry, pull, push, throw).

4. **Endurance.** The ability of your body to do work over an extended period of time.

5. **Body composition.** Although we usually think of this in terms of the percentage of body fat, we should really learn to think about total body composition—how much of you is muscle, fat, bone, and so on. (Look, your body composition really isn't the subject of this book, so let's just say that you are what you eat, and it is tough defending yourself or being your best if you're lugging around an extra 30 pounds.)

It is important to remember that karate practice involves the function of your body as a whole—your flexibility, strength, and endurance coordinated and combined. You will do specific exercises to develop each area, but the goal will always be to use them in harmony for the greatest total effect.

Getting Looser: You Need to Stretch!

No matter what type of exercise you do, it is always important to stretch first. No where is that truer than in karate! Flexibility is crucial to karate practice for three main reasons:

1. The more range of motion you have, the more effective you will be in applying your techniques. By increasing your flexibility, you increase your options. After all, you can't kick somebody in the head if you can't get your foot above your knee.

2. Increasing your flexibility increases your speed and strength because there won't be a lot of friction and resistance in your joints and muscles slowing you down. Instead, your body can work more smoothly.

3. The more flexible you are, the fewer injuries you will have—not only in karate, but throughout the day. At some point in your life, you will undoubtedly bend over to pick up your reading glasses and not be able to stand back up. In part, the purpose of your flexibility training is to help you put that moment off for as long as you can.

Some Basic Rules About Stretching

Now the bitter truth for some of you and a pleasant surprise for others: Everyone is not equally flexible, and they are not expected to be. You will find that you are looser than some and tighter than others. Not everyone can kick head high or do the complete splits. Regardless of your natural flexibility, your goal is to achieve your personal best and increase your natural range of motion. With that in mind, here are some important things to remember:

1. Make sure that you warm up before you stretch. For example, you can jog, run in place, jump rope, or do some other mild aerobic activity until you raise your heart rate and increase your body temperature and blood flow.

2. Don't rush. Increasing your flexibility is a slow and methodical process. You're not going to do it in two days.

Ouch!

Don't injure yourself when stretching! Make sure to warm up first. Don't rush and go for quick gains. Use static stretching (where you hold a position and breathe), not ballistic stretching (where you hold your breath and bounce) when you stretch.

3. Don't bounce in your stretch. Using a "static" stretch technique (where you hold the position, relax your breathing, and allow your muscles to loosen naturally) has been shown to be much more effective (not to mention safer) than ballistic stretching (where you bounce) to gain an increase in range.

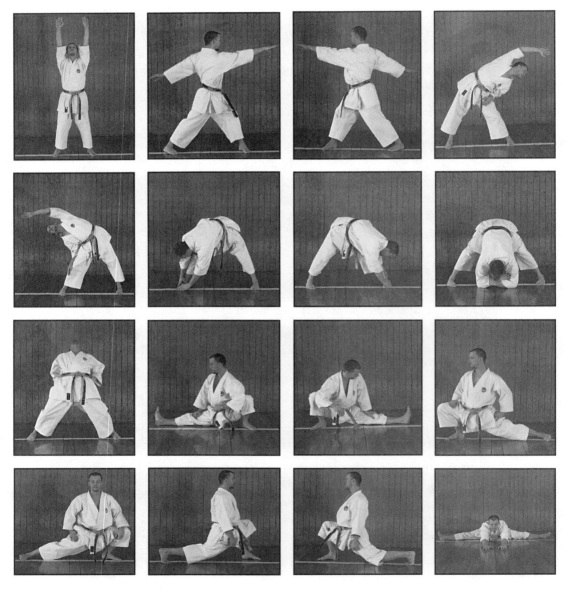

Warm-up and stretching exercises.

Getting Stronger

Being strong is always an asset, and karate training both uses and develops muscular strength. Keep in mind, however, that karate depends on synchronizing muscular interactions and body parts for strength, not by isolating them. For years, karate practitioners have strengthened themselves effectively solely by using the simplest strength exercises: push-ups, pull-ups, sit-ups, and squats.

Current practitioners and competitors frequently augment their training with weight lifting as well. If you choose to do this, we encourage you to remember that karate uses the whole body, and in karate the whole is greater then the sum of its parts. So be balanced! Choose a general strength program that develops all the major body parts instead of focusing on just a few.

Getting Faster

There's an old saying that when you and your hiking buddy are being chased through the woods by a hungry bear, you don't need to outrun the bear—you just need to outrun your buddy.

In a martial art such as karate, speed is important, but ultimately, speed is relative to your opponent. Usually, you need to get to, or away from, your opponent before he gets to or away from you. Also, the greater your speed, the more force you can generate with your techniques, and the more effective you will be at applying them.

Factors that will affect your speed are all related to your training habits. Some of these factors include …

1. How efficiently and quickly you start your techniques.

2. How well you relax the muscles you don't need while using only those you do need.

3. Your reaction time—the actual amount of time it takes you respond to a stimulus.

4. Your timing—how well your responce relates to what your opponent does.

5. Your confidence (nothing makes you as slow as indecision and apprehension).

Sensei Says

The study of karate usually takes two parallel paths. First, mastering what you can do well. Second, learning new skills (which you then go on to try and master). Don't focus on your lack of flexibility or strength or other limitations as you train. Focus on your strong points as you practice, even as you steadily try to improve your weak areas.

Lasting Longer

Your body thrives on activity. You gain energy from exertion and strength from effort. Typically, karate classes are from one to two hours in length and contain several periods of anaerobic and aerobic activity.

At first you may feel as if you're a few steps behind everyone else, but take heart. Your general physical endurance will develop as you continue your karate training, as will your ability to function under stress and hardship.

It Takes a Spark

Magic happens when the aspects of physical fitness merge into a synchronized and focused whole. Karate focuses on two key elements to create that magic: your ability to control and use your breathing, and your ability to project strength and confidence with your eyes.

Breathe Out Fear, Breathe In Strength

All Eastern physical disciplines, from yoga to various forms of meditation and to the martial arts, emphasize the importance of breathing for three main reasons:

1. Breath is life—literally. With air, you live—without air, you die. A well-known American karate champion of the late 1970s and early 1980s, Jack Clarke, jokes that he has studied Eastern philosophy and meditation for many years now and has finally figured out that, evidently, the secret to a long life is simply to keep breathing!

2. Many will find that controlling breathing is the doorway to controlling the emotions. If you think about times you've been excited, angry, scared, or nervous, and haven't been able to catch your breath, you will quickly understand the importance of breath control in emotional or stressful situations.

3. Being able to control your breathing is a very important tool in controlling your body. Good breath control will lead you to good physical control. Think of a boxer who uses his breathing to set the tempo of his punches when hitting a heavy bag, a gymnast doing a complex floor routine, a musician playing a trumpet, and a woman pushing to give birth to a baby. In all these instances, breathing affects how effectively you use your energy and can control the contraction and expansion of your muscles.

At times you will find yourself holding your breath as you practice basics—such as when doing your kata or sparring—and this is normal. Unfortunately, it is also wrong. Make sure that you breathe as you practice karate's fundamental techniques. A good place to start is to breathe out through your mouth when you do a technique, and breathe in through your nose to get more air.

The Eyes Have It

There's an old saying that "While you look out, the world sees in." Karate is not the place to look away demurely, to be shy, or to walk around with downcast eyes. It's okay for your therapist to know if you're nervous or insecure, but not your opponent—and certainly not that mugger in the parking lot. Your goal is to learn to use your eyes to
project strength and purpose.

To start, remember to keep your head up and your eyes forward and steady when training. When sparring, de-focus your eyes and look at the triangle that is formed by your opponent's head and shoulders.

Don't get into a staring contest, and don't look away. See your opponent by watching the area formed by their head and shoulders.

Okay, It's Time to Throw Your Weight Around

The explosive power and speed associated with all the basic karate techniques can be explained logically and scientifically. There is no more magic in karate than there is in the way Mark McGwire hits a baseball. Okay, bad example, maybe there is some magic, but it can still all be explained logically and scientifically.

Karate techniques are based on the principle of generating large amounts of force and momentum with the body center and hips, and then transferring that momentum to the faster or more precise actions of the arms and legs in as short a period of time as possible. Remember when we introduced this concept as "kime" (focus), "the pinpoint concentration of energy," as being essential to all karate techniques, way back in Chapter 3, "Karate Fitness Power: The Art of Contrast?" Well, basically, that's how focus works. In karate you will identify and study several methods of doing this. What may surprise you is that, once you give these methods some thought, they will not seem new to you. They are natural. As a moving, functioning human being, you use these all the time in a multitude of activities.

In the examples that follow, look for the relationship between the large or primary action of the hips, stomach, and body center, and the resulting effect on the action. Take some time and see if you can identify these actions in other areas of your daily life.

107

Twist It!

Twisting or turning the body, frequently called "body rotation," is one of the most frequently used body actions in karate. Twisting is used in the transition between blocking and counterpunching, punching in place, delivering midrange techniques, and circular kicks.

You can't hit a home run (or throw a pitch) without rotating your hips. Rotation is also used when boxing, playing tennis, golf, and Ping-Pong, or throwing a Frisbee, just to name a few.

Snap It!

Snapping, often called body "vibration," is another key method for creating power or speed with your techniques. You frequently use this method with striking techniques; when performing small, quick actions; and when you are close to your opponent.

Snapping—you've done this already, if you've ever snapped a whip, or tried to put a welt on your little sister's leg by snapping her with a dish towel.

Move It!

Moving, or "shifting," your hips from one point to another generates a tremendous amount of momentum. This is a biggie in karate. You will use this method when stepping, sliding, and moving forward, sideways, or backwards with either hand or kicking techniques.

A football player can't knock the other guy on his butt if he can't shift his weight.

Lift It!

You will use your legs to lift or drive your body weight up when you are close to your opponent, when he is taller than you, or when you are using jumping techniques. Lifting is frequently used in throwing your opponent or head-butting, when someone has grabbed you, or when using elbow techniques.

By using your legs to lift your body weight, you become stronger.

Drop It!

You will use the weight of dropping your body in close range if somebody grabs you and after you have thrown your opponent to the ground.

Dropping your body weight makes the job easier.

109

Compress It!

At times you won't be able to move, but by tensing and bracing your muscles against each other—often called "internal tension"—you will learn to generate force and power. This is frequently used with circular blocks, when using restraining holds and arm or wrist locks, and when you are close to your opponent.

Tensing his stomach and torso makes his arm 30 percent stronger.

Swing It!

Sometimes you will find yourself using your hips like a pendulum, lifting one hip to give your technique a little extra oomph. This is most commonly used when you use close-range kicking and for throwing your opponent to the ground.

The same principle is at work here. Work on how your hips move. As one hip goes down, the other hip goes up.

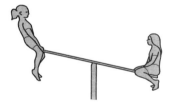

The Main Goal: Putting It All Together

A final point to keep in mind before you turn the page and start going through the chapters on stance, blocking, punching, striking, and kicking: Your initial goal as a karate-ka is not to learn thousands of techniques superficially, but rather, to start by learning a few techniques well. How do you do this? Well, by coordinating the principles we've discussed in this chapter—attention and concentration, the five aspects of physical fitness, correct breathing, eye-position, and the use of strong natural body dynamics—you will be on your way. Train hard!

The Least You Need to Know

➤ Bowing is a way to show respect and self-control.

➤ You use your whole body when you do karate.

➤ Knowing how to breathe correctly makes you faster, stronger, and more effective.

➤ There is no magic in karate. Everything can be explained logically and scientifically.

Stand Up for Yourself: Stances

Bottom line; your stances either make or break your karate techniques. But stances aren't just important in karate—stances are important in almost every sport or activity you do. If they weren't, we all wouldn't be trying to get an edge on the basketball court by spending $120 to wear the same shoes as Michael Jordan or Shaquille O'Neal.

Stand and Deliver!

You need a good stance for the same reasons you need a good friend. Your stances keep you balanced, they give you stability, and they help you move when you need to. You also can think of it this way: Stances connect you to the ground in the same way that a good set of tires connects your car to the ground. When the car in front of you decides to turn without signaling, can you brake in time? If there's another car right behind you, can you safely yank the wheel and go around the first car without losing traction and spinning out of control?

Stances are the foundation of karate.

Stances make you agile when you need to be fast, and stable when you need to be strong. In this chapter, you will learn the basic stances of karate. Some are long and low; some are high and short. You will notice that each stance has a specific purpose and a specific use. Ultimately, however, stances fall into three basic categories.

1. **Natural or "relaxed" stances.** You should be in a stance even when you aren't doing anything, even when you are waiting and watching, because although you aren't committed to anything you want to be ready. Think of a lifeguard standing at the edge of a pool filled with lots of excited children; a police officer approaching a suspect; you, waiting to cross a busy street: All are relaxed, balanced, and ready for whatever the situation calls for.

2. **Long, low stances.** These stances give you strength and stability when you actually need to make contact with someone or something. Whether you're blocking an attack, counterpunching, striking, or kicking, you will need to be braced and focused at the moment of contact. Think about when you set your feet to serve a tennis ball, tee off at golf, or help push a car that has run out of gas. When you get behind the car, lower your hips and set your feet—you are in a stance!

3. **High, quick stances.** These stances give you the balance that makes it possible to move quickly and smoothly to the front, back, side, and even up and down. Obviously this is useful in

Sensei Says

Usually, the longer and lower a stance is, the stronger and more stable it is. This is good, except for the fact that it's harder to move from these stances. Which is bad. To be a well rounded karate-ka, you will need to be able to use the right stance for the right job. Use long and low stances to plant your weight, and use high and short stances to be quick on your feet.

avoiding an attack or setting your distance and timing to counterattack. A bunch of kids playing a game of dodge ball naturally and instinctively make loose, relaxed stances so that they can move quickly to avoid being tagged by the ball. Usually, it's not simply the "fastest" kid, but the one that changes directions the most effectively, that lasts the longest.

Karate Minute

As a rule, most traditional karate schools will teach you the hard, low stances that you need to deliver strong blocks and counterattacks before they teach you the high, quick stances that you will need to move around with. The reasoning is that most real self-defense situations come out of nowhere, as a surprise. As someone who is untrained, you are more likely to get caught unaware, so you will need to respond with something that will simply stop your attacker—before you need to do a bunch of fancy moving, bobbing, and weaving. Also, low, strong stances are used to condition and strengthen your legs. Try standing in a low horse stance for 15 minutes at a time, and you'll see what we mean.

All stances share some common points—keep these things in mind:

➤ Maintain a good posture. Keep your back straight, your chin back, your eyes up, and your shoulders relaxed.

➤ Lower your body center. Think of the kid cruising down the street on a skateboard, drinking a soda: He's relaxed, steering with his hips.

➤ Even though some of these positions will be new to you, try to feel relaxed and natural. A good place to start is by breathing in a relaxed and natural way.

➤ Don't work too hard! Use only the muscles you need.

Talk the Talk

Dachi means "stance," **shizen tai** means "natural stance," **musubi dachi** means "attention stance," and **hachiji dachi** means "open-leg stance."

The word **yoi** means to "prepare." It is frequently used by the instructor to draw a class' attention together before beginning a **kata** or a sequence of exercises.

Ready for Anything: Shizen Tai, Natural Stances

Natural, ready, or free stances are the stances you use when you don't need a specific stance. You are waiting, you are alert, and you are ready, but you are not committed to a specific course of action—yet.

Be Official: Attention Stance and Open-Leg Stance

These next two stances, Musubi Dachi, the attention stance, and Hachiji Dachi, the open-leg stance, fall into the category of natural, or relaxed stances. They are used just prior, or right after, you jump into action. The first is a more formal stance, most commonly used when bowing—never bow with your feet apart! The second is used almost constantly in class; before and after doing kata, before and after sparring, and any time your instructor yells *"Yoi!"* to draw you and the rest of your class to attention.

In Musubi Dachi, the attention stance, you stand naturally with your heels together and the toes pointed out at a 45-degree angle. Your arms hang at your sides with your palms facing in. You will usually use this stance in formal situations and when you bow.

In Hachiji Dachi, the open-leg stance, you stand so that your feet are directly under your hips, with your toes pointing slightly outward. Be relaxed, but shift your weight slightly forward at the hips, onto the balls of your feet, so that you have to tighten your butt a little to maintain your balance. Keep your arms relaxed and your hands in a loose fist in front of your hips. You will use this stance before moving into an active position, before sparring with an opponent, and before starting your kata.

Anything Goes: Free Stance

Free stance is your sparring or fighting stance—your "GO" stance. From here you should feel like you can deal with anything that's coming at you, and be able to throw any technique in your arsenal. Everyone's free stance isn't the same. Some are higher, some are lower. As you gain experience, your free stance will change to accommodate your ability.

The free stance. Like the other natural stances, your body is relaxed and your breathing is natural. Keep your knees slightly bent, with your weight on the balls of your feet so that you can move easily. Keep your elbows close to your ribs, with your fists pointing toward your opponent. This stance is similar to a boxing stance, except that the feet are a little bit wider apart, and your arms are held lower so that you can deal with both hand and leg attacks.

Solid as a Rock: How Low Can You Go?

Low stances are used to deliver powerful and decisive techniques and to cover large amounts of distance. They are also used in training to develop strong legs and hips. These stances are frequently described as "outside tension stances" because once the legs are opened wide and the body is lowered, the stances become stronger when you use your feet to hold the floor and then push your knees away from each other.

Talk the Talk

Zenkutsu dachi means "front stance," **kiba dachi** means "horse stance," **kokutsu dachi** means "back stance," and **shiko dachi** means "square stance."

117

Front Stance: Zenkutsu Dachi

Because humans are designed to face the people we talk to, dance with, and fight, you will use the front stance a great deal. It is used against opponents who are in front of you.

Zenkutsu Dachi, the front stance, is as wide as your hips and twice as long. Keep both your feet flat on the floor, with the little toe of your front foot pointing forward, and your back foot at a 45-degree angle. Use your back leg to push your hips forward until your front knee bends over your front foot. Your back leg is doing most of the work, so the hamstring and buttocks of that leg should feel the strain and be tense. Remember your posture! Don't stick your butt out. Keep your hips under you just like in the natural stances.

Stepping: Moving from One Stance to Another

One of the most fundamental methods of moving front and back, and changing from one stance to another, is by stepping. The figure that follows shows stepping in and out of front stance. As you practice, keep in mind that stepping can be used with most stances and when applying almost all arm and leg techniques.

Crescent stepping involves moving front and back.

1. From a front stance with your left leg forward, keep your hips down and your body upright as you pull your right leg up to your front leg.

2. As your right leg passes by your front leg, continue your momentum as you drive your left leg into the ground, forcing your body center forward.

3. Continue driving forward with your left leg until you establish a new front stance with your right leg forward. Repeat this sequence going backward, too.

   Note: It is important that your hips stay down and that your legs scrape by each other as you step, tracing a crescent shape on the ground with your foot. Your foot should stay close to the floor. Don't stomp. This method of "crescent" stepping keeps you balanced, makes your step fast, and keeps you from making yourself into a bigger target than necessary.

Sensei Says

A few key points apply to all stances: Maintain good posture, keep your body center low, breathe naturally, and don't work too hard. Use only the muscles you need.

Sensei Says

Use your body and the body actions you learned about last chapter. If you don't rotate, vibrate, shift, lift, drop, swing, or compress your body as you use your stances to deliver your techniques, you'll be wasting most of the energy these stances are designed to generate.

Horse Stance: Kiba Dachi

The horse stance is used as a training stance from the front and as a fighting stance if you are attacked from either side.

Kiba Dachi, the horse stance, is just as long as the front stance. Both your feet are flat on the ground, with the little toe of each foot pointed forward. Keep your back straight as you bend your knees and push them outward, lowering your body. As the name implies, you should feel like you're riding a big horse bareback. The knees go out, around the body, and the toes turn in to hold you on.

119

Side-Stepping: Keeping the Same Leg Forward

Another method of moving from one stance to another is by side-stepping (sometimes called crab-stepping, or double-stepping). There are a ton of names for this one.

The following figure shows side-stepping in and out of horse stance. As with crescent stepping, keep in mind that this method of moving can be used with most stances and when applying almost all arm and leg techniques.

1. From the horse stance, keep your hips down and your body upright as you pull your right leg up to your left leg. Depending how far you want to step, you can bring your foot a little way up, or all the way past your left foot.

2. When your right leg reaches your left, drive it back into the ground so that your body and left leg again shoot forward.

3. Continue driving forward with your right leg until you establish a new stance with your left leg forward.

When side stepping, keep the same leg forward.

Back Stance: Kokutsu Dachi

Because most of your weight is on your back leg, this stance is very useful if you want to kick with your front leg or to stay away from your opponent. Make sure to keep your back straight and your back knee pushing back over your rear foot.

Kokutsu Dachi, the back stance, is the same length as the front stance and the horse stance, with both heels creating a straight line under the body. Be sure that the little toe edge of your front foot points forward and the little toe edge of the back foot is at 90 degrees and that the toes are pointed slightly forward. Notice that your front leg is slightly bent, while your back leg, which holds most of your weight, is deeply bent and torqued back.

The Sumo Square Stance: Shiko Dachi

In this form of side stance, the feet are turned out at 45-degree angles. This stance is used by sumo wrestlers when they prepare to clash or throw each other. It is very useful when you find yourself grappling with someone who is in front of you.

In Shiko Dachi, the square stance, position yourself into the horse stance and turn your feet out to a 45-degree angle. Notice that you can lower your body even more than usual in this stance.

Rooted Like a Tree: Rooted Stance, Fudo Dachi

This stance is kind of your "bring it on!" stance. You're locked to the ground, and you're not going anywhere until you finish business. Think of this stance as a cross between the horse stance and the front stance: Your body is low, your knees are twisted out, and your body is turned forward to face your opponent.

In Fudo Dachi, the rooted stance, start by assuming the front stance. Moving only your heels, change into a side stance position. Settle your weight and turn your torso back to face front. Shift your weight slightly forward and down, pushing your knees out.

Stick and Move: High and Quick Stances

High stances are used for fast movements and for changing directions and angles rapidly when you are close to your opponent. These stances are often described as "inside tension stances" because if your feet are close together and you want to lower your body center and make a stable base, you pretty much have to squeeze your legs in, toward each other. Of course, some instructors get the point of this stance across by telling their students to assume a position they would make after they had drunk two 48-ounce sodas in a row and can't find a bathroom. You get the idea.

EEEE-YA!!!

Talk the Talk

Neko ashi dachi means "cat stance"; **sanchin dachi** means "hourglass stance."

Light as a Cat: Cat Stance, Neko Ashi Dachi

In this stance, most of your weight is on your back leg so that you can quickly kick with your front leg and use your front knee to protect your groin (always a good idea).

In Neko Ashi Dachi, the cat stance, stand in attention stance and move your left (front) foot forward until your front heel is on the same line as the big toe of your rear foot. As you turn your back foot out to a 45-degree angle and bend your back leg, rest a small amount of your weight on the ball of your front foot. If you were to put your front heel down, it would be in line with your rear heel. Squeeze the knees and thighs lightly together. Feel that your front foot just lightly touches the floor so that it can move quickly.

Got the Time? Hourglass Stance: Sanchin Dachi

This stance is extremely useful for close situations and when someone grabs your arms or your body. Even though your feet are close together and your body is high, this can be an extremely strong and stable stance.

In Sanchin Dachi, the hourglass stance, stand in the open-leg stance and move your left (front) foot forward until your front heel is on the same line as the big toe of your rear foot. Turn your front foot in at a 45-degree angle. Point your rear foot straight forward. Drop your body weight and twist your knees in toward each other.

As you continue on through the next several chapters, which focus on blocking, punching, striking, kicking, and sparring, always keep in mind that stances are what make your karate techniques work. No stance—no karate. As you practice your techniques, experiment to see which stances work best with which techniques, and in which situations. With time and as you become more experienced, your body will learn to naturally choose the right stance for the right situation.

The Least You Need to Know

➤ Natural stances keep you ready for action.

➤ Long, low stances brace you and make you strong at the point of contact.

➤ High short, stances move you and make you quick.

➤ Posture, a low center of gravity, and leg tension are all crucial factors in a good stance.

Chapter 10

The Building Blocks of Self-Defense

In This Chapter

➤ The seven basic karate blocks

➤ The difference between "hard" and "soft" blocks

➤ The three keys of all blocking

Aside from all the other benefits of karate, remember that at its base, karate is a highly effective form of self-defense. This brings us naturally to the subject of blocking. Simply put, if you can't block or deflect somebody's attack when you need to, you can't defend yourself.

In Defense of Yourself

You will need to know several different basic blocks because you're preparing to defend against all kinds of attacks: punches, strikes, kicks, and holds. You never know until they happen whether these attacks are aimed at your head, your body, your groin, or your legs.

Clearly, then, your blocks are an absolutely crucial part of your karate arsenal. Think of them as your shield on the field of battle, the bumper on your car, the enamel on your teeth, or the force field on your starship. Practice them well. Depending on the situation, you will need to know how and when to use both "hard" and "soft" blocks, because each has a specific use.

EEEE-YA!!!

Talk the Talk

Uke-Wazi are "blocking techniques." The three main areas you will need to defend with your blocks are: **Jodan** (pronounced *joe-dahn*), which means "upper level," or the face, **Chudan** (pronounced *choo-dahn*), which means "middle level," or the stomach, and **Gedan** (pronounced *gay-dahn*), which means "lower level," or the groin.

This chapter introduces you to the basic karate blocks. Many other blocks are used in karate, but most are variations of the themes presented here.

When practicing, keep in mind some key points:

➤ Keep your arm and shoulder relaxed during the entire course of the block.

➤ Match the action (speed and timing) of your block with your opponent's attack. Remember, action equals reaction.

➤ Make sure that you hit the attack with the correct part of your arm or hand.

➤ Keep the blocking elbow close—so that it scrapes the side of your body—at the start of the block. If you become really, really skilled, blocking could be all the self-defense you need because if somebody can't hit or grab you, they can't hurt you.

Blocking is the heart of your defense.

Why Do We Block? No, It's Not What You Think

Well, why do we block? The answer is simple, right?

We block so that we don't get hit. Well, yes and no. Remember that everything in karate is related to everything else. Each action causes a reaction, and each situation demands a resolution.

Say that you're walking down the street and some-body—who has mistaken you for the guy who stole his wife, car, cat, dog, skateboard, homework, or whatever—suddenly jumps right in front of you and takes a swing at your head. Without hesita-tion, you block. Great. But now what? Both of you are still standing there, breathing on each other. While you pause to admire how effectively your first block worked, he's probably winding up to take another smack at you. Whoa! Here it comes! Quick, you block that one, too! Whew! That was close—where does it stop? Well, it only stops when you make it stop. When somebody is intent on at-tacking you, it is up to you to change his mind.

As you go through the blocks in this chapter, prac-tice while keeping the two laws of effective block-ing in mind:

1. Yes, an effective block deflects the attack—but that's only the beginning.

2. An effective block must also set you up so that you can immediately counterattack, es-cape, or in some way stop any further attack. If you can't do that, eventually you are going to get hit, kicked, grabbed, or choked.

Incoming! Hard Blocks

Most karate schools will probably teach you the "hard" blocks first: the rising block, for your face and head; the inside and outside forearm blocks, for your chest and stomach; the down block, for your stomach and groin; and the knife-hand block, for your chest and head. Some schools call these reaction blocks. It is extremely important to learn these beginning blocks well, because until you be-come more advanced and learn to shift, move, and respond with the timing of a black belt, these will be your first line of defense.

Ouch!

What happens if you don't follow the "Two Laws of Effective Blocking"? Well, its not pretty. Ignore the first law, and its—Bam! Right in the smacker. Ignore the second law, and its probably, Bam! Right in the smacker, too! Because you're going to get hit with whatever it is your opponent decided to throw at you right after the first thing you blocked.

Talk the Talk

These are karate's basic hard blocks: **age-uke** means "rising block"; **soto-uke,** which means "outside block"; **uchi-uke,** which means "inside block"; **shuto-uke,** which means "knife-hand block"; and **gedan barai,** which means "downward block."

127

Karate Minute

For some karate-ka, hard blocking is almost an end in itself. They have such strong blocks that they are able to convince the attacker to stop attacking them without doing anything else. Their blocks just hurt too much.

Ouch!

Sometimes blocking hurts for both the blocker and the blockee. Your arms, legs, and toes are probably going to get bruised as you first start practicing with your training partners or until you master your timing. As you get more advanced, however, you will bruise less, even as your blocks become stronger. Training hint: Tense the muscles in your arm tightly, exactly as you make contact with your opponent.

Hard blocks are the blocks you use in these situations:

➤ You are caught by surprise.

➤ You can't move to get out of the way.

➤ The attack is very strong and well-timed.

Hard blocks are just that—hard. You use the hard edge of your wrist or forearm to knock the attack out of the way. Use the same focus as you would in a punch or a strike. When doing these blocks, it is important to feel as if you are attacking and trying to hurt with your block.

By necessity, your blocks should be used and practiced from all stances. For simplicity, we suggest that you start by learning the blocks from the open stance. Notice that, as with punching and striking techniques, the hand that isn't blocking is almost always drawn strongly back to the hip. This is done for two reasons:

1. It gives power to the block.

2. It prepares the drawn-back hand to counterattack (the second law of effective blocking).

Block here! These are impact areas for the hard blocks.

Oops! Cover Your Head!

Clearly, the rising block (age-uke) is a biggie. The rising block protects your head, the part of your body that houses four out of five of your senses, maintains your consciousness, controls your thoughts, and contributes to a great deal to what you think of as your appearance. Also, typically this is the first target most attackers go after.

1. Start by placing your left hand on your hip and your right hand in the blocking position, as shown in the figure.

2. As you start to block with your left hand, simultaneously draw the right hand down toward your hip. Keep the arms relaxed and close to the body, and keep the palms turned toward the body, as the elbows of each hand pass close to each other.

3. As the block finishes, stay relaxed, but snap the left wrist and elbow sharply into the new blocking position. Impact with the attack takes place in the very last instant of the block—as the wrist is snapping into place. The bicep of your elbow should be about one fist from the side of your face, and your wrist should be about one fist from your hairline (unless you're bald, in which case, just pretend).

Age-uke, the rising block.

129

Hey! Protect Your Body!

The next three middle-level blocks (Chudan-uke) protect your chest, ribs, solar plexus, and stomach. Notice that you use both sides of the wrist, as well as the edge of the open hand, in these blocks. Be sure that you keep your posture upright so that by reaching for one attack, you don't open yourself up for something else.

1. Stand with your left arm pointed out in front of you and your right hand in a fist, at your ear, with the little finger pointed up. (As if you were holding a telephone upside down.)

2. Pull your left hand to your hip, and snap your right elbow around to the front of your chest so that the palm of your fist is facing you. As with the rising block, impact occurs at the little finger side of the wrist, precisely as the elbow and fist snap into place. The block should end with your elbow about one fist from your ribs, and with your fist in line with the top of your shoulder.

Soto-uke, the outside block.

The inside block covers the exact same area as the outside block, but with one major difference. It goes the opposite direction. Instead of starting at your ear and blocking with the little finger edge of your wrist, it starts under your arm, and blocks with the thumb edge of your wrist. You decide which block to use, depending on where your arms are in relation to the attack.

1. Stand with your left arm pointed out in front of you and your right hand in a fist, under your left armpit.

2. Pull your left hand to your hip, and snap your right elbow forward to the center of your chest so that the palm of your blocking fist is facing you. This block stops in exactly the same place that the outside block does; it just moves in the opposite direction. Impact occurs at the thumb edge of the fist, precisely as the wrist, elbow, and fist snap into place.

Uchi-uke, the inside block.

1. Stand with your right arm pointed out in front of you and your left arm with the hand open and straight to form a "knife hand," bent so that your palm is turned toward your ear. Your elbows should feel as if they are squeezing toward each other.

2. Pull your right hand back to your solar plexus, and snap your left elbow and wrist out so that the fingers of your left hand line up with your left shoulder, and your elbow is about one fist from your ribs. Impact occurs along the little finger edge of the hand. Be sure to flex the hand completely so that the edge is strong and hard.

Shuto-uke, the knife-hand block.

Ouch! Protect Down There!

The down block (Gedan-barai) is used against both hand and leg techniques that are directed at your lower stomach and groin. As with the other blocks, it is crucial that you keep your back as straight as possible and that you don't bend to "reach" for the attack. This is a very strong block that is often used against low kicks and in combination with long, low stances.

1. Stand with your left arm pointed out in front of you and your right arm, with the hand in a fist, bent so that your palm is turned toward your ear. You should feel as if your elbows are squeezing toward each other.

2. Pull your left hand back to your hip as you snap your right elbow and wrist down, as if slashing downward with a big sword. At the end of the block, your right hand should line up with your hip, and your elbow should be about one fist from your ribs. Special note of caution: Don't hyperextend your elbow as you do this block; there should just be the slightest bend in your arm. Impact occurs along the little finger edge of the wrist.

Gedan-barai, the down block.

Smooth and Easy: Soft Blocks

Soft blocks, or sweeping blocks, are an entirely different type of block. Where hard blocks are powerful and sharp, literally bashing the attacks out of your way, soft blocks are smooth and flowing, often deflecting an opponent's attack without them knowing it has missed, until it is too late. In general, soft blocks are considered a more advanced type of blocking technique. You don't need to block as hard because (theoretically) you have a more refined sense of timing. Well, yeah—with less power, you had *better* have better timing!

Talk the Talk

Nagashi-uke is a sweeping or deflection block, whereas **mawashi-uke** is a circular (hooking) block.

Remember the two laws of effective blocking? Well, they come into play here, too. With hard blocking, no matter how fast you are, you still will have to block and *then* counter. That's two actions. With soft blocking, the advantage is that you can block and counter at the same time—that's only one action. All things being equal, one action takes less time than two actions.

Sweeping blocks guide the attack past you by moving with the attack. Think of a broom sweeping leaves down the sidewalk. The broom and the leaves move together, at the same speed and in the same direction.

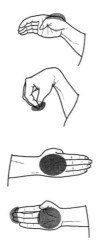

Block here! These are the contact areas for the soft blocks.

Sweep It Past!

The key to using sweeping blocks (Nagashi-uke) is to stay relaxed and to—get this—welcome the attack. It's true. The attitude you need in order to make sweeping blocks work is to want the person to attack. To make this block work, you will need to move *with* your opponent.

Sweeping blocks seldom work well if you are startled or caught unaware by the attack. (That's what hard blocks are for, and that's why we start with them.) Think of a pitcher throwing a fastball to a catcher. As the ball comes, the pitcher reaches out with his mitt and pulls it into him. He doesn't scream and jump out of the way, or throw his hands up in front of his head to avoid getting hit. He welcomes the throw, reaches for it, and takes it where he wants it to go.

1. Stand with your open right hand extended and your left fist drawn to the hip.

2. Keeping your elbow in line with the center of your body, draw your right hand back, just past your left ear. You are now blocking with the palm of your hand. Extend the hand out again, and then draw it back to your right ear. You are now blocking with the back of your hand.

Nagashi-uke, the sweeping block.

133

Guide It Around!

The key to circular blocks (Mawashi-uke) is to keep the elbow close to the body as you create momentum with the turning of the hand and wrist. You will bend the wrist sharply and make contact with the attack at the point where the back of the hand meets the wrist. Unlike the other blocks covered in this book, this block has a circular course and the smallest range of movement. All this means that your timing is crucial because there is less room for error.

1. Start with your left fist drawn to your hip and your right arm loosely at your side.

2. Bring your right hand up and across your stomach and chest, in a circular pattern. Form a hook with your wrist at the top of the circle, and continue around.

Mawashi-uke, the circular block.

Three Keys

By now you've probably noticed a set of key points or principles that apply to all the basic blocks. Understanding the key principles of any karate technique is important for two reasons. First, you will want to understand how the techniques relate to each other so that you can use them in conjunction with each other. Second, understanding something at the principle level is the first step to mastery. It gives you the ability to improvise and be flexible and spontaneous with your applications.

The Right Course

First, as obvious as this seems, the blocks need to go in the right direction, follow the right course, and cover the areas they are supposed to cover.

Sensei Says

When you have learned the blocks, always practice them in combination with other techniques. Every time you block, you want to be ready to counterattack.

Make sure that the course of your blocks is correct. Each block is intended to cover the shaded area.

Your Right Position

Second, the position of the elbow is the key to effective blocking. In general, the elbow should finish in line with your hip, or about one fist distance from your ribs. Imagine that you are arm wrestling with somebody. When you grasp your opponent's hand and put your elbow on the table, it is natural to pull your elbow close to your body for leverage. Blocking works the same way. If your elbow is in the wrong position or is too far from your body, you will have trouble covering the target or generating enough leverage to move the attack of a faster or stronger opponent.

The Right Angle

The final key point of blocking is the angle of the block in relation to the attack. The right angle gives you the most leverage. The most general rule of thumb for basic practice is that your block should finish at a 45-degree angle to your body. The angle changes somewhat with soft blocks, but the principle remains the same.

Make sure that your blocking angles and final elbow positions are correct—you need all the leverage you can get.

Get It Right! Timing: The Fourth Dimension

Clearly, the most important overall factor in executing a block that can actually protect you is timing. We will talk more about timing in Chapter 15, "Sparring: It's Different When You're Face to Face." For now, let's just say that it is just as bad to be too fast with your block as it is to be too slow. The karate-ka is able to move with the opponent, matching the timing of the block with the speed and intensity of the attack.

The Least You Need to Know

➤ Blocking is the beginning student's first line of defense.

➤ Blocks can be hard or soft.

➤ A good block will always give you the opportunity to counterattack.

➤ All blocks share a few common principles. Specifically, course, angle, position, and most importantly, timing.

Chapter 11

Punching In

In This Chapter

➤ Why karate uses punching so frequently

➤ How to make a fist correctly

➤ The different basic punches and their uses

When the authors of this book first started practicing karate, most people (us included) didn't have a very good understanding of what karate training was all about, or even what the techniques actually looked like. We knew that there was kicking and, more generally, we thought that the techniques would be tricky, exotic, and strange. Most of the karate we had heard or read about or saw in movies and on TV (mainly spy shows and professional wrestling) portrayed "chops" with the side of the hand and pokes with the fingertips to secret nerve centers.

It was surprising for most of us to find out that punching, in fact, is the heart of karate. The majority of traditional karate schools teach punching as one of the very first techniques you will learn. In general, when training, whether practicing basic techniques or kata, or sparring, you will probably use punching more often than any other family of techniques.

The Heart of Karate

In karate, punching is more than just balling your hand up and whacking someone in the nose with it. You can think of punching, or "tsuki" techniques, in terms of "thrusting." Punching and striking comprise the two main categories of karate's offensive arm techniques.

To help you understand the important distinction between punching—thrusting—techniques and striking techniques, picture yourself holding onto a knife. If you stab something with the knife so that the tip of the blade is the first thing to touch the target, and then drive with the handle, you are thrusting. On the other hand, if you slash, or cut, with the knife so that the side of the blade is the first thing to touch the target, and the handle of the knife "pulls" the blade, you are striking.

Okay, there's punching and striking. But why do we learn punching first and use it so much? Although both punching and striking are important, most traditional karate styles share the common belief that punching is the most natural and instinctive combative technique we have. By *natural,* we mean motions that are untrained and reflexive. It's the thing we do first, without thinking. So, clearly, it makes sense to build on that instinct.

EEEE-YA!!!

Talk the Talk

Tsuki means "punch."

Punching is the heart of karate.

Think, for example, of what you would "automatically" do if someone stood way too close to you and wouldn't move back, or if someone grabbed you and held on to you, or if someone pushed you until you got disoriented, scared, or angry. You would naturally put your hands up against them, and shove them—thrust them—away from you. Or, if you are the aggressive type, you might ball your hand up and punch out at someone. If you've ever seen two-year-olds fight over a toy, you've seen them do both things, naturally. It is natural for them to push at each other by extending their arms and thrusting—and if they are really mad, they punch at each other.

Many schools also feel that once your hands are up, all things considered, punching is the most direct, fastest, and most powerful path to your target. They feel that if you are well trained, you will be able to respond with a punch more quickly than you will with anything else.

This chapter covers the fundamental punches of karate. You will notice that although they vary in course, use, and fist position, they all share the same key, fundamental principles. Try to remember the following points as you go through the various punches:

➤ Keep the arm and shoulder relaxed.

➤ Match the action of the punching arm with the action of the drawn-back hand and the movement of the body. Remember, action equals reaction.

➤ Make sure that your fist is tight and that the wrist is correctly aligned at the moment of contact.

➤ Keep the punching elbow close so that it scrapes the side of your body at the start of the punch.

➤ Wait until the very last instant to snap your fist over into position. This snap is what helps give the punch its focus.

A Solid Fist Is a Happy Fist

Because karate punches can generate so much force, and because karate-ka don't wrap the hands and wrists to protect them, the way boxers do, making a proper fist is very important. One of the things you will learn through practice is to keep the fist tight on impact while the arm stays loose and relaxed during the punch.

When dealing with force, shock and momentum, alignment is everything. That's what the last chapter on stances was all about—how to align the large and heavy parts of the body to make momentum. Alignment of the fist is equally important because that is the point where the momentum transfers from you to your target. For basic punching, you

Sensei Says

The saying goes, "Ten thousand for one." This means that it takes 10,000 repetitions of a technique before you have one that works. Don't rush when practicing these techniques, Take your time and get them right, but once you have them, work them like crazy. Repetition is the byword of karate.

Ouch!

The two most common injuries you are likely to get if you punch something are a sprained wrist and sore knuckles. Make sure that your fist is tight on contact and that your fist is aligned with your wrist to absorb the shock of the punch. Also, hit only with the first two knuckles of your hand because the knuckles of your little finger break pretty easily.

want to generate as much force as you can to as small a point as possible—in this case, the first two knuckles of the fist.

1. Start by tightly bending the fingers and knuckles of the hand.

2. Lock the thumb over the index and middle fingers.

3. Keep the wrist straight, and line the first two knuckles up with the bones in the forearm.

4. Make impact with only the first two knuckles of the closed fist.

Making a fist.

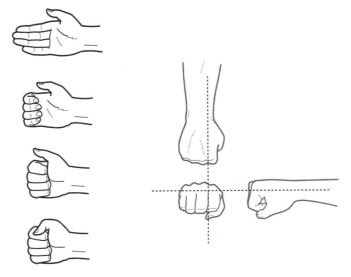

One important thing to realize with punching is that there is no "one size fits all" fist. Sometimes you will need to modify your fist depending on the target you are dealing with.

Here's a quick cheat sheet to help you remember which fist you should use and when:

1. Middle-knuckle fist for straight attacks to small targets

2. Index-knuckle fist for round attacks to small targets

3. Fore-knuckle fist for attacking targets such as the throat and the sternum

Talk the Talk

Choku-zuki means "straight punch."

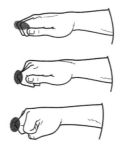

Sometimes you will use a special fist for special targets.

Straight In

Choku-zuki, or the straight punch, is the most commonly used punching technique. Additionally, it forms the basis for all the other punches. As you will see, this technique can be done with either hand and can be directed to the head or the body.

1. Stand in the open stance, with the left arm and fist extended toward the solar plexus.

2. Simultaneously draw the left hand back to the hip as you thrust the right hand out. Make sure that the elbows of both hands scrape along the sides of your body.

3. Turn the right wrist over at exactly the same time as the punch locks into place; the left hand should lock onto your hip.

EEEE-YA!!!

Talk the Talk

Gyaku-zuki means "reverse punch"; **oi-zuki** means "lunge punch"; and **kizami-zuki** means "short punch or jab."

Choku-zuki, the straight punch.

141

Reverse Punch

The reverse punch (Gyaku-zuki) is a very powerful way to apply the straight punch. It is frequently used in competition and in actual self-defense situations following a block or a defensive action. This punch is delivered with the rear hand, from the forward or free stance, and benefits from the strong rotation of the body.

1. Start in a forward stance, with your front hand and hip extended.

2. Turn the hips forward, breathe out, and punch simultaneously.

   Note: Practice this punch as you do each of the blocks you learned in the last chapter, including the rising block-reverse punch, the down block-reverse punch, and so on.

Gyaku-zuki, the reverse punch.

Lunge Punch

The lunge punch (oi-zuki) is a unique karate technique. With practice, it will allow you to attack someone with a punch from a long distance away. It also trains you to start large actions and cover large distances quickly. Although it feels awkward at first, this punch is deceptive to people who don't have any karate training because they usually aren't ready for how quickly you can cover the distance between you and them.

1. Start in the forward stance with your front hand extended.

2. Without moving your upper body or front foot, quickly step forward with your rear foot into the front stance. Be sure to stay down throughout the action, and draw your legs together (crescent step) as you go forward.

3. Punch at the very last instant of the step (exactly when your foot hits the ground—not before). Your body, back leg, and punch should all lock at the same time.

Oi-zuki, the lunge punch.

Note: Okay, this is the hard part. Hold your body square to the front at the end of the punch so that the full momentum of the body is able to transfer into your technique.

Short Punch

The short punch (kizami-zuki), is the karate version of the jab. It is a very effective and versatile punch. As with the jab used by boxers, the short punch is used as a quick, sharp punch to keep someone from coming close to you. The short punch can

143

Talk the Talk

Mawashi-zuki means "round punch," and **ura-zuki** means "close punch."

also be used as a fake to distract someone while you attack them with something else; as a counter to someone else's attack; and, if you become good enough, as a technique that can finish a bad situation all on its own.

1. Start from a relaxed free stance.

2. Simultaneously snap your front fist forward as you drive your front hip, front knee, and front foot in, toward your opponent. Draw your other hand strongly back to your hip. After you fully extend, snap back to ready position.

Kizami-zuki, the short punch.

Ouch!

Be selective. Don't hit anything harder than your own fist. Punching someone in the knee, elbow, or head usually hurts you more than them. Also, at some point you undoubtedly are going to smash fists with someone. Yes, it hurts! But it hurts less if your fist is tighter than your opponent's fist.

Go Around

The round punch (mawashi-zuki) is the karate version of the boxer's hook. It can be used with either the front or the rear hand, and because of its course, it is used when you are closer to your opponent than you are when you use a straight punch. Be careful not to swing your arm too far away from your body when you throw this technique. Remember, even with this punch, your elbows stay close to your sides at the beginning of the technique.

1. Stand with your left fist extended in front of you at head height. Turn your wrist so that the back of the fist is turned toward your face and so that your fist is pointed into your opponent's ear.

2. Draw the left hand back as you punch with your right hand in a shallow curve. Wait as long as possible to snap over your fist.

   Note: This punch doesn't need to go "around the block" to get there. Practice by having somebody hold his fists up in front of his face while you punch (narrowly) around his hands, toward their jaw or temple.

Mawashi-zuki, the round punch.

Up Close

The close punch (ura-zuki) starts out as a straight punch and then stops short. The target, whether it is the groin, stomach, ribs, or chin, must be close to you. It is especially important to start this technique as quickly as possible because there is very little distance for you to generate any momentum.

1. Stand with your left fist extended, palm up, and your elbow close to your ribs. Be conscious of your arm squeezing close to your body.

2. Snap your right punch out while you draw your left hand back.

Ura-zuki, the close punch.

Note: With the close punch, you don't snap your wrist over. In fact, try to twist it slightly backward at the point of impact so that your arm and torso lock more strongly together.

145

Karate punches are extremely fast, strong, and versatile. They can be used independently, in combination with any of the blocks we discussed in the last chapter, or with any of the strikes and kicks that are coming up in Chapters 12, "Striking Out," and 13, "Kicking Back."

The Least You Need to Know

➤ Punching is your first line of defense.

➤ There is more than one kind of fist and one kind of punch.

➤ Effective punches can be delivered with either hand and from just about any stance.

Striking Out

Karate's striking techniques are both fast and strong. Strikes come in all shapes, sizes, directions, and angles. They can be applied against opponents who are in front of you, to the side of you, behind you, above you, and below you. Clearly, this makes striking very effective for self-defense situations. As you will see in this chapter, you can strike effectively while going forward toward your opponent, while backing away from him, and while moving obliquely to the side. You can apply striking techniques while jumping through the air, while dropping to the ground, or even while being knocked off balance. Additionally, striking uses a wide variety of open-hand and closed-hand positions and impact areas.

In short, striking techniques are extremely versatile.

Striking Forward

As we discussed in the last chapter, the thing that distinguishes striking from punching (thrusting) is the way in which the force and momentum of a strike are generated. When striking, your elbow leads, in a sense pulling your technique to the target. Keep this in mind as you learn and use the various karate strikes.

Striking gives you 360 degrees of effectiveness.

Talk the Talk

Uchi means "striking."

Ouch!

Make sure that you don't hit with the wrong part of the hand. For example, hitting with the knuckle of the little finger instead of the back of the first two knuckles when back-fist striking is one of the most common self-inflicted injuries people get when striking. Slowly practice hitting something soft until your hand naturally learns the correct position.

In fact, if you are at all active, you probably do a striking type of action as you participate in lots of different sports and activities: executing a backhand in tennis, throwing a Frisbee, hitting or throwing a baseball, chopping wood, pounding a nail, and so on. With each of these actions, the elbow goes first, pulling the arm and hand into the movement. So, a simple rule for striking might be to make sure to always point your elbow directly at your target as you strike.

One big advantage that striking offers over punching is that your opponent doesn't have to be right in front of you for a strike to be effective. Also, you don't need to be as planted or balanced to get off a good striking technique.

A disadvantage to striking is that in order to strike, you often need to wind up or cock the strike, the same way that you wind up to throw the Frisbee. Sometimes this extra movement takes more time than you have.

You will discover that there are two main types of striking techniques: snapping—also called whipping—and sticking—also called locking.

What's the difference? Why would you decide to use one instead of the other? Is one better than the other? Well, not really. Usually it just comes down to the target and the opportunity.

As a general rule snap strikes are sharper and faster. This means that the moment of contact is very short and doesn't leave a lot of time for the momentum of the technique, or the force, to transfer to the target. These strikes are something like what you use when you hit a volleyball. They are ideal for small, tight targets, such as the face and the side of the head. Usually, when doing snap strikes, you will hit with hard points, such as the side of the hand or the back of the first two knuckles.

Locking or sticking strikes, on the other hand, are heavier. They take a little more time to apply because you need to commit more of your body weight to the technique. (Think back to the body actions we talked about in Chapter 8, "How to Practice Karate.") It simply takes more time for all the energy in these techniques to leave your body and go into something (or someone) else. Think of how it would feel to drive a stake into the ground with a sledge hammer—you don't tap with it, you whale into it. These techniques are used for bigger targets such as the ribs, the collarbone, the back of the neck, or the solar plexus. Frequently, with locking strikes, you hit with the bottom of your fist so that you don't damage your hand.

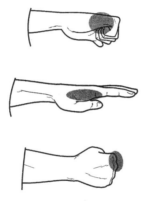

Striking hand positions.

Striking uses a wide variety of open-hand and closed-hand positions. Be sure to use the right area for the right technique.

Whip It

In general, when something snaps in karate, the beginning and end points of the action are the same. So, the first thing you need to know about snap strikes is that they start and end in the same place. Also, you will usually turn or snap your body, using either body vibration or rotation, to give your technique power.

Be sure to pay attention to the fundamental principles that apply to all the snap strikes:

➤ Keep the arm and elbow relaxed during the strike.

➤ Don't just use your arm to strike. Match the strike with a strong drawn-back hand and body movement. Just as with punching, action equals reaction.

➤ Make sure that your fist or hand is tight at the moment of contact.

➤ The snap back is more important than the extension of the technique, so snap back quickly—sort of like you are snapping a towel or a whip.

➤ Don't hyperextend your elbow. The snap back should occur just before your arm is fully extended.

➤ Most important, aim with your elbow. Always point your elbow exactly at the target you want to hit.

Ouch!

Don't hyperextend your elbow when doing a snap type of striking. Make that sure your elbow doesn't lock all the way out. Always use your muscles and tendons to stop a technique, not the joint itself.

Sensei Says

Use everything! Remember, the reason karate techniques are so effective is that they coordinate the strength and energy of the entire body in each movement. Breathe with your techniques, and make sure to always use your body.

Stick It

If you use your imagination, it is easy to understand lock striking if you think of hitting something with a stick. Your body turns, your elbow leads, and you swing through the target (hmmm, sort of sounds like what the golf or tennis pro at the country club might tell you). Now continue using your imagination, and lose the stick. Your body turns, your elbow leads, and you swing through your target, locking and bracing your body and stance at the moment of impact.

Just as in hitting something with a stick, your technique, whether it is a knife-hand strike or a hammer-fist strike, and your body go in the same direction and stop at the same time.

Remember these key points of lock striking:

➤ Keep the arm and elbow relaxed during the strike.

➤ Move, turn, or shift your body with the technique.

➤ Brace your body and your stance (breathe out) when you make contact.

➤ Make sure that your fist or hand is tight at the moment of contact.

➤ Always point your elbow exactly at the target you want to hit.

Closed–Hand Strikes

Depending on the target, most strikes can be done with either an open or a closed hand. We give examples of two closed-hand strikes, one snapping and one locking. Again, be extra careful of where you hit. Make sure that you use the right part of the hand against a vulnerable target.

The Back–Fist Strike

The back-fist strike (Uraken-uchi) is probably the most commonly used striking technique in karate. It is very effective as both an offensive and a defensive technique, and it is often used in combination with other techniques. Its usual target is the front or side of the face or the head.

1. Bend the arm sharply, and stretch the elbow out toward the target.

2. Snap the fist to the target. Be sure to make contact only with the back of the first two knuckles of the fist.

3. Sharply snap back to the starting position.

Talk the Talk

There are two basic types of closed-hand strikes: **uraken-uchi,** which means "back-fist strike," and **tettsui-uchi,** which means "hammer-fist strike."

Uraken-uchi, the back-fist strike.

The Bottom Fist Is a Hammer

The bottom-fist strike and the hammer-fist strike (Tettsui-uchi) basically involve the same technique. It just depends on which course the strike takes. If you swing the strike in a parallel line with the ground, like a tennis backhand, it's a bottom-fist strike. If you bring it straight down, like a hammer, it's a hammer-fist strike. As we mentioned earlier, because this is a locking technique, you will usually use it against heavier target areas, such as the back of the neck, the ribs, the collarbone, and areas of the torso.

1. Start with your striking arm raised high, with the elbow by your ear.

2. As you draw your other hand back to your hip, strike down, extending your arm as you hit.

Tettsui-uchi, the hammer-fist strike.

Open–Hand Strikes

You usually will apply open-hand striking techniques to smaller, more specific targets than you will with the closed-hand techniques. In general, if you're surprised, caught off-guard, or rushed, you might just strike or punch out automatically. But if you have a moment to think, to choose your target, and to formulate a strategy, you might use an open-hand technique to attack or counterattack.

Open-hand techniques are selected over closed-hand strikes in two main instances. First, open-hand strikes are used to attack parts of the body that are difficult to reach with the rounder, more cumbersome fist—for example, the throat, the side of the neck, or the groin. Second, open-hand techniques are frequently used in closer distance situations, where it is natural to grab, control, or throw your opponent after striking him. As with closed-hand techniques, open-hand strikes can either snap or lock. The next sections give examples of an open-hand snapping strike and two locking strikes.

Talk the Talk

Two open-hand strikes are: **shuto-uchi,** which means "knife-hand strike," and **haito-uchi,** which means "ridge-hand strike."

The Knife–Hand Strike

By now, you've probably noticed that karate uses the names of numerous tools and weapons to communicate a general impression and understanding of the technique. When using the knife-hand strike (shuto-uchi), make sure that your hand is as knife-like as possible. Make the edge of the hand sharp and straight. Flex the fingers, squeeze them tightly together, and *don't* cup the palm of your hand!

The knife-hand strike (snapping) works very much like the back-fist strike. However, since the impact area of the knife hand is so much narrower than the back fist, it is easily used for attacking the throat.

1. Bend the arm sharply, and stretch the elbow out toward the target.

2. Snap the hand to the target. Be sure to make contact only with the side of the hand, not the edge of the little finger (ouch!).

3. Sharply snap back to the starting position.

Shuto-uchi, the knife-hand strike (snapping).

The knife hand-lock strike can be used in a variety of ways. The two main applications are, first (as shown in the following figure), to the side of the neck, and second, in a downward course to the collarbone or back of the neck, in the same way you would use the hammer fist.

1. Place the fingertips of the striking arm at the ear, with the elbow pointing back and away from the target.

2. As you draw the other hand to your hip, snap the elbow of the striking hand forward, exactly as if you were throwing a baseball (elbow first, then wrist, and then fingers). Lock the elbow and wrist into position, with the palm turned up, parallel to your opponent's shoulder.

Shuto-uchi, the knife-hand strike (locking).

153

The Ridge–Hand Strike

The ridge-hand strike (haito-uchi) probably will remind you a little of the round punch. The ridge-hand strike is a very strong and surprising technique because, as anyone who has ever been hit with it says, "It seems to come out of nowhere." The ridge-hand strike is formed by folding the thumb down across the palm of the hand and hitting with the area from the index finger to the thumb joint. This technique is frequently used to go around your opponent's defenses and hit him at right angles to you. Actually, you see a variation of this technique if you watch football or professional wrestling. There they call it a "clothesline."

Talk the Talk

Empi-uchi means "elbow strike."

1. Stand with one hand extended to the height of your opponent's head, and the other (in ridge-hand position) resting on your hip with the palm up.

2. Use a curved course to bring your hand, palm up, to the side of your opponent's head as you draw the other hand back to your hip. Snap the hand over, into position, at the very last moment.

Haito-uchi, the ridge-hand strike.

Or Just Smash It: Elbow Strikes

Elbow strikes (empi-uchi) are used when you are close to your opponent. These strikes are very strong and can be used in several ways. To get maximum force from these techniques, make sure to start the movements quickly and to hit with the tip of your elbow, not your forearm.

Karate Minute

Many techniques are defined by their use. When necessary, strikes can be used as blocks, and blocks can be used as attacks. Notice that many techniques share the same starting positions and body actions, depending on how you use them. For example, the upward elbow strike makes a really good defensive block against a round punch. Just ask a boxer defending against a hook.

Elbow strikes can be used in five main ways:

1. Going up
2. Going across
3. Going to the side
4. Going to the rear
5. Going down

Empi-uchi, the elbow strike.

The overwhelming advantage of striking techniques is that they can be used in so many different ways and in so many different situations. If you want to be as effective as possible, be sure to strive for accuracy, as well as speed and power, as you practice.

The Least You Need to Know

➤ Strikes are very versatile—they can be used to the front, side, and rear.

➤ Strikes either lock on contact or snap back to their starting point.

➤ Strikes can be used as defensive or offensive techniques, and they also can be used in combination with other techniques.

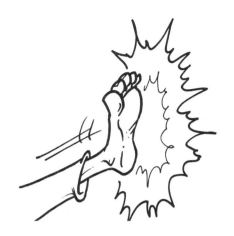

Kicking Back

If you're like most people, when you think of karate, you think of kicking. Because as everyone knows, kicking is one of the things that makes karate so special.

You may visualize yourself getting to the end of this chapter, jumping up, throwing down the book, and starting to snap out head-high kicks with ease. Or, you may envision yourself using kicks to stop muggers and assailants as they approach you from the front, rush you from the side, or sneak up on you from behind. Depending on how strong your imagination is, you may even see yourself kicking around corners, over tables, through walls (well, at least through doors), and as you leap through the air.

On the other hand, you may be a bit more pessimistic, figuring that since it makes you grunt just to bend over and pick up your socks, you're not going to be kicking anyone, anywhere—ever.

Setting Kicking Straight

For most of you, the reality lies somewhere in the middle. Regardless of what you see on TV and in the movies, everyone cannot—and will not—be able to kick someone in the head. Thankfully, as you will see, kicks don't need to be high to be effective. They do, however, need to be done correctly.

*Kicking gives you range,
power, and versatility.*

Kicking techniques add tremendous versatility and range to your karate arsenal. First of all, your legs are longer then your arms—and usually your opponent's arms, too. This gives you greater reach. Second, your legs are stronger than your arms. This gives you more power. Third, most people (regardless of how much professional wrestling they watch on TV, or how many karate video games they play) don't expect you to kick them. This gives you the element of surprise.

Let's not fool ourselves, though—mastering kicking is tricky. For most people, the biggest problem is usually flexibility. Make sure that you warm up and then stretch before you start kicking—every time you kick. This way, you won't injure yourself as you train, and your kicks will keep getting better as you practice, developing more range and speed.

Usually, the second biggest problem is balance. Let's face it—sometimes it's hard enough just to keep your balance while standing on two feet, especially if you're trying to deal with a fast, strong opponent in the dojo or an attacker on the street. And now we want you to do it on one foot?

Don't worry! Although it's not easy, you *can* do it. Just remember karate's one true secret—practice. Like everything else related to karate, getting good at kicking requires lots and lots of practice.

Follow these steps for learning how to kick properly:

1. Use the ball of the foot for front and round-house kick.

2. Use the instep for round-house kicks, leg kicks, and low front kicks.

Ouch!

Without a doubt, some of the most common self-inflicted injuries in karate are the amazingly bruised shin and the totally smashed toe. Kicking is easy; the problem is getting your foot through your opponent's arms and over his knees as you try to hit the target. That's why most people do a lot of basic sparring and kicking exercises with a partner—to learn where the foot should (and shouldn't) go. Otherwise, your foot will find out how hard an elbow can be.

3. Use the side edge of the foot for side snap and side thrust kicks.

4. Use the heel of the foot for back thrust kicks.

5. Use the sole of the foot for sweeping techniques.

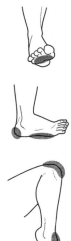

Make sure to use the right part of your foot when you kick.

Remember these points. They will help you get a good start in learning your kicks and will help you kick more effectively.

➤ Be accurate. Be sure to kick with the correct part of the foot to an open target. Nothing is worse than breaking your own toes or foot on your opponent's body, knee, or elbow, as you try to defend yourself. Ow!

➤ Stay loose as you kick. Pay special attention to keeping your shoulders and arms relaxed.

➤ Don't hold your breath. Breathing will help your balance and affect how well you control your body.

➤ Use your hips to kick. Make that sure your hips move in the direction of the kick.

➤ Keep the leg you are standing on bent and your foot flat on the floor (for most kicks) as you kick. This leg is both your shock absorber and your stance. The kicking foot may hit the target, but your power and speed start and end with your hips and support leg.

Ouch!

The second most common self-inflicted injury is probably pulling a muscle by trying to kick too high, or kicking without warming up. First of all, low kicks can be very effective. Second, flexibility takes time to develop. Learn to incorporate stretching into your karate life.

➤ After you learn the kicking course, be sure to practice all the kicks as one smooth movement. Everything—hip, knee, and foot—starts and ends at the same time.

➤ Keep your kicking leg soft and loose during the kick. The looser the leg, the faster the kick. The faster the kick, the stronger the kick.

This chapter focuses on karate's five basic kicks and one basic sweeping technique (a sweep is when you use your leg to knock someone else's legs out from under him). Remember that you can use most of your kicks from almost all your stances, so when you practice, kick from a variety of positions, and be sure to use both your front and your back leg.

Karate Minute

Many of the kicking techniques used in traditional karate are actually new and were once frowned upon. Before the late 1940s, all karate kicks were low. They were aimed to the knees, legs, groin, and low stomach of the opponent. Gradually, people started experimenting with higher kicks and a wider variety of targets. They also developed new kicks, including the round-house kick, jumping kicks, and the reverse round kick. Naturally, the traditionalists of the day were shocked by these new techniques, so for a while, these new techniques had to be practiced in secret.

Snap It or Lock It?

Remember when we divided your offensive arm techniques into two categories—punching and striking? Well, we're going to do the same thing with your kicking techniques. Basic karate kicks also fall into two major categories—snap kicks and thrust kicks. It will be important to understand this distinction as you practice and apply your kicks.

Snap It!

In the same way that the elbow leads, or pulls, your strike, so does the knee lead, or pull, your snap kick. As you will see, in each of the three snap kicks you learn in this chapter—front-snap kick, side-snap kick, and round-house kick—the knee points to your target.

This one principle makes aiming these kicks pretty easy. Want to side-snap kick someone in the shin? Well, that's where you point your knee. Want to roundhouse-kick toward the face? Same thing, point your knee. Want to front-kick somebody in the stomach? Well, you get the idea.

Snap kicks are meant to be very sharp and fast. When you get the technique down, try to build up the speed of the kick so that it would be impossible for someone to grab your foot before it snaps back. Also keep in mind that snap kicks are extremely versatile. One of the surprising (to your opponent, not to you) advantages of snap kicks is that they can be used at very close *or* very long distances. If you can point your knee at the target, you can kick it!

1. Notice how the elbow of the striking technique points to the target at the beginning and at the end of the technique.

2. Now notice how the knee of the snap kick also points to the target at the beginning and end of the technique.

Elbow or knee, it's all the same—point to the target when you snap.

Lock It!

Whether it's with the arm or the leg, thrusting is thrusting. When you thrust with your arm (see Chapter 11, "Punching In"), your elbow drives the fist. When you thrust with your leg, your knee drives your foot. Make sure that you do two things when you practice the side thrust and the back thrust kick discussed in this chapter. First, pull your knee close to your body (in the same way that you cock your arm to punch). Second, lock your knee out at the end of the technique. Make sure that you breathe out, kick, and move your hips all at the same time.

Thrust kicks are most effective at full length and are extremely effective at stopping someone who is rushing at you.

1. Notice how the elbow of the punching arm draws back before the punch.

2. Now notice how the knee of the thrust kick also draws close to the body before and after the kick.

With thrust kicks, strongly cock the knee before you kick, just like you cock your elbow before you punch.

Talk the Talk

First of all, **keri,** means "kick." The five most basic karate kicks are: **mae geri,** which means "front kick"; **mawashi geri,** which means "round-house kick"; **yoko geri kekomi,** which means "side-thrust kick"; **yoko geri keage,** which means "side-snap kick"; and **ushiro geri (kekomi),** which means "back (thrust) kick."

Let's Kick It Around

With good kicking techniques, you can defend yourself in all directions. The five kicks that follow are the most basic karate kicks. We will look at the front-snap kick, the side-snap and side-thrust kicks, the back-thrust kick, and the round-house kick. And, to jazz things up a bit more, we also will introduce a basic foot sweep.

To the Front

The front-snap kick (mae-geri) is the easiest and most natural kicking technique we have, and it is probably the first kick you will learn as a new karate student. We are designed to raise our leg and knee to the front—that's how we walk, how we run, and how we climb. Also, if we are in danger or in a conflict, we will usually turn to face our opponent, putting our opponent in front of us. All this makes the front kick a natural. This kick is especially well suited to attacking your opponent's groin, stomach, and hip.

1. Standing straight with your support leg slightly bent, raise your knee to your chest as you rock your hips slightly forward. Keep your toes back (you're going to kick with the ball of your foot), and keep the heel of your foot as close to your butt as possible.

2. Let the foot snap out as your knee and hip extend forward.

3. Snap your kicking foot back to its starting position.

   Note: This whole action should be done in one smooth, flowing action. Nothing stops. The knee, hip, and foot all start and end together. Start by practicing *slowly,* and then gradually speed up.

Mae-geri, the front-snap kick.

To the Side

The side-snap kick (yoko geri keage) works a lot like the front-snap kick. The knee points to the target, but this time it moves to the side. For some, getting the foot in the right position is the hardest part. Remember, you want to hit with the side edge of your foot, not the joint of the little toe. If getting into the right position turns out to be a battle, try walking around the house on the side edges of your feet that can be attacked (do this in private—it looks pretty strange). The usual target for this kick is almost any part of the body that can be attacked from an upward angle, or under the chin.

1. Stand straight, with your support leg slightly bent.

2. Raise your knee toward an imaginary target to your side, as you rock your hip slightly up. Be sure to set the side edge of your foot as you raise the knee.

3. Let the foot snap out as your knee continues to extend toward your target.

4. Snap your kicking foot back to its starting position.

   Note: As with front kick, this whole action should be done in one smooth, flowing action. Nothing stops. The movement of the knee, hip, and foot all start and end together. Practice *slowly* at first, and then gradually speed up.

163

Yoko geri keage, the side-snap kick.

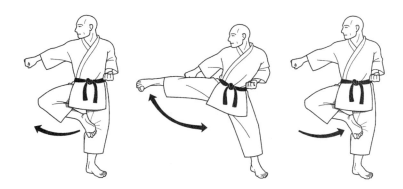

The side-thrust kick (yoko geri kekomi) is an extremely powerful kick. More important, it is your first thrust kick, which means that you will need to concentrate on using the knee and hip to forcibly drive the kick into the target. When you practice, make sure that the knee works as a piston. This kick is usually used in two ways: It is used against a target who approaches you from the side, and it also is frequently used as an attack with your front leg. (Try it using the cross-step from Chapter 9, "Stand Up for Yourself: Stances.") The side-thrust kick works effectively against almost any target you can see. In self-defense situations, you will drive it down against your opponent's knee (be very careful to keep control when you practice this with a partner). It is also an effective kick against the hips, stomach, ribs, chest, and head.

Sensei Says

Kick everywhere. Gain control over your legs. Kick all the time. You don't just have to kick in class. Kick over the toilet while you're brushing your teeth, or over the couch while you are talking on the phone. Can you close a cupboard (gently) with a round kick? Or, try standing with two totally full glasses of water in your hands (do this in the yard) and not spilling any while you execute a front, side, or round kick.

1. Raise the knee as high to the chest as you can. (Remember to bend the leg you are standing on, and to set your foot position.)

2. Smoothly use the hip to drive the knee to the target. You want the knee and hip to lock into place at the end of the kick.

3. Pull the knee back to the starting position, and then step down, forward, or back.

Yoko geri kekomi, the side-thrust kick.

From the Back

Pound for pound, the back-thrust kick (ushiro geri) is probably your strongest technique because it carries a lot of oomph. The trouble is that your target is usually behind you, and at first it's hard to aim. But once you have it down, your opponents had better watch out!

You probably will start practicing this kick from a standing position, kicking back against a target that is behind you. As you become more advanced, though, you will learn what is called a spinning back kick, which lets you use it to the front. The back kick is good against almost any part of your opponent. Its strength, however, is that it's surprising to someone who isn't expecting it.

1. In one smooth movement, bring your knee to your chest, your heel to your hip, and your hip to your target. Glance over your shoulder.

2. Continue the movement by thrusting your knee out to your target. Try to keep the foot pointed down. You are kicking with the heel of your foot.

3. Strongly pull the knee back to your starting position.

Ushiro geri, the back-thrust kick.

All Around

The round-house kick (mawashi geri) is extremely versatile. Depending on your ability and strategy, you can use the round-house kick to attack your opponent from his ankle (as a sweep) all the way up to his head—and everywhere in between.

The special characteristic of the round-house kick is that it hits at a perpendicular angle to your opponent. So, for example, if his hands are up between you, you can use this kick to go around them. This is a snap kick, so the knee points to the target, and the heel snaps back to the hip.

1. Raise your knee to the side of your body. As you do this, form one level plane with your knee, your hip, and your heel. It's okay to lean your body, but try to keep your shoulders level with the ground.

2. Turn your hip and knee to the target, snapping your foot out and back.

3. Return to the starting position.

Mawashi geri, the round-house kick.

It's Time to Sweep the Floor

Contrary to what we've said all along, sweeping is neither a snapping or a thrusting kick. But that's okay, because it isn't really a beginning technique, either. We just thought we'd throw it in!

Sweeps are used to attack your opponent's stance and balance. Sometimes a sweep will actually topple your opponent off his feet and onto the floor. That's good! Sometimes it will just break his balance and concentration enough to let you follow up with a punch or a kick—and that's good enough!

This kind of sweep works kind of the way a golf club works: It swings through the target. Usually, because of the leverage involved, the lower you hit your opponent on the leg, the more effective your sweep will be. Think of sweeping with a broom—the closer it stays to the ground, the more effective it is.

Karate Minute

Aside from the kicks covered in this chapter, karate has many other more advanced kicking techniques. As you progress, you will undoubtedly learn jumping front and side kicks, crescent kicks, hook kicks, ax kicks, inside-snap kicks, inside-round kicks, and inside sweeps. Often, more advanced students can use many of these kicks as blocks and defensive techniques, as well as attacks.

Make sure to sweep from a stable stance. You don't want to knock yourself off balance trying to knock someone else down. Also, be sure to turn your foot sideways so that you hit with the sole of your foot.

1. Start from a stable front stance. Swing your leg out in a circular course so that the sole of your foot contacts the ankle at a right angle.

2. Brace your body and hips after you hit so that your opponent moves sideways, but you continue your forward momentum as you attack. You don't want to lose your own momentum after the technique.

The outside foot sweep.

Make Them Work: It's the Momentum!

At the beginning of this chapter, when we said that "the second biggest problem (of kicking) is keeping your balance," we used the term *balance* incorrectly, mainly because you didn't know anything about kicking. Now that you're a kicking pro, we'll use the right term: "The second biggest problem (of kicking) is failing to use your *momentum*." Balance is static; it is about standing in one place. Momentum is about movement, energy, speed, and power.

As we've said before, the thing that gives karate kicks their power is how effectively you move your hips with the kick. Except for very few instances when you will kick from very close range, try to shift your body center so that it is between your driving foot and your opponent, not perched over your support leg.

Momentum creates force.

Drive off your support leg when you kick. Drive your hips into the target as you make contact.

This chapter completes our overview of karate's basic principles and techniques, which in addition to kicking include stances, blocking, punching, and striking. As you continue on with upcoming chapters on kata, sparring, weapons, and self-defense, continue to reference back and study the fundamentals. In karate, as in all physical and intellectual pursuits—hard work and a strong basic foundation are the key to brilliance.

The Least You Need to Know

➤ Kicks give you extra range and power.

➤ Kicks don't need to be high to be effective.

➤ You need to be able to use both "snap" and "thrust" kicks to be versatile.

➤ You can kick to all directions.

Part 4

Let's Put It All Together

With a good grasp of karate principles and a working understanding of basic techniques, you're now ready to start "using" your karate. No, not by, as Bill Cosby used to say, "walking down the street with $20 bills hanging out of your pockets, hoping that people will jump out and attack you." Instead, you'll put together the techniques you've learned in ways that make sense, that build on each other, and that help you achieve your karate goals.

Try thinking of learning karate in the same way you think of learning a language. (After all, when people are throwing kicks and punches at each other, they are communicating!) At first, as a child, you learn basic words that cover basic situations: "Mommy," "ball," "potty," "NO!" Gradually, as you mature, your vocabulary grows, and your ability to communicate more complex and subtle ideas develops. Eventually, you are able to speak fluently and to express yourself precisely in a variety of situations. You are able to find the right words at the right time and without hesitation.

When you learn the language of karate, you do the same thing. You go from simple to complex, basic to subtle, conscious to spontaneous. The goal ultimately is to become fluent with your technique—to be able to find the right techniques, at the right time, without hesitation.

In Part 4, we look at kata—forms and sets of movements used for individual practice and technical development; sparring—methods for learning to apply your techniques safely in combative situations; controlling your techniques—how to avoid painful mistakes and accidents; kobudo—the use of karate's ancient weapons; and self-defense—using karate on the street in real situations.

Chapter 14

Karate's Dynamic Deadly Dances of Death: Kata

In This Chapter

➤ What a kata is and where it came from

➤ The importance of kata practice

➤ How kata practice improves both mind and body

➤ Learn a simple kata

Each of the major styles of Japanese karate has its roots in the old forms of Okinawa-te, the Okinawan fighting arts that were formulated largely from Okinawan and Chinese systems of combat. In its early stages of development, Okinawa-te was a system of all-out combat. There were no sport competitions—each encounter was a matter of life and death. As the systems became more stylized, the masters developed routines of self-defensive and symbolic movements to provide an avenue of practice for the trainee without actual combat. These routines, in turn, became highly stylized within each school and came to be known as kata, which means "form" or "formal exercise."

What Is a Kata?

A *kata* is a choreographed routine of sequential techniques performed along specified lines of movement, in which you defend yourself against multiple imaginary opponents. A kata kind of looks like a gymnastics floor routine using punches, kicks, strikes, and blocks instead of tumbling. It also resembles complicated dance sequences, which is why kata sometimes are called "dances of death." Each kata is a unit within itself, and each is designed to practice and demonstrate specific body movements.

Some kata are slow and graceful; some are fast with short, hard movements.

Some kata are slow and graceful, with long, sweeping movements, while others are fast, with short, hard movements. Some are designed to practice expansion and contraction of specific body muscles, and some are designed to practice control of breathing. All the kata practiced for competition by the major Japanese karate organizations have one ultimate test of correct performance: The point at which you begin must be the same point at which you finish.

In karate kata, regardless of style, you can almost always sense beauty, coordination, and grace.

Karate Minute

Kata are one of the three major divisions of karate training. The other two are **kihon** (basic techniques) and **kumite** (sparring).

Name That Kata

Every style of karate practices a unique set of kata, and most styles of karate have several kata in common with each other. Counting all the traditional styles of karate-do, at least 60 kata are practiced regularly. Counting the smaller, lesser known styles, there probably are more than 100 kata in existence.

To keep it all straight, each kata has a name, and the names most often indicate something about the nature of the kata. *Heain* for example, means *peaceful* and is derived from the idea that people who have mastered the Heain kata are capable of defending themselves in all normal situations and, therefore, have peaceful minds. *Jutte* means "10 hands," indicating that mastery of the kata will give you the strength of 10 hands. *Tekki* ("horse riding" or "iron horse"), *Gankaku* ("crane on a rock"), *Empi* ("flying swallow"), and *Hangetsu* ("crescent") are named for the resemblance of their distinctive movements to commonly observed objects and actions. *Jion,* on the other hand, is the name of a temple where some people think the kata came from. *Bassai* ("to penetrate a fortress") is typical of a kata whose name creates an image of the kind of overall movement seen in the kata. The idea of penetrating a fortress conjures up an image of charging, driving, sweeping attacks, and that's what the techniques of Bassai look like.

Still other kata are named for people, such as *Kushanku,* and some are named for the number of steps or techniques or directions they have. Some examples of those types of kata are *Niseshi* ("24") which has 24 distinctive stepping motions; *Gojushiho* ("54 steps"); and *Hyakuhachiho* ("108 steps"). That's a really long kata, though. Most kata have somewhere between 25 and 45 movements.

Talk the Talk

Kata means "form" or "formal exercise."

Sensei Says

A kata should not be viewed as a number of connected techniques, but rather as a single technique in and of itself.

Karate Minute

When Gichin Funakoshi introduced karate to Japan, he changed the names of many of the kata from their Okinawan names to more meaningful names for the Japanese. Among others, *Seisan* (thirteen) became *Hangetsu* (crescent); *Chinto* (name of a Chinese envoy) became *Gankaku* (crane on a rock); and *Kushanku* (name of a military envoy) became *Kanku* (viewing the sky).

Physical Kata Training

Because kata encompass so many of the physical techniques of karate-do, they are invaluable to student and master alike. Kata are the very essence of all karate training. They are the most effective way of practicing by yourself, and they are unsurpassed as physical conditioning exercises. The best way to develop the muscles needed for a particular technique is to practice the technique itself, and kata force you to do just that. By regularly practicing kata, you will develop strength, agility, coordination, and control over your body because the kata techniques are performed in many different directions and with highly varied timing.

When trying to learn a new kata, try to view the kata in its entirety. Then, following the movements of a leader, perform the kata slowly several times. You'll probably have to break it down into smaller segments and gradually add more movements as you memorize the pattern. This will give you a feeling for the general direction and timing of the kata. When you have the direction and timing more or less memorized, you can start giving attention to the individual techniques, and you'll find yourself growing stronger in the kata each time you practice it.

Ouch!

Kata is the most important part of karate training because you can learn basics and sparring from kata, but you can't learn kata from basics and sparring. Kata has it all.

From the beginning, it's important that you understand the meaning of each movement in the kata and imagine that opponents are actually attacking you as you perform the movements. After all, you want the kata techniques to work in a real emergency.

As you progress through the ranks and learn more kata, you should not practice one kata exclusively and disregard the others. A well-rounded knowledge of all the kata is essential for a well-rounded understanding of the techniques of karate-do.

Mental Kata Training

Kata practice is excellent for developing continuity between the actions of the mind and the actions of the body. Serious kata practice can actually provide you with solutions to certain problems—solutions that otherwise you might not find. For example, in karate you are expected to be bold and confident, and at the same time humble and gentle. Under stress, you are expected to display a calm and steady demeanor. These things are very difficult to learn just through sparring alone because when you spar with an opponent of greater skill, it's very easy to display humility and gentleness, but very difficult to be bold and confident. On the other hand, when you face an opponent of much lesser skill, it's easy to be bold and confident, but overwhelming your opponent doesn't teach you anything about humility and gentleness.

In kata practice, though, you always control the opponent. You create him, you make him do what you want him to do, and you make him do things that you wouldn't want an actual opponent to do to you. Using your imagination, you can make the opponent bold or shy, strong or weak, fast or slow, and you can learn how to deal with many different kinds of opponents. When you face an actual opponent, there's no time to stop and think and feel what should be happening in your body and mind. In the kata, however, you can do all these things because you are sparring with your own imagination. You face whatever your imagination creates, and you can face a devastating opponent again and again, suffering defeat without damaging physical effect. And if you keep facing that opponent repeatedly, you might eventually defeat him. The sense of accomplishment and overcoming of fear derived from this type of training is stored in your intuition and memory, and can be called into action in an actual combat situation.

You can take this very seriously if you remember that fear of an opponent does not lie in the opponent or his actions, but only in the mind of the one who is afraid. That would be you. Fear is similar to imagination—with discipline, you can learn to chase it away. So, be serious in your kata practice, and use your best imagination to create and deal with vicious opponents.

If you are conscientious about training this way, your sparring will become an extension of your kata. Remember that what you face in your imagination is stored in your intuition and memory, and you can bring it out to deal with an actual opponent in sparring. In fact, if you're very serious about it, the biggest things you will have to learn from sparring are timing and distancing, and even those will be easier to learn from a position of physical strength—the physical strength you will gain from practicing kata.

EEEE-YA!!!

Talk the Talk

Bunkai (pronounced *boon-kah-ee*) means "application" and is the word used to describe the practical application of techniques in the kata.

Kata and Kinesthesia

The kinesthetic sense is the movement sense. It's the sense that tells you whether you are right-side up or upside down. Even with your eyes closed, you are aware of your body's movement because sense organs in the muscles, tendons, and joints respond to movement just like the eyes respond to light. Your eyes interpret light in terms of light, shadow, color, hue, and intensity, and your kinesthetic sense interprets movement by sensing tension and relaxation in your muscles, balance, posture, and position.

Each sense has its own set of corresponding art forms that use the materials of that sense as their media. The auditory (hearing) sense has a corresponding art form—music—whose medium is sound. Similarly, one of the kinesthetic sense's corresponding art forms is karate, whose medium is movement.

In any art form, learning a technique centers on gaining mastery of the instrument and the medium. So, in music, you learn to control the instrument to produce subtle variations of sound, and you learn to hear in a highly sensitive manner.

In karate, the body is the instrument, and movement is the medium, so karate training centers on gaining control over the body and its movements. The main elements of movement are space, time, and energy; if you practice karate, you will be able to feel these things in a highly sensitive manner. Movement is the main material of karate, and kata practice is the best way to turn your body into an instrument of the art of motion. More than any other part of karate training, kata practice helps you develop feelings of movement, time, space, and energy, and the feelings that you develop by practicing kata can help you in every other physical activity that you engage in. Kata puts you in touch with your body.

Karate Minute

In some dojos, instructors sometimes have their students try a kata while blindfolded, to help them develop their kinesthetic sense.

The Elements of Kata

To fully appreciate the complexity of kata performance, it is important to know what the underlying elements of good kata performance are.

The Terms You Need to Know

Here are some of the terms that are used for different elements of performance in the dojo and competition.

➤ *Rei* is a ceremonial bow performed at the beginning and end of each kata. It is performed in musubi dachi (attention stance, heels together, toes pointing outward). Throughout the bow, keep your eyes fixed straight ahead. The bow is used to signify respect for one's opponents and symbolizes one of the most famous sayings in karate: "Karate begins with courtesy and ends with courtesy."

➤ *Kamae* is the yoi, or ready posture, from which the fist movement begins. The purpose of kamae is to show the opponents a state of relaxed awareness. In karate kamae, breathe slowly in the lower stomach and concentrate on building your fighting spirit.

➤ *Zanshin* is the perfect finish of the kata and literally means "remaining mind." When you finish the kata, you must not relax your concentration. Your spirit, mind, and concentration must remain until you complete the ending bow.

➤ *Kiai* is a shout from the abdomen that occurs once or twice during the kata. Its purpose is to indicate the climax of a series of movements and to help tense the body muscles through contraction of the diaphragm and the forceful expulsion of air.

➤ *Embusen* is the performance line of the kata. Basic kata follow a line on the floor that is like a large "I" or "H." All movements are performed on these lines or at specific angles to them. Advanced kata, of course, follow much more complex lines of movement.

Kata's Big Three

Three important technical points apply to every kata:

1. **Power control.** Each kata is different and is designed to demonstrate and practice different aspects of body movement, so it is very important to understand where and how to apply proper strength and power in the kata. The movements are not to be done with equal power; they are to be done with *proper* power.

2. **Expansion and contraction of muscles.** This principle also involves *proper* expansion and contraction of body muscles, and in the proper order. The kata are very dynamic and complex, and performance of them must be fluid and smooth. Improper tension and relaxation will make the movements jerky and unbalanced.

3. **Speed and rhythm control.** Each kata has a different rhythm; while some movements are performed slowly, others are performed very fast. Proper control of speed and rhythm is essential to the performance of each kata.

EEEE-YA!!!

Talk the Talk

Bunkai oyo means "expanded application" of kata techniques. In other words, use your imagination when trying to figure out the meaning of kata techniques.

To really make your kata performance shine, you need to work on these points, too:

➤ **Eye intensity:** A strong gaze will indicate strong concentration.

➤ **Attitude:** Your attitude should be serious and intense.

➤ **Deportment:** You should display an air of dignity and a sense that the kata you are performing is important.

177

➤ **Position and posture:** Your posture should be erect and relaxed to indicate good body control.

➤ **Continuity from one technique to another:** The kata should be smooth and flowing, not jerky.

Do Kata Techniques Work?

Yes, they do. Each and every movement of each and every kata has a practical meaning and a self-defense application. However, because no single, universal standard defines the precise meaning of each kata technique, practical interpretations of the techniques vary widely. One person might look at a downward blocking motion in a kata, for example, and see a downward block against a front kick. Another person might see a downward bottom fist strike against a wrist grab. Still another might see the windup for the block as a sweeping forearm block against a punch.

So, who's right? They all are. The meanings of the techniques in the kata have been handed down from generation to generation orally, for the most part, so there is no real way to be sure of the meanings intended by the originators of the kata. To make things even more complicated, several kata are clearly copies of old Okinawan folk dances, which means that they might not even have been related to actual combat techniques in the beginning. The best thing for you to do is to listen to your instructor and ask questions about the meaning of each movement. The final answer is this—the meaning of each kata technique is whatever your instructor tells you it is.

Who Makes Up the Kata?

Today, nobody makes up a kata. The kata have been handed down, some for several hundred years from generation to generation, and they are highly revered links to karate's origins. Many of them were created by people who actually had to defend themselves against repeated violent attacks, and it would be hard to duplicate that experience today. Most of the kata practiced today in Okinawan and Japanese karate-do can be traced (at least, their roots can be traced) to the late 1600s and early 1700s. There have been many changes to the kata over the years, of course, but most of them are still recognizably linked to their old predecessors.

In the years when Okinawa-te was being created, kata were being created along with it. Also, it appears that many kata were imported to Okinawa from China. As the techniques of Okinawa-te progressed, more kata were created, and more were modified. When karate became available to the public around 1900, though, the various styles organized themselves in a logical fashion so that karate-ka could present their art to the

Sensei Says

Kata are your living links to the past. Study them carefully to understand your roots, and never change them.

178

public in a coherent way. When that was done, the kata of each system were pretty much set in stone; although there have been some modifications of kata since then, very few new kata have been created.

A Beginner's Kata: Heain Shodan

Heain Shodan is a beginner-level kata taught as the first kata in many different styles of karate. In some styles, it is known by its older name, *Pinan*. See? We told you things change.

The techniques of Heain Shodan follow the big "H" pattern on the floor. There are also techniques at the end of this kata that go at angles to the H. There is no jumping in this kata, nor are there any complicated techniques, so you should be able to get a good idea of what performing a kata is like by following along with the pictures. All the techniques in Heain Shodan can be found in this book.

Kata Heain Shodan.

The Least You Need to Know

➤ Kata are choreographed sequences of techniques handed down from the past.

➤ Kata practice greatly enhances both physical and mental abilities.

➤ All kata techniques have practical self-defense applications.

➤ Mastering karate's kata can improve your performance in all other sports and physical activities.

Chapter 15

Sparring: It's Different When You're Face to Face

In This Chapter

➤ Different types of sparring exercises

➤ How timing and distance make your techniques effective

➤ Controlling your techniques

➤ Using impact equipment

Soon after you start practicing karate, and probably before you even learn your first kata, you will start doing some sort of sparring practice. Right now, some of you are probably are reading this and saying, "Oh boy! Sparring, finally!" Others of you might be saying, "Hmmm, sparring. I'm not so sure about this. What if I get hurt? What if I'm not ready? Maybe I can just do kata?" In every dojo, there are people who love to spar and people who hate it. But, love it or hate it, sparring is a very important aspect of your karate training.

What Is Sparring?

The traditional concept of sparring, or *kumite,* is sometimes a little difficult to grasp until you start getting the hang of martial arts culture and philosophy. No, sparring is not simply about getting out there and kicking someone's butt. It's a little more complicated than that. Sparring is a training method in which you try to improve your techniques by testing them against someone else's techniques. More fundamentally, in sparring, you try to improve yourself by being tested against someone else.

Now you may be saying "Okay, fine, but really, that just sounds like a fancy way to talk about kicking someone's butt." Well, to be honest, it's a little of both.

The key thing to remember about sparring is this: Sparring is *not* fighting. Sparring is practice for fighting. And, like any other activity that trains you to compete (or fight) against someone else, you use specific and structured training methods to prepare yourself. After all, football teams don't just get out there during practice and beat the tar out of each other before the big game—they scrimmage and run plays. Boxers don't pound the daylights out of each other before a fight—they wear helmets, they practice combinations, they do bag work, and they spar with "partners." The military doesn't just hand out guns and the keys to fighter jets and tanks, and say "Go get 'em boys!"—they train, they test equipment continually, they develop and practice battle plans, and, most importantly, they develop discipline. Karate is no different.

Talk the Talk

Kumite means "sparring."

Sparring is not fighting—sparring is practice for fighting.

Sparring will do two things for you. First, it will teach you basic strategies and help you develop a sense of distance and timing so that you can actually put your blocks, punches, strikes, and kicks where you want them to go when you want them to go there.

Second, as you become more advanced and the sparring becomes more intense, it will teach you to control your feelings and emotions when you are under pressure—always a useful personal tool. Remember that initially, karate was developed so that you could defend yourself from someone who really wanted to hurt you. Believe us, this can be very stressful. If you can't control your emotions in these situations, you're going to have a hard time defending yourself.

Remember, too, that karate should be safe to practice. It is a structured activity that gradually increases in intensity as your abilities and confidence grow. Sparring should be controlled. No good karate school will put you in a position in which you are at risk, or in which you haven't been trained to deal with what's coming at you. As we've discussed elsewhere in this book, statistics show that there are fewer overall injuries and far fewer serious injuries in karate than in almost any other organized sport or athletic activity.

But, this isn't to say that accidents won't happen, or that you shouldn't expect to regularly get some bangs and bruises as you become more advanced. After all, this is an art that focuses on developing personal courage, using split-second timing, and getting your arms, legs, fists, and feet to fly around the room as fast as possible. Also, let's be honest, it is much better to find out that your blocks need work, or that your timing is late, by getting "popped" in the dojo once or twice, than to find out late at night, on the way to your car.

As we will cover in this chapter, there are many different methods of kumite practice in traditional karate, from very basic and prearranged sparring to free sparring. Depending on your ability, the lesson or technique being taught, your dojo's philosophy, and your instructor, you will practice some or all of them. At the right time, they all have their place, and all are valuable.

We will start with the simplest and most fundamental sparring exercises and gradually move to the more advanced. As you will see, each type of sparring teaches a main point or principle that will help develop your abilities.

Start Simple

Basic sparring exercises and drills are designed to teach you how the techniques work and to get you used to working with a partner or opponent. Start simple. Both you and your opponent should know exactly what the other is going to do and when. Surprises hurt!

Sensei Says

Be aware of what's going on. When training, think of a "partner" as someone who is working with you, to help you and your technique get better. That person may help you stretch, act as a target, or stand there and allow you to try a technique. Think of an "opponent" as someone who is trying to make himself and his technique better, at your expense. To get good at karate you will need both.

Sensei Says

Control is very important in karate, and it isn't just about not hitting each other. Control also means being able to control your feelings and emotions in times of stress and intensity. For some, this will mean not losing a temper; for others, it will be not giving into fear and insecurity.

The first skill you will need to learn if you're going to spar is to control your techniques. Practice throwing your kicks, punches, strikes, and blocks with speed and power, but stop just short of contact. This will allow you to master the use of your techniques and will increase your ability to work with others.

Simple exercises might include kicking or punching at each other as you stand in place. After that, you can practice those same techniques as you move forward and back. From there, you can move to exchanging basic attacks and blocks, and you and your opponent agree on who is going to punch, strike, or kick, and who is going to block. Again, focus on control. If you get hurt at this stage, you may decide to stop training before you have had a chance to actually learn anything of value.

Start simple. Try standing at arm's length from each other. One person punches, while the other person blocks. Start slowly! Both people should start and end their technique at the same time.

Step by Step for Self-Defense

The most common type of sparring practice is basic sparring. This is a prearranged exercise in which both the attacker and the defender know what the other is going to do. Basic sparring usually is practiced in five-step, three-step, or one-step variations.

Traditionally, the attacker announces a target and a technique or series of techniques such as "Lunge punch, face" or "Front kick, stomach" and then they attack. The defender then blocks and counterattacks. As in all sparring exercises, start slowly until you have the timing and distance down. But, once you know what you are doing, let 'er rip!

As you look around your dojo, you will notice that basic sparring isn't just for beginners. Intermediate and advanced students practice it, too, because it develops your techniques, speed, and timing. People also sometimes think that basic sparring is mainly to help the defense person, but that's not true. Both people are trying to make their techniques as good as possible. You have to figure that once you get good enough to stand in front of somebody, tell them what you're going to do, and then go ahead and do it without the other person being able to stop you, you really have a technique that works.

Karate Minute

Almost everyone who wants to learn self-defense wants to free spar. But real self-defense situations are hardly ever like free-sparring. People who attack you outside a dojo or a tournament are very unlikely to move or "bob and weave" before they attack you. There is usually no faking, either. They walk or run up and attack you. Bam! The bottom line is that basic sparring, if you really practice with effort and intensity, is what will prepare you for self-defense more then anything else.

Be sure to be precise when you do basic sparring. You are training to deliver good karate techniques. Use good form, good stances, and the right distance. Most basic sparring exercises and drills start with the attacker in a forward stance, down block position, and the attacker standing in a natural stance position. As the attacker, you should start from a distance where you can hit your opponent if he doesn't move or block.

Three Steps

In basic three-step sparring, or *sanbon kumite,* the attacker uses three stepping attacks as the defensive person blocks three times and then counterattacks. As the attacker, this type of exercise is meant to help you learn how to deliver a sequence of more then one strong technique in a row and how to break the attacker's distance. As the defender, this exercise teaches you to cope with a series of attacks and to end up at the exact distance you need to be, in order to counterattack effectively. Although you can use any attacks in three-step sparring, and although you can vary them, it is most common for beginners to use the same attack throughout the series.

Sensei Says

To break your opponent's distance is to move in a way that prevents your opponent from being able to keep up with you or to respond to your movements smoothly.

185

Talk the Talk

Sanbon kumite means "three-step sparring." **Gohon kumite** means "five-step sparring." **Ippon kumite** means "one-step sparring."

These are the steps that are involved in three-step sparring, or sanbon kumite:

1. The offensive person assumes the front stance, while the defensive person remains in the natural stance.

2. The attacker lunge-punches to the face; the defender steps back into the front stance and executes rising blocks.

3. Do this again …

4. … and again.

5. After the third attack, the defender counterattacks with a reverse punch to the stomach or *sanbon kumite*.

Three-step sparring, sanbon kumite.

Five Steps

Basic five-step sparring, or *gohon kumite*, continues in the same vein as three-step sparring. When you develop a functioning skill level, try to vary the attacks and counterattacks. Again, both people are trying to improve their techniques and abilities. Start slowly, but build to a point at which you feel that you are being tested.

If you really try to score with your punch or kick, your opponent will have to block harder and move more quickly. This way each of you gets better.

One Step

Basic one-step sparring, or *ippon kumite,* offers you the greatest opportunity to safely use a wide variety of techniques. Make sure that, as the attacker, you announce what your attack is going to be. Be creative. To make basic one-step sparring as realistic as possible, the offensive person should always attack as quickly and strongly as possible. The defender should always try to block and counterattack before the attacker has a chance to get a second attack off.

With one-step sparring, you want to start from the same starting position that is used for three- and five-step sparring.

1. The offensive person attacks with a front kick to the stomach. The defender side shifts and executes a down block.

2. The defender counterattacks with a reverse punch, as the opponent finishes his kick.

3. The attacker performs a round-house kick to the head. The defender uses an inside forearm block ...

4. ... and counters with an elbow to the stomach.

One-step sparring examples.

Surprise!

After you have practiced a lot of basic sparring, you will be ready to go on to what is commonly called semi-free sparring, or *jiyu-ippon kumite*. In this type of sparring, both opponents are allowed to move from the free stance in order to gain an initial advantage. Basically, this is the same way that you see boxers move. There are many variations of this kind of sparring. Sometimes the attacker will announce the target and technique he is going to use, and sometimes you just know who is going to attack next.

Free for All

Free sparring, or *jiyu-kumite,* is kind of like a free-for-all mixed with a chess game. When you first look around a dojo and see free sparring, it often looks wild and random. Arms and legs are going everywhere. People are kicking, punching, and yelling. Every now and then, someone gets swept to the ground and punched. At first you may not really be sure about what you're looking at.

After a while, things start to get a little clearer. You start to notice certain things. First, you notice the control. For all the punching and kicking that is going on, you don't see anyone getting hurt (okay, a little bruised sometimes, but not hurt). Second, you notice that in general, the more advanced people—usually the black-belts and sometimes one or two of the brown-belts—seem to be calmer. Even though they are faster and stronger, and even though they are able to get more techniques in, they don't seem to be working as hard. In the midst of all this chaos, they seem almost relaxed. Third, you notice that, even in the same dojo and the same style, everyone doesn't spar the same way. Some people are aggressive, while some seem to be counterattackers. Some kick a lot, and some just punch. Some are faster and quicker, and some are stronger and more solid. Some get scary expressions on their faces, while some seem almost neutral and passive. Everyone seems to have an individual style.

It's All in Your Head

Free sparring is where it all comes out. You can move, fake, attack, and counter. You can kick, punch, strike, sweep, and throw combinations. Your goal is pretty simple: Use what you have to catch your opponent with a good technique before he catches you.

At one time, beginner and intermediate students were never taught to free spar. In fact, it was uncommon to do any free sparring until a student reached the brown-belt level. (You could do it in secret, of course, but you didn't want your instructors to see you.) In most dojos today, though, some beginners (as early as six months after they start training) and most intermediate students are given some free sparring instruction if they want to compete in tournaments.

Whatever your level, it is always best to start sparring slowly and to be comfortable with what you are doing.

Have a Plan: Strategy

Having a strategy is crucial to being successful in sparring. As you become more experienced, you will see that there is no one right strategy for every situation. You also will see that many very good karate-ka use very different strategies in different situations and against different opponents. The size, speed, and experience of your opponent are all factors that will affect your strategy at a given moment.

In the next sections, we look at the three most basic strategies you can use. Realize that no one strategy should ever be used exclusively (if it were, it wouldn't be much of a strategy, would it?). Generally, strategies are mixed and matched, until someone scores a decisive technique. As with everything else in karate, the goal is to be spontaneous and effective. Start simply so that what you are doing gradually starts to feel natural.

The Best Defense

The saying goes, "A good offense is the best defense." One strategy for sparring is to see the opening and attack, known as *Sen No Sen.* That's it—just attack. As soon as you get in range of your opponent, attack. As soon as your opponent gets in your range, attack. If you are not in range, get there and then attack. If your opponent blocks your first attack, attack again.

Now, we admit this isn't fancy, but if you are focused, intense, and aggressive, it works.

Come and Get Me

A second strategy is to encourage your opponent to attack you, known as *Go No Sen.* Why would you want to do that? So that you can counterattack! Position yourself so that your opponent thinks you are open, or throw out a fake technique to give him some bait. As he attacks, you shift, block, and counterattack. Again, this is very simple in concept, but it requires a lot of practice.

Take Your Best Shot

A third basic strategy, and an especially good one if you don't know what else to do, is to "match" your opponent, hoping to beat him to the punch (or kick). This is simple to do, in theory. Set a distance between you and your opponent, and when he attacks, so do you. Be first (and strongest) to the target, and you win. When you see this strategy being used by two advanced people, it really becomes a thing of beauty because it is almost impossible to tell who moved first.

EEEE-YA!!!

Talk the Talk

Jiyu-ippon kumite refers to "semi-free sparring." **Jiyu-kumite** refers to "free sparring." **Sen No Sen** means to "take the opening to attack." **Go No Sen** refers to counterattacking.

Everything but the Kitchen Sink

As you become more advanced, you will start to use combinations of techniques instead of using one technique at a time. Basically, combinations are techniques that are strung together like the words of a sentence. When beginners start to do combinations, they usually just start by throwing anything they can think of. This is not a combination; it is karate gibberish.

A combination should first break your opponent's timing, distance, or concentration. This is the fake. Then, it should follow with a major, or series of major, techniques, which are the main point of the combination. Always be sure to finish your combinations from a strong defensive position so that you can protect yourself if the combination didn't work the way you wanted it to. As you become more advanced and adept at using your body, you will be able to develop a wider array of combinations that you can use.

Here's a suggestion for a combination that you might try once you become able to put some techniques together:

1. Start with a round kick to the head.

2. Finish with an elbow attack.

3. Or, start with a front kick to the stomach.

4. As your opponent blocks, continue with a punch to the head.

Even simple combinations can be very effective.

In the Nick of Time: Timing

In a sense, effective karate comes down to just three things: First, how good are your techniques? This is what we've talked about in Chapters 8 through 13. Can your stances move and brace you? Do your blocks, punches, kicks, and strikes actually work?

Second: How good is your sense of timing?

Third: How effectively do you use distance?

Think of it this way: The factors that separate a major league home run hitter (with a multimillion-dollar contract) and a lumber jack, who cuts down trees for a living, is simply timing and distance. Both guys are strong. Both swing a stick. But one guy can whack the heck out of a tiny little ball as it zooms past him at 95 miles an hour, while the other guy stands there and whacks a big tree. Offense or defense, single techniques or combinations, karate or other sports, driving without getting squished or just making it across the street—it all comes down to timing and distance.

Now let's discuss three different types of timing and talk a little about distance.

Better Late Than Never

The most fundamental timing involves someone doing something and you responding—one, two. This is usually thought of as basic timing, reaction timing, or beginners' timing. It is practiced most in the first type of sparring you do—basic sparring. One person attacks, and the other person blocks and counterattacks.

Now, as you get more advanced, you don't stop practicing this type of timing be-cause, although it is not as glamorous as free sparring, this type of sparring (and tim-ing) is what really happens in most real self-defense situations. You're walking down the street, and someone lunges out at you from nowhere. Surprise! You block and counter (hopefully). There is no bobbing, weaving, or even faking—the opponent at-tacks, and you defend.

One for One

Next, when you have learned to move, to block and counter, and, to some extent, read an attacker's intentions, you will find that you are also able to match the attack—you block, or shift, and hit the opponent at the same time that he is trying to hit you. This type of timing is very sophisticated and is usually done with a combi-nation of fancy footwork, soft blocking, truly good timing, and lots of experience (not to mention a little intuition).

With good timing, your opponents will never get a chance to finish their attacks.

The Sooner, the Better

The most sophisticated type of timing is to be able to counterattack your opponent or to defend yourself in some other way—before the attacker actually attacks you. This doesn't mean that you can read minds or predict the future. It does mean that you are aware of your surroundings, people's intentions, and the messages people give off with their bodies, facial expressions, and movements. It also means that you can react to that information before you find yourself in true danger.

The true beauty of having this type of timing is that, in most cases, you will never have to actually use your karate. In most cases, you will be able to move, evade, escape, or avoid a situation almost before your opponent actually has had time to formulate a plan of attack.

Hey, Just Stand There for a Minute, Will Ya?

Now, distance is the flip side of timing. At one time or another, you will wish with all your heart that you could just get your opponent to stand still for a moment. But you can't. All techniques have an ideal range or distance, the one point where all the karate dynamics come together and the punch, kick, or strike is most effective. The problem is that people just keep moving. Worse, they keep trying to hit you while you are trying to deliver this perfect technique.

As you train, try to identify and really understand the distance you need to throw certain techniques. That way, if your timing is good, when your opponent is at the right distance, you will have the right technique for the job.

From Kissing Range to Kicking Range

One of the most common mistakes you will make (along with everyone else) is not recognizing what range you are in, and attempting to use the wrong technique at the wrong time. Remember the adage, "Always use the right tool for the right job." Learn to use a variety of techniques, both for long and short distances, so that your response matches your opportunity.

Know your distance. For example, this is not a great distance to start kicking from.

R.E.S.P.E.C.T.—Find Out What It Means to Me

As you train, kumite provides three different ways for you to test yourself and your technique. There will always be opponents who are weaker or less experienced than you, there will be those that are equal to you, and of course, those that are stronger and more experienced than you. Each presents you with a different opportunity to show your respect for yourself and your opponents. Try to approach each from this perspective:

1. With the less experienced, go hard. Always try to improve your technique, but don't be a bully. Role model intensity, effort, and most importantly, control. Bring the opponent up to your level, don't go down to theirs.

2. With your equals, go hard. Each encounter is an opportunity to improve, to raise your self from where you are, and a challenge for your opponent to do the same.

3. Finally, with your seniors, go hard. There is nothing more respectful than effort, and to give someone else the opportunity to show you their best.

Safety's Great, but I Gotta Hit Something

In addition to all the different sparring exercises and training methods, you are also going to have to use stationary and moving impact equipment, if you really want to develop timing distance and focus. Otherwise you will miss out on a very important part of punching, striking, and kicking—the hitting part.

While traditional karate places great value on control and safety when you are sparring, it also places great value on making sure that your techniques actually do what they are supposed to do. Specifically, you want your techniques to deliver significant shock (focus) to your target when you hit something. Soon after becoming a karate student, you will probably start using different types of impact equipment designed for this job.

Remember, you want to hit this stuff, but not the people you train with.

You will test your techniques on all different types of equipment.

As we have cautioned you throughout the book, start each new activity with discretion, and give your body time to catch up with your intentions. When it comes to hitting the equipment, let your body learn—don't try to kill the bag at first.

Some people are under the misconception that karate practice is supposed to make your hands big and hard. This is not true. Everything you hit in the dojo is flexible; it is meant to give and to absorb the force of your techniques. Remember that the goal is to coordinate the strength of your entire body into each technique, not to smash your hands, feet, or head into immovable objects.

Ouch!

Children's bodies are still growing and forming. They should never hit hard surfaces with their fist, and extreme caution should be shown when they kick hard things as well. It is much better to let them practice kicking soft impact targets and bags.

The Makiwara: The Heart of Karate

In many traditional dojos, the *makiwara* board, or punching post, holds a place of special significance. This simple device is felt by many to be karate's most important training aid.

The makiwara is a beveled wooden post that is mounted in the ground. The part you hit is wrapped in a material that is soft but firm (the most traditional makiwaras are wrapped in straw) and allows you to build up to hitting it with considerable force.

Like other impact devices, the makiwara should be flexible enough to absorb the blow, yet provide enough firmness for resistance.

Hitting the makiwara regularly will improve your technique.

Big Bags and Little Bags

Impact bags come in all shapes and sizes. Some, like the heavy bag, hang independently, while others are held by your instructor or your training partners as you hit them. Try to get comfortable working with a wide variety of kicking bags. Some build your power, and some improve your speed. All are important.

Kicking bags come in all sizes.

Shields and Moving Targets

Using moving targets will not only help improve the power of your techniques, but they also will teach you about timing and distance. Start slowly, but eventually build up to being able to hit just about anything that's put in front of you.

195

Have someone move with you as you spar with the moving targets.

Boards and Bricks

We admit that it's pretty impressive to see someone smash through boards, bricks, or a bunch of tiles. But by now you realize that breaking things is not what karate is all about. When karate was first introduced to the West, breaking something was a very clear way to show that, with training, anyone could develop a great deal of power. Karate guys were breaking things all the time. In fact, in the 1970s, a dojo in Great Britain demolished a condemned house with their bare hands as a demonstration of what karate could do.

Usually, breaking will not be a regular part of your training. However, some schools use board-breaking as part of the promotion process. Of course, as you become more advanced, you may get to break boards if you and your dojo do a demonstration somewhere.

Sometimes you will break boards at a promotion or demonstration.

As we stated at the beginning of the chapter, sparring is not fighting. Sparring is practice for fighting. So as you work out with partners and opponents, and use the impact equipment to perfect your distance, timing, and technique—remember your goal. You want your techniques to come to you automatically—when you need them. To this end, be sure to use all the training methods of karate; the basics, the kata, and the material in this chapter with equal intensity. Don't just focus on the ones you find the easiest, the most fun, or the most exciting.

The Least You Need to Know

➤ Sparring is not fighting—sparring is practice for fighting.

➤ There are many different types of sparring training methods such as basic, semi-free, and free-sparring.

➤ It is important to control your techniques so you can practice with speed and power, and so no one suffers unnecessary accidental injuries.

➤ Using impact equipment will teach you to make your techniques more effective.

The Ancient Weapons of Karate: Kobudo

While the Okinawans were developing karate for self-defense, they by no means limited themselves to empty-handed techniques. Indeed, they displayed great ingenuity in turning their farming and fishing implements into deadly weapons. Undoubtedly, the Okinawans began developing the use of farming and fishing implements as weapons even before they began systematically developing empty-hand techniques.

The Okinawan arts of weaponry are today known as *kobudo,* and they are practiced by many styles of karate as an adjunct to regular karate training. Practicing with weapons builds physical strength and improves coordination.

History and Traditions

It seems that there are just as many theories about the history of Okinawan weaponry as there are researchers studying the subject. Some historians believe that kobudo weapons developed as extensions of the punches, kicks, and strikes of karate techniques. Others suggest that the weapons were simply copies of Chinese weapons.

Sensei Says

Karate weapons are not used as weapons today. They are used as an extension of the arms and the body.

Talk the Talk

Kobudo literally means "old (ko) martial (bu) ways (do)." Today it is the term used specifically to describe karate weaponry.

Talk the Talk

A **Gaff** is a sharp prong that is usually tied to the end of a stick, and is used to help land big fish. It is a common fishing tool.

Some believe that the weapons were developed by members of an elite stratum of society and were more for demonstration than for actual self-defense.

In fact, virtually all the tools and implements turned into weapons by the Okinawans were in general use throughout Southeast Asia, but it was the Okinawans who showed the greatest ingenuity in developing those implements into weapons.

The problem with studying the history of Okinawan kobudo is that there are almost no written records covering the subject. Diligent researchers are digging up more documents every year, but such documents are still scarce. Oral histories and traditions about kobudo, however, are not scarce at all. They are abundant in the extreme, so that is where we have gone for our information about kobudo.

According to legend, the weapons of kobudo came from two primary sources: Okinawan fishermen and Okinawan farmers.

Weapons from the Fishermen

From the fishermen came two popular weapons that could be wielded with deadly accuracy and effect. The *nunte* and *sai,* both used as gaffs during the day, were turned into deadly weapons of self-defense. The nunte was a cast-iron implement about two feet long, about one-inch thick in the center, and tapered to points on each end for piercing effect and to provide balance. On each side of the nunte was a sharp tine, pointing toward each end of the shaft.

The nunte could be used effectively against a swordsman by catching the blade of the sword in one of the tines and then jerking the sword away from the swordsman with a sharp snap of the wrist, or, in a more fluid motion, pinning the sword blade to the ground. Some fishermen carried two nunte, concealing one in their clothing or hanging another from their waist sash behind their back. In this fashion, one nunte could be used for parrying a sword attack, and the other could be used to stab the opponent.

The nunte, also known as "manji sai."

Karate Minute

Originally, nunte and sai were made of cast iron, but today they more often are made of steel; some are even chrome-plated.

In many instances, the nunte would be tied with fishermen's knots to a long staff (bo) and would be wielded like a spear or halberd. Used in this fashion, the nunte was extremely effective against armed warriors because it gave the fisherman an important edge in distance from the attacking swordsman.

A variation of the nunte was the sai, similar in construction, but with both tines pointing toward the sharpened end of the center shaft.

The sai, a pronged weapon and fishing tool.

The sai in action.

The shaft of the sai also had one shorter, blunted end, which could be used to punch at an opponent.

The main advantage of the sai was that it could be held with the pointed end lying along the forearm, and the blunted end extending outward from the hand. With a flip of the wrist, the fisherman could snap the long end of the sai forward, catch a swordsman's blade, twist it away from him, and either stab the attacker with the sharp end, strike him with a flipping action of the long shaft, or retrieve the long end and jab him with the short, blunt end. Furthermore, holding the sai along the forearm enabled the fisherman to block or parry a sword slash at close range with his iron-protected arm and then move in for the kill. As with the nunte, fisherman often carried the sai in pairs, for the same reasons and with the same results.

Ouch!

Never try to use a nunte or a sai without proper instruction—they are made of very heavy metal and can easily bruise you or even break your bones if you don't handle them properly.

The first thing most people think of when they see a nunte or a sai is that they are throwing weapons, but in reality these weapons were rarely thrown, except as a last resort. Fishermen carrying three sai might throw one to distract the opponent, but both the nunte and the sai were far more effective as hand-held weapons than as projectiles.

Another contribution of the fishermen to kobudo was the *eku,* or the long oar.

Eku, a long oar.

Although it was a heavy and somewhat cumbersome weapon, the eku nevertheless could be used to great effect in sweeping the opponent off his feet, deflecting strikes from other weapons, and jabbing and striking.

Comparatively little creativity was required to use the eku as a weapon, and as a formal system of weaponry, it is today almost extinct. In the hands of an Okinawan fisherman, though, the eku was a very effective weapon.

Karate Minute

While millions of people all over the world have used a boat oar as a weapon at one time or another, only the Okinawans formalized its use and created carefully choreographed exercises with it.

Weapons from the Farmers

For all their ingenuity, Okinawan fishermen were overshadowed in the development of weapons by Okinawan farmers. Farmers had many more tools at their disposal than fishermen and, therefore, were able to develop a larger arsenal of weapons.

One such weapon, the *bo,* was a nearly six-foot staff of hardwood that could be conveniently whittled from almost any tree or branch of sufficient size.

The bo, a hardwood staff.

As a fighting instrument, the staff has been used since antiquity—and in fact, the Japanese martial arts recognized hundreds of different schools of *bo-jutsu,* or *arts of the staff.* Almost all the Japanese schools of bo-jutsu, however, utilized a thick, heavy rod of wood, called *rokushaku.* The Okinawans, on the other hand, developed a thinner, lighter, tapered shaft for the bo, and this provided superior speed and flexibility in the application of their techniques.

Of all the arts of Okinawan weaponry, the bo was probably the most highly developed and carefully studied. Kata (formal exercises) from the various masters of the bo today number in the hundreds, and entire styles of bo-jutsu have been created in accordance with the principles developed by the early Okinawans.

It is likely that the tapered bo was a natural outgrowth of the use of gaff handles and plow handles as staves. Whether by design or chance, the tapering of the bo into a lighter staff was of great importance in the development of Okinawan staff techniques, and it served the Okinawans well in combat against the Japanese.

Sensei Says

Even with their weapons banned, the Okinawans still could carry their long staffs in daylight by holding them across the back of their necks with a bucket of grain or water on each end.

In addition to the bo, the farm people also made extensive use of the *kama* (a sickle), the *tonfa* (a handle from a rice grinder), and the *nunchaku* (a wooden flail). Of these three weapons, the kama was probably the most effective and versatile.

The sharpened, curved blade of the kama was attached to a short, wooden handle in a perpendicular fashion. Not only could this weapon be used to slash and cut, but it also could (much like the sai) be held along the forearm to protect the arm and then to whip out at an opponent with blinding speed.

The kama, a sickle.

The kama in action.

205

Ouch!

Don't try to practice with a real kama until you have lots and lots of training. A real kama has a very sharp blade and can easily lop off fingers or even hands. Unless your instructor tells you otherwise, always practice only with 100 percent wooden kama. Those can bruise, but they can't cut.

Two kama, one held in each hand, could be waved and whipped around the body and the head in a circular fashion, providing protection from a multitude of attacks from multiple opponents. This short kama (about 2 feet long) usually consisted of a wooden handle and an 8-inch or 10-inch slightly curved blade, sharpened on one side.

A longer, sturdier version of the kama exhibited a straighter blade sharpened on both sides. This kama often was lashed to a long pole and used in the fashion of the Japanese halberd (*naginata*). Not only was it an effective weapon at longer range, but it also proved very effective in slashing the legs of horses ridden by heavily armored samurai.

Another variation was called *nichigama,* and it consisted of two short kama tied together by a long rope or piece of chain.

Kusarigama, a chain that was attached to a sickle.

This enabled the farmer to throw one kama, ensnaring the opponent and drawing him close, and then hack him to pieces with the other blade. Another more advanced technique involved throwing both blades at once while holding onto the center of the rope or chain. Used in this fashion, the kama would scissor past each other in the air and return to the sender in boomerang fashion. As might be imagined, this technique was at the apex of kama technique in terms of difficulty of execution and the degree of skill required of the user.

A kama attached at the end of the handle or the base of the blade to a long chain with a lead weight on the other end was called a *kusarigama* and could be used in bolo fashion to trip a man or a horse, drag him near, and kill him with the blade. The attachment of a chain or rope to a kama also made it possible to throw the weapon and retrieve it easily.

As an instrument of versatility, the tonfa also ranks high among indigenous Okinawan weaponry.

Tonfa, a rice-grinder handle.

The tonfa in action.

The tonfa was a square shaft of oak, about two feet long, with a four- or five-inch handle set perpendicular to the shaft, about five or six inches from one end. The tonfa was an integral part of the millstone used to grind rice, so it was a very common implement among farmers. The millstone used by the Okinawans consisted of a stone that was rolled over the rice as it lay in a shallow groove. The tonfa was inserted in a hole cut in the grinding stone and was used to move the stone back and forth across the rice. Thus, it was easily removable, and the short handle could be grasped to turn the tonfa into an effective weapon.

207

Karate Minute

Many modern police forces use a nightstick weapon called PR24 or Enforcer. Except for the fact that it is made of high-impact plastic, it is an exact replica of the Okinawan tonfa.

A farmer holding a pair of tonfa could use one lying along his forearm to block or parry a blow, and because the ends of the weapon extended beyond both the fist and the elbow, he might use the other to jab, punch, or even strike with the end protruding past the elbow. By grasping the short handle in a light grip, the farmer could also spin the long end of the tonfa toward an assailant, either tightening his grip to make a forceful strike, or letting the tonfa continue to spin in a raking motion across the opponent's face.

In close combat, the long end of the tonfa could be grasped, and the short, protruding handle could be used in grappling hook fashion to grab an opponent's knee and unbalance him.

Of all the weapons derived from Okinawan farming implements, the most popular today is the nunchaku, or the flail. When harvesting rice, Okinawan farmers would cut the grain with a kama and then separate the grain from the chaff with a wooden flail.

EEEE-YA!!!

Talk the Talk

Nunchaku (pronounced *noon-chah-koo*) is the proper name of the Okinawan flail. In the 1970s and 1980s, they came to be called "noonchucks," "num-chucks," or just "chucks." Be aware that these silly variations are irritating and even insulting to real experts.

This flail was made of two tapered sticks of wood, each about one-inch thick, connected at the tapered ends by braided horse hair, or sometimes by a thick, sturdy vine called kanda. In modern times, horse hair has been replaced by heavy cord or a length of chain.

A little-known fact in the Western world today is that there were many different kinds of nunchaku, and many of them had three (san-setsu-kon nunchaku) or four (yon-setsu-kon nunchaku) pieces.

Neither were the pieces of the nunchaku all of uniform length. *So-setsu-kon nunchaku* was composed of one section only half the length of the other, and *san-setsu-kon nunchaku* sometimes displayed one piece of normal length attached to two smaller pieces. Some nunchaku were octagonal in shape (*hakakukei nunchaku*), some were round (*marugata nunchaku*), and still others were only half-round (*han-kei nunchaku*).

The nunchaku, a flail.

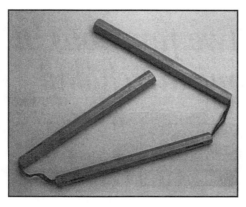

San-setsu-kon, a three-section nunchaku.

No matter what shape or form the nunchaku took, it proved to be a very deadly weapon in the hands of a skilled farmer. Holding one end firmly, the wielder of the nunchaku could generate tremendous force in the other end of the weapon by swinging it in deadly patterns at his assailant. Particularly effective in disarming an opponent, the sticks of the nunchaku could also be grasped, either singly or together, and used as a cudgel or a truncheon at close range. Other effective close-range uses of the nunchaku included using it as a garrote for strangling the opponent and as pincers against the limbs or the head.

The nunchaku in action.

Because the nunchaku was easily concealed in a person's clothing, and because it could be used effectively even by those with limited skills, it quickly became the most popular weapon among the Okinawan peasants.

Possession of weaponry was prohibited, so kobudo experts had to practice in secrecy, and their skills were passed on to others by word of mouth and in the form of kata (formal exercises) containing the techniques and movements of each expert's individual style. Many of these kata are still practiced today.

In addition to the primary ones mentioned previously, other weapons were used by the Okinawans, but their use was never systematized or passed along from generation to generation in as formal a manner as the others. These included, among others, the *suruchin* (a rope weighted at both ends and used as a bolo), the *kumade* (a common rake), and the *masakari* (ax).

One semi-formalized combat system was known as *timbe,* and its practitioners used a small shield of leather stretched on a wooden frame. The shield was called a *to-hai,* and it had a peephole cut in it for the fighter to look through. Parrying with the to-hai, the fighter would counterattack with a *hera,* an implement normally used for harvesting rice.

Modern Uses

In today's world, we aren't often chased by mounted samurai or accosted by sword-wielding assailants (thank goodness!), so there is limited usefulness for the weapons of kobudo as actual fighting instruments. Like the empty-handed techniques of karate, kobudo today is practiced as an art form.

Primarily, the techniques of the various weapons are practiced in set patterns of formal exercises called kata. Each kata uses only one weapon at a time, and great emphasis is placed upon precise movement and control of the weapon.

Many tournaments have kobudo divisions in which contestants perform their kata and vie against each other for trophies or medals. A very small number of organizations promote actual kobudo fighting—weapon against weapon—but even with padding on the contestants and on the weapons, the practice is very dangerous and has not become popular on a widespread basis. Generally speaking, almost all Okinawan styles of karate practice at least a little bit of kobudo, while kobudo practice is less prevalent in Japanese styles of karate.

Modern kobudo practice is an excellent method of physical conditioning that promotes strength, co-ordination, and concentration. Consequently, in the 1990s, numerous empty-handed styles of karate and even other martial arts have sought out instructors of kobudo and have started training in these ancient ways.

As an art form, Okinawan kobudo has become highly stylized and technical and can be divided into three main lineages:

➤ The Shinken Taira lineage

➤ The Shinpo Matayoshi lineage

➤ The Yamani-ryu lineage

The differences among these major schools of thought are highly technical and center on stances, application of techniques, hand positions, gripping methods, and many other technical points. If you don't know anything about kobudo, you probably won't be able to easily tell the differences among them, so you should let your instructor be your guide.

Ancient Weapons and Modern Laws

Just remember this: A kobudo weapon is a potentially deadly weapon and is viewed by law enforcement and the courts as such. Before you even think about purchasing a kobudo weapon, you should check with your state attorney general's office and with your local police department to find out what laws are in effect in your area. Generally speaking, kobudo weapons are treated just like guns—if you

Sensei Says

Even though kobudo is now practiced as an art form, it is most important to remember that its implements are still very dangerous weapons. Extreme care must be taken at all times.

Ouch!

How dangerous are kobudo weapons? Well, a particularly creative criminal once robbed a bank using nunchaku. He smashed things and broke the arm of a security guard. In a final bold gesture, with the money under his arm, he leapt into the air, swung the nunchaku at a chandelier, missed, and hit himself in the head. He was still unconscious when the police arrived.

wouldn't walk down the street waving a gun in your hand, don't walk down the street beating the air with your nunchaku. Both citizens and police frown on that kind of behavior.

The laws vary widely from state to state and precinct to precinct, so it is impossible to list all of them here. Just take a little time to find out what is permissible in your area and what is not. Even in states that ban the sale of weapons such as nunchaku, exceptions are frequently made for karate schools that teach kobudo as part of their regular curriculum.

The Least You Need to Know

➤ Karate weapons were developed from the farming and fishing tools of the Okinawan people.

➤ Modern kobudo is practiced as an art rather than a method of actual combat.

➤ Modern kobudo practice promotes strength, balance, concentration, and coordination.

➤ Check with your local law-enforcement agencies before purchasing kobudo weapons.

Chapter 17

Samurai Strategy: Defending Yourself

In This Chapter

➤ How to avoid dangerous situations

➤ Safety tips to keep you safe

➤ How to handle a sudden attack

➤ The laws governing self–defense

One of our favorite self-defense stories is about Tsukahara Bokuden (1490–1572), one of Japan's greatest swordsmen. Bokuden wanted to test the self-defense abilities of his three sons, all of whom he had trained in the way of the samurai. To do this, Bokuden placed a pillow over the curtain on the door to his room so that when the curtain was raised, the pillow would fall on the head of the person entering.

Bokuden first called his oldest son, who saw the pillow, took it down, entered the room, and replaced the pillow over the curtain.

As the second son entered, the pillow fell, but the son caught it in his hands and placed it back over the curtain.

As the youngest son rushed in, the pillow fell squarely on his head, but the son cut it in half with his sword before it hit the floor.

To the first son, Bokuden gave his sword, saying, "You are a great swordsman."

To the second son, he said, "You will one day become a great swordsman, but you must yet train very hard."

To the third son, he said, "You are a disgrace to this family, and are not qualified to even hold a sword." So saying, he took his youngest son's sword away from him and cast him out of the house.

This story has been told to countless karate students by karate instructors, in one form or another, for as long as karate has existed. The reason is that it perfectly illustrates the essence of self-defense—because of their potential to deliver extreme impact force, karate techniques should be used only as a last resort against surprise attacks. What Bokuden's sons faced was a surprise attack, and the eldest son displayed the perfect defense—he avoided the situation entirely. In other words, the more you increase your awareness of potentially dangerous situations, the more you decrease your vulnerability to being attacked. It's not easy to accomplish this, of course, but we have some ideas that we think will get you going in the right direction.

Karate Minute

Tsukahara Bokuden's test of his three sons was a little harder than it seems at first glance because, in those days, Japanese pillows were cylinders made of solid wood. So, the test carried some real danger.

Common Sense First

Over the years, we have heard one question repeated again and again: "What should I do if I get in my car, and someone hiding in the back seat grabs me by the throat or puts a gun to my head?" The correct answer has always been the same: "If a mugger is lurking in the back seat, don't get in the car." This is not a facetious answer because the plain fact is that there is little or nothing you can do when you're caught in a certain situation. Oh, sure, there are certain techniques you could execute against a mugger in the back seat, but their success would require a high degree of awareness of lapses in the attacker's attention. If you had that kind of awareness, wouldn't you have been aware of the danger before you got in the car?

If you practice karate seriously, you will be able to defend yourself in almost any situation, but not on the basis of physical ability only. The most important aspect of self-defense is to understand your position at all times and to become aware enough of yourself and your surroundings to be safe.

Avoidance is always the best method of self-defense, but to avoid danger, you have to be aware that the danger exists. The heightened awareness necessary for successful self-defense is not something mystical. In fact, it is mostly a matter of paying attention and using common sense.

Remember that karate-do is a lifetime art and that it can make you just as successful at self-defense at the age of 80 as it can when you are young and strong. Even young, skilled athletes can't escape from a surprise attack if they are not aware of the attack until it hits. Once hit, the body might be too injured to respond. So, the essence of karate self-defense is awareness of the attack before it hits.

To clarify this idea, think of attacks in two categories:

➤ Contemplated attacks

➤ Surprise attacks

Contemplated attacks are attacks that you see coming, have time to think about, and can respond to from a strong defensive position. The techniques and training of a first-degree black-belt are more than adequate to take care of almost any contemplated attack.

Surprise attacks are all types of attacks that are initiated before you become aware of them. Again, the skills of a first-degree black-belt generally are adequate to defend against many surprise attacks. The black-belt usually will be able to counter at least part of the force of an attack with superior reflexes, timing, and coordination. But these physical responses have their limits, and the limits shrink with age. So, the goal to strive for is to relegate all potential attacks to the level of contemplated attacks, and this is a big part of the *do* of karate-do.

So, how do we do it? We do it by consciously training the mind along with the body. Awareness is not a quantitative thing that can be learned; it is a state of mind.

Try some of the following exercises to see if you can increase your awareness.

Sensei Says

Awareness and vulnerability go hand in hand. The more aware you are of potential danger, the less likely you are to be vulnerable to it.

EEEE-YA!!!

Talk the Talk

Zanshin means "remaining mind" and is the word used to describe the keen state of awareness of a person who trains seriously in karate-do.

Samurai Strategy on Your Own

Using the example of the mugger lurking in the back seat of your car, take a few minutes to place the image of the car in your mind. Visualize yourself walking toward the car, lowering your breathing to your center to calm your mind, and looking in the back seat. Visualize the back seat empty, and see yourself get in, calm and secure. Now visualize an attacker in the back seat, and see yourself walking (or running!) away to call the police or find help. Then, when you actually walk to your car, do the same thing, and you'll find that you will have a sense of calmness and a general feeling of well-being.

Before we go any further, let's get it straight that the aware mind is not a paranoid mind. Paranoia is full of fear, but the aware mind is almost empty of fear. The simple exercise of looking in the back seat every time you get in your car will develop strength rather than fear. Think about it: You're not afraid that there might be somebody in your car; you're afraid that he might attack you if you get in. Therefore, you can overcome that fear completely by not getting in.

Sensei Says

If you are worried about a particular kind of attack, use your imagination, and visualize yourself being attacked that way over and over. When you can visualize a proper defense, you will not be worried anymore.

This kind of thinking is what we mean by "samurai strategy." The samurai warriors of old placed high importance on their position in any situation and the strategic use of that position for self-defense. In the case of the car, your physical position is very important. The best possible position that you could be in when you perceive the danger is outside the car because you are then able to run and avoid the confrontation altogether. Being inside the car when you perceive the danger is the worst possible position to be in. If you get in the car and then realize that you forgot to check the back seat, turn around immediately and look. That would put you in a better position for defense than if you were driving when you perceived the danger.

Samurai Strategy in a Crowd

To take another example, assume that you have just entered a room full of people, most of whom you don't know. This could be a PTA meeting, a cocktail party, or maybe a theater lobby. Someone you know calls out to you from the other side of the room and motions you over. If you simply walk through the crowd to your friend, you have thrown away an opportunity to increase your awareness. Instead of mindlessly walking through the crowd, pause for a couple seconds when you enter the room, and exercise your mind with samurai strategy. Drop your breathing to your center, and first observe the approximate number of people in the room. Second, see where the exits are, and look at the windows to see whether they could be used as exits. Third, observe whether people are in small groups or are scattered. Fourth, consider the atmosphere—is there tension and arguing, or do the people mostly seem happy? What you are doing is determining your position in terms of self-defense.

Samurai strategy is a diverting and pleasant game that also helps you develop a sense of well-being and increases your powers of observation.

If there is a large group of people between you and your friend, the best strategy might be to walk around the group rather than through it. Maybe one small group is arguing and another is joking. It would be better to walk through the happy group, even if you have to walk farther. On the other hand, maybe nobody calls to you. In this case, it might be better for you to take a position as close as possible to an exit.

If you sit down, think about the chair in terms of self-defense. Is it a stuffed chair in which you would sink down and be unable to rise from quickly? Does it have arms that could restrict your movements? If it has arms the same height as the table next to it, don't pull it up to the table and box yourself in. Will the legs of the chair slide on the floor, or will they stick? Is it possible to sit with your back to the wall? If you sit on a sofa, it is better to sit on the end so that you can't be attacked from both sides at once.

Consider the manner in which you sit. If you bend far over and grasp the chair with both hands to pull it to you, you are vulnerable to attack. Bent over, looking down with both hands behind you is a poor position for self-defense. Practice sitting straight down and standing straight up while maintaining a firm center.

Keep in mind that samurai strategy is a game, but it's a game that helps protect you from danger. As you exercise the strategy, forget about fear. Fear has no part in it. You are training your mind to be aware; you are not worrying about being attacked.

In a larger sense, self-defense is defense of the human organism against all threats. In this sense, it includes the common-sense act of looking both ways before crossing the street. Common-sense self-defense also tells us not to slice a tomato by holding it with one hand and raising the other hand high over the head to quickly slash downward with a sharp knife. Our training and experience have taught us the danger in these acts, so we avoid them.

In the same way, the samurai strategy game trains us to be alert to potentially dangerous situations and to avoid them.

Still not convinced? Okay, we admit that some of this might seem a little silly at first, but we want you to take it as seriously as if you were blind. The goals of the samurai strategy game are similar to the goals of training a blind person. Blind people seem to hear better than the rest of us, but in fact they simply are more aware of sounds. Their perception of sound is heightened because they are forced to rely on it for most of their vital information. Samurai strategy is a method of heightening all perceptions and making you less vulnerable to attack. Try it; you'll like it!

Safety Tips

When you realize that the foundation of self-defense is awareness and avoidance, you can improve your position and decrease your chances of being attacked by following the commonsense safety tips found in Appendix F, "Self-Defense Safety Tips." Preparedness and precaution are as much a part of karate self-defense as sweating on the dojo floor is.

Defend Your Body, Not Your Ego

Okay, now that you've implemented all of the tips in Appendix F and done everything possible to avoid a self-defense situation, it's time for a quiz. Let's say that you're driving along on a sunny day, singing along with the radio and just generally thinking about how good life feels. You stop at a red light, and while you're sitting there, some maniac in a pickup truck plows into the rear end of your car. You're not hurt, so you get out to inspect the damage, and you find that while your trunk is pushed up above the back window, the only damage to his truck is a tiny scratch on the bumper. Undoubtedly, you are by this time thinking about exchanging insurance information and calling the police. As the driver of the truck approaches you, though, he starts yelling obscenities, waving his arms and stomping his feet. He loudly asserts that you are a moron and that your mother was an unmarried dog. He says that your IQ is just one level higher than an avocado and that if the state had any brains at all, they never would have given you a driver's license in the first place. You try to speak, but he shouts, "Listen, you (pick one: short, fat, skinny, stupid, little) so-and-so, I oughtta ram your head in that trunk with my bumper!"

Oh, boy! Now you're mad, and it's time for self-defense! Your cheeks turn red, and your blood boils. You're thinking that you were minding your own business and sitting still, so why is this guy calling you names and threatening you? So here's your quiz question: What do you do? Do you break his nose with your best reverse punch? Do you kick him in the stomach and whack the side of his head with a knife-hand strike when he bends over? Or do you drop into a stance and wait for his attack so you can block and counter? The answer is: None of the above. The reason you do none of the above is that he has not actually attacked you; he has attacked your ego.

In a situation like this, it's time to remember that karate techniques are for defense against surprise attacks against your body—not your ego. This lunatic has done everything he can to make you mad, and has he ever succeeded! He's called you names, called your family names, and threatened to bang your head, but the key point for you to remember is that he has not actually attacked you. And after all his shouting and posturing, if he did attack you now, it certainly wouldn't be a surprise. He's told you that he's thinking about it, so you have time to take defensive action without hitting him or waiting for him to hit you. You might actually be able to get back into your car and lock the doors while waiting for the police. Or,

Ouch!

If you respond emotionally to a threat, you almost certainly will lose because your mind won't be clear enough to see the attack clearly and decide on an appropriate response.

you might be able to maneuver yourself around to the other side of the car, to put it between you and him. You might even look around for something that could be used as a defensive weapon, such as a stick or a rock.

The most important thing, though, is to remember that if you execute karate techniques against another person in defense of your ego, you are executing them for exactly the wrong reasons and with exactly the wrong state of mind. You've probably heard of someone being "blinded by his own ego." That usually means that a person has gotten so full of himself that he can't see straight anymore. More to the point, responding with techniques against offense to your ego means that you are emotionally out of control when you execute those techniques. Remember what we said earlier about stable emotions: If you don't have stable emotions when you're under attack, you can't possibly succeed. Sure, it makes you mad when somebody acts so completely moronic as that truck driver. But remember that karate techniques rely as much upon emotional control and concentration as they do upon body mechanics.

Sensei Says

If your hand goes forth, withhold your anger. If your anger goes forth, withhold your hand.

So, if you get really mad and want to argue and yell and scream, it's okay as long as you put your karate techniques away and forget about using them. On the other hand, if you are forced to use your techniques for self-defense, you absolutely must put away your anger and control your emotions. Doing it any other way will make you more vulnerable than you were before.

Talk the Talk

Goshin-jutsu means "self-defense techniques."

Talk Your Way out, but Stay Alert

If you practice karate seriously, you probably will be able to learn to keep your emotions under control in a self-defense situation, and this will enable you to exercise your most powerful weapon—your mouth. No, not as a biting machine (although teeth can be pretty powerful weapons in an emergency), but as a reasoning machine. If you can keep enough control over your emotions to not be drawn into an argument when somebody like that truck-driver friend calls you names, you probably can deflect most, if not all, of the unstable emotions of your attacker.

The key here, as in every other aspect of self-defense, is stable emotions and a calm mind. The best self-defense strategy is to remain calm enough in the face of shouting and hateful talk to deflect it or go around it. For example, when the truck driver makes pointed statements to you about your intelligence, calmly try to divert the subject. If he says "You're a moron!" and you say "Am not!" and he says "Are, too!" then you're definitely headed for a fight. On the other hand, if he says "You're a moron!" and you respond with "That was quite a jolt. Are you okay?" you have a very good chance of calming him down. If he persists with questioning your family heritage, you can persist with "I'm just glad you weren't hurt." Of course, at this point, you really couldn't care less whether he was hurt. In fact, the idea of him being unconscious after banging his head on the windshield is probably seeming more like a pretty good idea to you.

For this to succeed, though, two things have to come into play. One is that you stay calm enough, no matter what, to gently try to bring him down from his fever pitch. The other is that you stay alert enough to be aware of your position so that you can confidently drop him on his butt with a reverse punch if he just won't have it any other way.

By maintaining eye contact and keeping your body relaxed, your center firm, your breath under control, and your voice and facial expression calm, you will exude confidence, and this is usually enough to diffuse even the most potentially violent situation.

Sensei Says

No matter what happens in a dangerous situation, be sure to stay focused on your opponent, not yourself. If your attention lapses for even an instant, you create an opening for the opponent to attack.

The Company You Keep—It Isn't Always Strangers

Up to this point, we have considered scenarios in which the attacker is a stranger—somebody unknown to you who suddenly appears out of nowhere and tries to rearrange your face. But the fact of the matter is that very few of us will ever be mugged. Most of us don't get mugged because we avoid places where something like that might happen. We could give you all kinds of advice, like, "Don't go walking in dark alleys in strange neighborhoods at night." Duh! Even an idiot wouldn't do something like that! Because we assume that you aren't going to be in dark alleys in strange neighborhoods, we want to offer this interesting piece of wisdom: You are far more likely to find yourself defending yourself against someone you know than against someone you don't know. That's right, if you are a man, you are more likely to be attacked by a good friend than you are by a mugger. Granted, your friend isn't as likely to attack you as violently as a mugger would, but a couple cocktails have been known to turn good friends into dire enemies.

If you are a woman, there is more than a 50 percent chance that a man who assaults you will be someone you know. Very reliable statistics indicate that between one half and two thirds of all sexual assaults against women occur in either the victim's home or in some other private residence, and that at least 50 percent of all attackers are known, at least slightly, by their victims. The attacker could be—and often is—a relative, a friend, an employer, a co-worker, or some other trusted acquaintance. The reason for these alarming facts is that we are most likely to be attacked when we are relaxed and vulnerable. At home and among friends, we are the most relaxed—therefore, we are the most vulnerable. A woman tends to leave her guard down around her husband's friend who drops by to return a tool he borrowed, or the friendly fellow at the office who drives in the carpool, or good old cousin Clarence, whom she sees about once every 10 years.

Karate Minute

When Gichin Funakoshi ate with his students, he would sometimes shove their chopsticks into their mouths if they let the chopsticks point straight toward their faces. If they failed to hook one finger over the front lip of their soup bowl, he would sometimes dump the soup on them. He said, "I am your friend, but what if a friend has too much to drink and becomes your enemy? You must be aware and prepared at all times."

The point of all this is, once again, that the more relaxed and less vigilant you are, the more vulnerable you are to attack. Keep your guard up and your awareness radar finely tuned, and you will not be vulnerable to attack.

Karate at Home: Domestic Violence

Each of us has experienced a situation in which a new or prospective student has come to us because they wanted to learn karate to defend themselves from their husband, boyfriend, father, stepfather, brother, uncle, wife, sister-in-law, or whatever. They were getting beaten up at home, and they wanted to either stop the violence, or in some cases, have the skill to "teach the person what it feels like."

Listen carefully: This is nuts! It is crazy thinking! It is contrary to everything the martial arts are about. Violence is bad. Period. Controlling others with violence or the threat of violence is bad. Exposing yourself to this kind of risk is wrong. If you feel that you need karate to defend yourself from the people you live or associate with, you need to leave, to call the police, or to get counseling. Do something, but please don't share a living space with a violent person, or have social relationships that are not safe.

The only karate principles that apply to this kind of situation are distance—lots of it—and timing (as in leave now).

Do What Works

There is an old saying in karate that anything clever or fancy you do to defend yourself will work, but only half the time. For example, women frequently are encouraged to carry a whistle on their key-chain and to blow it if they are attacked. Well, that might work half the time, but what about the other half, in which the attacker beats them to death to make the noise stop? Sticking your keys between your fingers and jabbing them at an attacker's face might work half the time, but what about the other half where it makes him so mad that he beats you to death because you cut his face? It might work to spray an attacker with mace or pepper spray, but if the wind is blowing the wrong direction or if you can't get the thing out, aimed, and fired before the attacker grabs you (which is very likely), you might end up getting sprayed yourself. So, what's the answer? Basics, basics, basics! Do what works, and do what has the most chance of working without backfiring on you.

By basics, we mean the basic karate techniques of blocking, punching, striking, and kicking. And we mean the basic body mechanics such as rotation, snap, movement of the body center, and so on. Instead of blowing a whistle, try a loud kiai and a sharp elbow to the side of the head. If you miss, or if it doesn't work, try it again. If you execute a strong reverse punch to the attacker's nose and it doesn't work, at least he can't take the punch away from you like a can of mace and use it against you. From your basic training in karate, you will amass a sizeable arsenal of strikes, punches, and kicks very quickly, and you will have these at your disposal all the time. If you train hard, you will soon realize that every block can be a powerful strike, and every strike, kick, and punch can be a powerful block. Basic techniques—not weapons or tricks—are the karate student's best friends.

It's the Size of the Fight in the Dog

Which kind of dog scares you the most, a 200-pound English Mastiff or a tiny little Chihuahua? Well, if you're smart, you'll tread much more lightly around the Chihuahua because, except for the cute ones that sell tacos on television, Chihuahuas are not known for the gentle nature that is a hallmark of the giant Mastiff. Indeed, they originally were bred for their viciousness and tenacity. That's why so many of them are skittish and seem to enjoy biting so much. Would you rather have a nudge from the giant head of a Mastiff or a vicious bite on the ankle from a Chihuahua? Ouch! Bulldogs and Pit Bulls aren't particularly large dogs, either, but once they latch onto you, it's all over! Our point is that it's not the size of the dog in a fight that matters so much; it's the size of the fight in the dog. And that's just what we want you to remember if you are ever faced with a serious self-defense situation: The outcome will be determined by how much tenacity and fighting spirit you have.

No matter how big the opponent, and no matter how seemingly hopeless the odds, you have a good chance of prevailing if you defend yourself with tenacity and spirit. Even if you think you can't win, you still might if you overwhelm your opponent with your fighting spirit, your willingness to keep fighting until it's over, and your intention to win, no matter what. Miyamoto Musashi, Japan's most famous swordsman, said that the spirit of a real fight is the spirit of fire—so if you are attacked, fight back with fire, and keep flaming until the attacker sizzles! At the very least, your screaming, slashing, flashing, and terrorist attitude might convince the attacker that you're crazy and that he doesn't want anymore to do with you. As we said before, do what works!

Talk the Talk

Jissen means "fire," and it is the word used in karate to describe the nature of a real fight.

Law and Order

Because karate techniques are extremely powerful and potentially lethal, it's important to understand that you can't go around using them on people without consequences. While the laws about the use of force for self-defense vary from state to state, county to county, and city to city, the general idea is that you have a right to use a reasonable amount of force to defend yourself when in fear of death or serious injury. What is and is not "reasonable," of course, is the sticky point. We're not lawyers, so we can't speak with authority, but we can tell you about a couple instances of people we know who used karate for self-defense and what the consequences of their actions were.

Let's start with an easy example. A young Japanese university exchange student was spending a year in the United States and took a job tending bar late at night to earn some cash to supplement his scholarship. He didn't have a car, so when his shift ended at 2 A.M., he walked six blocks to a bus stop, where he caught the last bus of the night back to the university dormitory. One night, while walking with his jacket over his shoulder, he realized that he was being followed by three men. He was a second-degree black-belt in karate, so he knew what to do. He crossed the street and tried speeding up, but they started chasing him in earnest. He ran as fast as he could and suddenly turned a corner to try to get away.

Unfortunately, he had turned into a blind alley. Surrounded by brick walls on three sides, he had no choice but to turn and face his attackers. As they spread apart in front of him, he saw that the leader had a stiletto knife in his hand and that one of the other two was rattling a length of chain. After some name-calling, the leader suddenly lunged forward with the knife. Clearly, they were going to rob him, and they appeared to be willing to kill him in the process. The student swung his jacket at the attacker's knife hand and simultaneously dropped into a strong stance and executed the strongest reverse punch he could at the man's face, hitting him in the forehead. Without pause, he executed a side thrust kick at the second man. Both men fell heavily to the pavement. The third attacker took a look at what was happening and quickly ran away into the night.

When the police arrived, they found that the first attacker had died instantly from a fractured skull that had lacerated his brain. The second man had several broken ribs and a bruised heart from the kick. It was a terrible tragedy all around, but an easy one to interpret in terms of self-defense law. There was no question that the young man had reasonably felt that his life was in danger, and he was justified in using even lethal force to defend himself.

Now for a hard one: An American karate student was out on the town with his wife at a country music lounge. Drinks were flowing, the band was playing loud, and everybody was having a good time. A partially inebriated patron came over and offered to buy the karate student's wife a drink, which she declined. When he persisted, the karate student told him that he was bothering his wife and very pointedly told him to go away, which he did. When his wife got up to use the restroom, though, the karate student saw the same drunk reach out and pinch her rump as she walked by. That did it! The karate student got up, pulled the offender out of his chair, and popped him on the end of the nose with a palm heel strike. He didn't hit him hard enough to do any serious damage, but a bloody nose was more than enough to settle the guy down. By the time his wife came back from the bathroom, the police had arrived and arrested the karate student. In court, the karate student was convicted of assault, was forced to pay medical expenses for the "victim," and was placed on probation for a year. Remember when we told you to defend your body and not your ego? This is a perfect example. The student reacted to an offense to his ego rather than to a threat to his or his wife's body. Not only is it stupid; it's also against the law.

And now for a *really* hard one: Another karate student found himself at a party at a friend's house. His friend called him into the living room to help him with a guy who was trying to crash the party. The karate student told the guy who was trying to force his way through the front door that he wasn't welcome at the party and should go away. As the argument escalated, the intruder forced his way in and grabbed the karate student by the throat. Reacting instantly, the karate student broke the intruder's hands away from his throat, grabbed the sides of the guy's head, and smashed his nose with a head butt. Then he gave him another one for good measure and threw him out. The intruder later sued the karate student, and the judge ruled that although the karate student had every right to use the head butt to defend himself against being choked, he had no right to hit the man a second time. The first head butt was reasonable force. The second one was excessive force, and it cost the karate student $7,000 in fines and medical expenses for the intruder. It also cost him a year of probation for battery.

Ouch!

If you are forced to hit somebody to defend yourself, be sure to hit only hard enough to stop the attack, and don't hit the person twice if you don't have to. If you hit your attacker too hard or more than is necessary to stop him, you might end up going to jail for assault!

So, the moral to our stories is that self-defense is a very serious matter and that karate techniques are very serious weapons. Always defend yourself, but don't overdo it.

The Least You Need to Know

➤ Increasing your awareness decreases your vulnerability to attack.

➤ Your most powerful self-defense weapons are common sense and reason.

➤ Karate techniques are for defense against surprise attacks.

➤ Spirit and attitude mean the difference between successful and unsuccessful self-defense.

➤ You have a right to defend yourself with karate, but you must use restraint.

Part 5

Let's Test Ourselves: Belts, Rank, and Competition

As in life, we are tested regularly in karate. And while these tests may take many forms, only two standards are ever really used. First, in ranking, we are tested against ourselves. Second, in competition, we are tested against others.

Ranking in karate is an evaluation of your progress toward the physical and mental mastery of the art. Because there are so many different karate organizations, there are many different kinds of rankings and ranking systems. Almost all of them, though, believe that ranking should not be awarded solely on the basis of physical ability. This makes good sense because karate-do is a method of physical, psychological, and spiritual development all in one.

Karate-do encourages the unlimited development of your physical and mental powers. The ranking system is like a long staircase, on which every step up is a measure of your progress toward the top, which is perfection. Because none of us can actually be perfect, the staircase really is endless, and because we can never reach the top of the stairs, we have to focus on continuously progressing, rather than achieving some limited goal.

Karate competition, on the other hand, is where karate's philosophy and techniques merge with good, old-fashioned, get-out-there-and-win, scream-your-lungs-out-from-the-stands, "thrill of victory, agony of defeat" sports. In both kata and sparring competition, you can compete as an individual or on a team. As in all sports, there are rules you'll need to know, mistakes you'll need to avoid, and goals you'll need to set.

White Belt Black Belt

Bat Belt

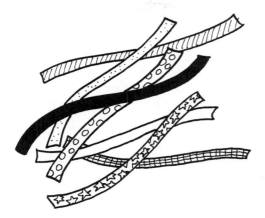

Chapter 18

All the Colors of the Rainbow

In This Chapter

➤ What colored belts mean

➤ How to prepare for your first test

➤ The importance of attitude in karate ranking

➤ The difference between novice, middle, and advanced rankings

➤ How to set goals at each level of ranking

➤ How to be a good advanced student

If you visit 10 different karate schools, you might see 10 different systems of colored belts. Almost always, though, you will see that the systems start with a white belt to indicate a beginner and end with a black belt to indicate expertise. Some systems, on the other hand, might have just white and black belts, while others might have some red and white or pure red belts to signify mastery beyond the black-belt level. We know it sounds confusing, but almost all the systems share some common traits.

Why Belts?

The main purpose of wearing a belt with a karate uniform is to keep the jacket of the uniform closed. No mystical, ancient, or secret meaning here. In karate, a belt is just a belt.

When people originally studied karate in Okinawa, they trained in their underwear, so belts weren't necessary at all. Only when karate became more formalized, around the turn of the twentieth century, were karate uniforms invented. Because karate was being introduced into the elementary and middle schools, it was natural that a uniform of some sort would be necessary, just as a uniform of sorts is necessary for any physical education activity. In Chapter 7, "Dressed to Kill: The Uniform," we explained the origin of the uniform and its practical and aesthetic design—the belt was just one part of that.

Talk the Talk

Obi (pronounced *oh-bee*) means "belt."

Nobody knows for sure why belts became designated for rankings, but it is probably because Japanese traditions in court and in religious ceremonies used sashes of different colors to indicate the relative importance of the officials involved.

Karate Minute

When karate was practiced in secret in Okinawa, men usually practiced in their underwear. When karate was introduced to the schools as physical education, though, the uniform was invented, and the belt was used to keep the jacket closed.

The first formalized use of the type of rank belts worn in karate today appeared in 1882, when a famous Japanese educator, Jigoro Kano, founded the art of judo and introduced it into Japanese schools. The uniform that Kano designed for judo practice looked a lot like a modern karate uniform, except that it was very heavy, was doublewoven, and had specially reinforced collars, sleeves, and knees. This was necessary to withstand the constant grabbing of the uniform that is so common in judo grappling. At the same time, because judo was a sport, Kano adopted a formal ranking system to indicate achievement and experience. Judo had gained such popularity in Japan by the time karate came along that the karate masters copied Kano's system of ranking, in the hope that it would lend more credibility to their own art.

What the Colors Mean

It's hard to say what different colors indicate because different organizations believe different things. Some say that individual belt colors are reflective of various phenomena in nature. A yellow belt, for example, would represent the rising sun to them, and the next ranking, an orange belt, would represent the setting sun. In other words, a person with an orange belt has more experience and has been around longer than a person with a yellow belt. Others believe that the various colors are directly related to Buddhist ceremonies in which the various colors of sashes and robes indicate the status and position of the participants.

Whatever you choose to believe, one thing seems to be pretty much standard across the board: Lighter-colored belts indicate lower ranking, and darker-colored belts indicate higher ranking. So, beginning and novice students usually wear white, yellow, gold, or orange belts; intermediate students usually wear blue, green, or purple belts. Almost universally, a brown belt indicates an advanced student preparing for black belt, and a black belt indicates some sort of expertise or mastery.

Symbolically, the beginner's white belt indicates an empty canvas. People wearing white belts are just entering into karate and know nothing. As they progress, their belts get darker and darker, just as they would if they were never washed. Increasingly dark color, therefore, indicates more experience. The students' experience keeps growing and growing until the belt is completely black, which indicates that the students have taken the first step toward mastery of their art.

How Long Until I'm a Black Belt?

This is the big question to which almost everybody who starts karate wants to know the answer. In most schools, the time required to obtain a black belt is directly proportional to how much time you spend studying and practicing. Karate techniques are not easy to master, but as with any other physical skill, practice is cumulative—that is, the more you practice, the better you become. If you practice karate only in class at the dojo, it's going to take you a long, long time to reach the black-belt level. On the other hand, if you put in some regular practice time at home, polishing what you learn in class, you might rise to the black-belt level relatively quickly. Most organizations have strict time-in-grade standards for all rankings, but most also recognize an outstanding individual who dedicates extraordinary time and effort to the art. While we can't say exactly how long it will take you to earn a black belt, we can say that in a good karate dojo, it usually takes somewhere between two and five years, with three

Sensei Says

Rankings in karate are never just given. They must be earned.

EEEE-YA!!!

Talk the Talk

Shiro (pronounced *shee-roh*) **obi** means "white belt." **Kuro** (pronounced *koo-roh*) **obi** means "black belt."

years being about average for someone who attends class regularly and practices regularly at home.

Everybody wants to be a black belt, but it's not possible for everybody to achieve that goal. Most people quit before they obtain a black belt, and some just never dedicate enough time and effort to reach that level. The black belt is a symbol of achievement, and it doesn't come automatically. You have to work for it!

Why Can That Brown Belt Kick Higher Than That Black Belt?

Let's say that you start training in karate, and about a month or two down the road, it becomes clear to you that a couple of the brown belts are obviously kicking higher, punching harder, and generally making a lot more noise than the senior black belt who has been helping you with your techniques. This can be mystifying to a beginner, but it is not at all uncommon because ranking in karate-do is not just about who can kick higher or punch harder or make the most noise. It's about individual growth and achievement.

Ouch!

Never compare your own ranking progress to the progress of others. You are not in competition with them, and you are not being compared to them when you take a test. If you concentrate on others, you won't be able to concentrate properly on yourself—and you won't move up in ranking.

Here's another quiz for you: If an 18-year-old athlete starts karate and can kick high over his head, but uses only 10 percent of his potential to do it, and a 72-year-old sedentary person starts at the same time and can kick only as high as his own knee, but uses 90 percent of his potential to do it, which one is the better karate student? The older guy wins, hands down! Karate ranking is supposed to be an evaluation of the whole person—physically, mentally, and spiritually— which means that everything possible is taken into consideration by the examiner. There is a saying in karate: "Your only opponent is yourself." This means that your journey in karate-do is a personal journey toward self-perfection. You are the only one who can stand in the way of your development, and you are examined individually for ranking without being compared to anybody else. Only you can ensure your success—by training hard and always trying your best. Likewise, only you can ensure your failure—by not training hard and by not giving it your best effort.

When Can I Test?

Different schools have different standards about when tests are conducted and how much time is required in one grade before you can move on and try for the next level. Many specify a certain number of class hours that you must complete before trying for the next level, and a few schools don't have tests at all. In that case, the instructor just gives you the belt when she thinks you're ready for it. That's highly unusual, though, and most schools offer rank tests about every three months.

Who Tests Me?

Depending upon the rules of the school or the organization to which it belongs, rank examinations usually are conducted by the chief instructor of the school, along with a panel of high-ranking students. Some schools are required by their parent organization to have an examiner from outside their school, but even then, the examiner usually has the higher-ranking black belts from the school sit on the panel. The idea behind the panel of examiners is that these are black belts with long experience in karate and that, if they pool their knowledge and experience, they will be unbiased in their judgments and evaluations.

Who Tests Them?

As with other technical matters, the answer to this question of who tests the examiners varies widely from school to school and from organization to organization. If the school is a member of a large, well-organized organization, the answer is easy. In that case, very strict protocols will be in place to determine who can conduct rank examinations and who cannot. Some groups have examiner licensing procedures in place, while others say that any black belt can promote anybody to a ranking one or two levels below his own rank. If the school is not a member of a larger governing body, the instructor might invite black belts from other schools to sit on the panel, or she might just give the examinations herself.

Schools usually issue certificates of ranking or require you to have a passbook into which they enter your ranking and technical qualifications. This isn't always the case, though. Some schools simply issue a new belt. The question of who ranks your instructors is one we address more completely in Chapter 5, "Find the Right School," and is something you should consider before you even join the school.

The Kyus to Success: Up the Rank Ladder

In karate-do, rankings below black belt are called *kyu* rankings, and black belt rankings are called *dan* rankings. Kyu means *class*, and dan means *grade* or *step*. Taking into consideration that different schools and organizations might have widely different standards, there are usually 8, 9, or 10 kyu rankings and up to 10 dan rankings. Kyu rankings are attempted in descending numerical order, while dan rankings are attempted in ascending

Talk the Talk

Kyu (pronounced *kee-yoo*) means "class," and **dan** (pronounced *dahn*) means "grade" or "step."

order. That is, tenth kyu is the lowest rank, and first kyu is the highest rank on the kyu rank ladder. First dan is the lowest dan ranking, and tenth dan is the highest. The ninth and tenth kyu rankings generally are reserved for students who can perform only the most rudimentary of basic techniques. Beginning no later than eighth kyu, kata (formal exercises) and kumite (sparring) usually are added to the examination.

The First Test

Because the standards for ninth and tenth kyu vary so widely, and because many organizations do not have ninth or tenth kyu rankings at all, we can't really say what the tests for these ranks might be, except that they usually cover the simplest and most basic of techniques. For our purposes here, we will consider eighth kyu to be the first rank test most people take.

Preparing for that first test can be the most nerve-wracking experience you can imagine. First of all, you'll be out there on the floor with one or two other people, facing the examination board. Or, you might be out there all alone. No matter, though, because even though that big bunch of black belts looks fearsome, they really are on your side. In fact, they are the best friends you have in the room. Their goal is to be good teachers and seniors, and good teachers and seniors produce good students. So, trust us on this—they want you to succeed as much as, if not more than, you want to succeed.

Sensei Says

Use the examiner like a mirror to see the reflection of your development.

The best thing you can do to prepare for your first test is to breathe deeply into your stomach, try to find your center, and try to calm your mind. Remember that you are not being compared to anybody else—not even the people who are testing with you. Your only enemy is you, and you are the only one who can defeat you.

How Much Do I Need to Know?

How much you need to know depends, of course, on the policy of the school, but in general, you probably will need to know one kata, some basic techniques performed at the level of complexity of the techniques in the kata, and some simple, controlled sparring. At the eighth kyu level, the sparring usually is done in three or five steps, and usually it is done by the examiner's count. A school using the techniques found in this book probably would require you to perform at least the following:

➤ The basic kata, Heain Shodan

➤ Three-step or five-step sparring

➤ Lunge punch, three or more times

➤ Rising block, three or more times

➤ Outside block, three or more times

➤ Knife-hand block, three or more times

➤ Front kick, three or more times

➤ Side-snap kick, three or more times

➤ Side-thrust kick, three or more times

The examiners usually assign a point score to your performance of each item and then either average the scores or total them to decide the outcome.

Under the Microscope: Karate's Three Ks Plus the Kun

So, now that you know what you will be required to perform for your first test, it might be helpful to know what the examiners are looking for. In some cases, the examiners are just looking for an overall impression of your attitude, your spirit, and your techniques. In other cases, they are looking at specific points within each technique. In all cases, though, you can be sure that the examiners will, in their own way, carefully examine your attitude, karate's three Ks—kihon, basic techniques; kata, formal exercise; and kumite, sparring—plus the Dojo Kun (Principles of the Dojo).

The Dojo Kun are …

➤ Character.

➤ Sincerity.

➤ Effort.

➤ Etiquette.

➤ Self-control.

As an example of an examination conducted on specific points within each technique, consider this. If you were being examined on the basic techniques presented in this book, specific examination points the examiner would look at might include a review of distinct elements within each technique. We've provided a list for you to refer to in Appendix D, "Elements of Technique Evaluation."

Talk the Talk

The beginning levels of ranking include **jukyu** (tenth class), **kukyu** (ninth class), **hachikyu** (eighth class), and **shichikyu** (seventh class).

Karate Minute

Rank examinations in karate-do are not just physical. In addition to examining kihon (basic techniques), kata (formal exercises), and kumite (sparring), examiners also consider how well you understand the Dojo Kun (principles of the dojo).

Sensei Says

Don't be too happy or too sad about the results of a rank examination because each examination is just one small step in the lifelong journey of karate-do. Pass or fail, there is still much more to be learned.

When Will I Get the Results?

In many schools, the results of the examination are announced right away, often with great fanfare and applause from the audience. This is particularly true in schools where a high percentage of the students are children. Parents love to applaud. In some schools, a formal ceremony is conducted, either immediately or at a later date. In many traditional karate schools, though, the results of the examination are not posted for a week or two. This is the old Japanese tradition, based upon the idea that the results of an examination are not important; only the process of the examination is important. So, if your instructor doesn't tell you the results of the exam right away, don't ask! Remember that the point of training in karate-do is progress, not achievement.

What If I Don't Pass?

The examination process in karate has been likened to looking in the mirror when you get out of bed in the morning. The mirror tells you what you look like right then. You might look great, and if so, that fact will be reflected in the mirror. If your hair is out of place, or if you have a red streak across one eye, the mirror will tell you that, too, and you will proceed to fix those problems right away. In karate, the rank examiner is your mirror. You look into that mirror and find out how your karate looks right then. If some things don't look so great, you are expected to proceed with fixing them right away. If you think about the examiner as a mirror, it really is true that you can't actually pass or fail an examination, just like you can't pass or fail the mirror you look at in the morning. Like the mirror on your wall, the examiner can reflect back to you only what you look like today. It is an evaluation more than an examination. You might get a high evaluation, a medium evaluation, or a poor evaluation. It is up to you to move quickly and confidently to improve your reflection the next time around.

What If I Do Pass?

Because karate-do is a lifetime art in which the journey is more important than the destination, you are expected to accept your new belt with humility and a renewed sense of purpose. Naturally, you'll be very happy to receive a new belt and move up in the ranking system, but more than anything else, you should be humble about it and be sure to be in the next class, doing your best to move forward. Don't miss the next class after passing a rank examination! That will tell the instructor that you really don't understand the purpose of karate-do training. Set a goal of physical improvement for your next period of training, and move forward!

Typical Novice and Middle-Level Tests

We already have given you the contents of a typical test for eighth kyu. In addition to doing everything you did for your last test, you will face increasing complexity in the techniques and usually will have to perform a new kata. Some things you might be asked to perform in typical tests for novice and middle-level rankings can be found in Appendix E, "Novice and Middle-Level Rank Examinations."

Setting Goals in the Novice Ranks

The novice ranks are tenth, ninth, eighth, and seventh kyu. These are the rankings in which you learn the most simple external actions and techniques, and where you learn the underlying principles of karate-do. When you are a white belt, your physical goal should be to attend as many classes as possible and to set aside at least a few minutes every day for practice on your own. In other words, make

Ouch!

If you don't receive a promotion after your rank examination, remember that it is considered very impolite to ask your sensei why you didn't pass. Good manners dictate that you simply ask your sensei what you should concentrate on to improve.

Sensei Says

Pass or fail, be sure to attend the next class and practice hard. This will show that you understand that the journey of karate-do is more important than the destination.

EEEE-YA!!!

Talk the Talk

Shoshin (pronounced *shoh-sheen*) means "beginner."

consistency and attentiveness your goal as a novice. If you learn the fundamentals well, you will progress much faster at higher levels.

Setting Goals in the Middle Ranks

The middle ranks are sixth, fifth, and fourth kyu, and these sometimes are called the intermediate ranks. Each of these rankings requires a more sophisticated development and application of techniques in combination. As a novice, for example, you first had to master the basic idea of performing a front kick standing still and then moving. As a middle rank, you will have to learn to perform two front kicks in one movement, kicking first to stomach level and then to face level. Then you will have to put the front kick together with other techniques and learn to perform them smoothly. You might be required to execute a front kick, followed by a round-house kick, followed by a reverse punch, moving smoothly forward. Then you might have to try a front kick in combination with a side kick and a punch. The possibilities are endless.

When you were sparring as a novice, you mostly had to concentrate on proper form, basic timing, and correct, basic distancing. You also always knew what attack was coming and when it was coming. In the middle ranks, though, you will be required to learn how to shift out of harm's way quickly, in many different directions, and how to counterattack without hesitation from many different angles. You will learn how to defend against multiple attacks, and you will learn how to do it without knowing in advance what might be coming at you.

Your goal for the middle ranks, then, is to work with as many different people in the dojo as possible, to broaden your base of experience. When you look at that green belt who moves like lightning and scares you to death, your goal should be to work with that person as often as possible to improve your own speed and learn how to handle fear.

Brown Belt: The Black Belt's Apprentice

There is a common saying in karate: "A brown belt is the world's most dangerous animal." This saying is not too far off base because a person who reaches the brown belt level knows just about everything needed for a first-degree black belt, but that person doesn't know how to control power like a black belt does. People who attain a brown belt have the ability to defend themselves, and, if their organization participates in sport karate, they know how to compete. Their techniques have power, and their bodies and minds are strong. What they usually are lacking are the refinement and control displayed by a black belt.

The brown belt represents a pivotal point in a person's karate development because, although the technical differences between each of the middle ranks are relatively small, the technical differences between a brown belt and the middle ranks are relatively huge. At the same time, the gap between a brown belt and a black belt is also huge, so the person who attains a brown belt is kind of stuck in the middle between people of distinctly lesser ability (the middle ranks) and people of distinctly superior ability (the black belts). This causes the brown-belt rankings to suffer two very unpleasant distinctions: a lot of inflated egos caused by looking down on middle-ranking students, and a very high dropout rate caused by looking too much at how far they have to go to get the black belt. A lot of people at the brown-belt level decide that, even though they have come so far, they still have too far to go, so they quit. Also, at brown-belt level, they are forced to interact more directly with black belts, and their initial inability to handle the higher-level training offered by the black belts is sometimes discouraging.

People who decide to rest on their laurels after achieving a brown belt or to quit karate training altogether simply do not understand the meaning of the brown belt. A brown belt signifies an apprentice black belt, which means that they now have to really "turn it on" and get doubly serious about their training and their position in the hierarchy of the dojo. They are kind of like molten steel that must be hammered strongly on the anvil to be useful.

Generally, there is not a lot of difference among the tests for third, second, and first kyu brown belt, and some organizations don't test people at all after they attain the brown belt. In those organizations, a person promoted to third kyu brown belt just keeps training until he is ready to try for first-degree black belt. If a student doesn't get the black belt when tested, second or first kyu are awarded as kind of a consolation prize. On the other hand, some organizations consider the brown-belt levels to be very important and distinct from each other, and testing for them sometimes turns into an endurance marathon. Either way, though, the brown belt in karate represents a lot of hard work, dedication, and strong techniques. A person achieving the first kyu brown-belt ranking is expected to be able to execute all fundamental body movements and all hand and leg techniques with power and proper application.

A brown-belt ranking examination is very difficult, and the complexity of techniques and sparring increases dramatically. In addition to all the other things tested in the middle rankings, some of the more difficult things tested at the brown-belt level might include these:

Sensei Says

The brown-belt level is the level at which you must decide whether you are going to seriously pursue karate-do for years to come.

EEEE-YA!!!

Talk the Talk

Brown-belt levels are advanced levels and include **sankyu** (third class), **nikyu** (second class), and **ikkyu** (first class).

Brown-belt kihon:

➤ Multilevel kicking using the front leg first, while rooted in a strong stance

➤ Complex combination techniques requiring complete changes of momentum while moving forward, such as a side-thrust kick, followed by a round-house kick with the other side of the body, followed by a reverse punch with the original side of the body

➤ Multiple kicks using the same leg without putting it down, moving forward, and following with punches

➤ Multidirectional kicks with one leg while balancing on the other, such as a front kick to the front, a side-snap kick to the side, and a side-thrust kick to the side, all with the same leg and without putting it down between kicks

➤ A test of punching and/or kicking control, such as punching or kicking at a moving object, such as a pencil or a paintbrush, controlling full-power techniques so that they stop just short of contact

Brown-belt kumite:

➤ Defenses executed in a freestyle stance

➤ Self-defense techniques against grabbing or holding

➤ Defense against difficult techniques, such as a back kick

➤ Sometimes free sparring

The bottom line on karate's brown-belt ranking is that it represents a very high level of achievement, but it is the turning point at which you must decide to really get serious about karate or forget about it.

EEEE-YA!!!

Talk the Talk

Ren-waza means "combination techniques."

The Least You Need to Know

➤ Karate rankings below black belt are divided into novice (seventh kyu and lower), middle (sixth, fifth, and fourth kyu), and advanced (third, second, and first kyu brown belts) levels.

➤ Karate rank examinations usually consist of tests of kihon (basic techniques), kata (formal exercise), and kumite (sparring).

➤ Lighter-colored belts represent less experience, and darker-colored belts represent more experience.

➤ Character development, spirit, and attitude are just as important in the ranking process as technique.

➤ The brown-belt ranking is an apprentice black-belt ranking.

Chapter 19

The Point of the Pyramid: First-Degree Black Belt

In This Chapter

➤ The true meaning of the black belt

➤ Your chances of earning a black belt

➤ The difference between expertise and mastery

➤ The meanings of each of the black belt levels

When karate was spread to the world outside Japan after World War II, about the only thing English-speaking people knew—or thought they knew—about it was that it was mysterious, that its experts were able to break boards and bricks with their hands and feet, and that an expert was identified by the black belt he wore. Judo was already being practiced outside Japan long before the war, so when karate expert Mas Oyama toured the United States as a professional wrestler, announcers found it convenient to describe his slashing hand attacks as "judo chops." Believe it or not, karate was so new and unknown that the word *karate* was considered too difficult to pronounce!

As you will see, there is nothing mysterious at all about karate, and a black belt does not necessarily designate an expert.

The Real Question: What Is a Black Belt?

The use of a black belt to signify expertise today really is an outgrowth of martial arts going public in Japan during the Tokugawa period (1600–1867). Prior to that time, martial arts were taught in private by masters of each *ryu* (school or style), who

Talk the Talk

Yudansha means "a person with grade," and is the word used to indicate that a person has a black belt. **Mudansha** means "a person without grade" and is used to indicate a person who has not yet attained the black belt ranking.

carefully guarded the secrets of their arts from outsiders. When the ryu felt that the students had achieved a certain level of mastery, it gave them a certificate of proficiency, and that was that. As Japan became more peaceful and martial arts became less necessary for battlefields, the warriors turned their arts away from arts of war and self-protection to arts of self-perfection. As the arts became more open to the public, it was necessary to institute a system of controls and balances to be sure that not just everybody would take a little instruction and then start their own ryu for profit. The system that was gradually adopted was the *kyu-dan* system of ranking that karate uses today. In fact, the Japanese have dan rankings for almost everything from karate to flower arranging.

Karate Minute

When karate was introduced to the United States in the 1950s, people thought the word *karate* was too difficult to pronounce, so they frequently called it judo. Dojos also often were known as "judo karate schools."

The first-degree black belt is the point of a pyramid.

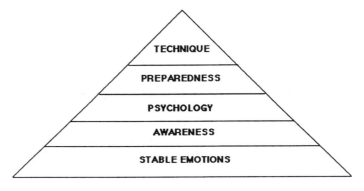

SHODAN
1ST DEGREE BLACK BELT

TECHNIQUE

PREPAREDNESS

PSYCHOLOGY

AWARENESS

STABLE EMOTIONS

Today, we think of a first-degree black belt as a symbol of accomplishment, but it is a long way from mastery. The idea is that when a student enters the dojo for the first time, she knows almost nothing about karate. She doesn't know the language, the ritual, the formalities of bowing, or anything else. It's as if she is surrounded by a huge amount of information that's spread out all around her. What she eventually discovers is that this vast sea of knowledge is like the base of a huge pyramid of knowledge. As she struggles forward and trains through the years, she gradually acquires the knowledge at the base of the pyramid and moves up to a higher, smaller area. Step by step, she moves up the pyramid as she acquires the knowledge and abilities of each level. After a long and difficult climb over a period of years, she realizes that the point of the pyramid is the first-degree black belt. She also realizes that she doesn't want to "get" a black belt; she realizes that her goal is to *be* a black belt. But what does that mean, exactly?

Physically, a first-degree black belt is a person who knows all the basic body movements and techniques, and who can apply those movements and techniques with enough extended force to neutralize an opponent of equal size, weight, and strength. Physically, that's it.

Sensei Says

A first-degree black belt is awarded to those who have mastered the basics of karate-do, both physically and mentally.

First-degree black belts can't leap tall buildings with a single bound or slash through 30 attackers like Bruce Lee. What they can do—and do very well—is defend themselves in almost all common self-defense situations. They know how to fight, and they know how to compete. They have several years of experience in facing many different people of varying levels of skill. In other words, physically, a first-degree black belt is a person who has mastered the basics of karate. Of course, the basics are much more difficult at the first-degree level than they are at brown-belt level. A first-degree black belt (shodan) test usually will include (in addition to all the things tested at the brown-belt level) at least the following:

Shodan (first-degree black belt) kihon:

➤ Multilevel kicking using the front leg first, in combination with arm and hand movements

➤ Complex combination techniques requiring complete changes of momentum and stance while moving forward and backward, such as an outside block in front stance, followed by a sideways elbow strike in side stance, followed by a sideways back fist strike, followed by a reverse punch while changing back to front stance

➤ Complex combination techniques combining leg and hand movements, beginning with the front leg, such as a front leg side-thrust kick, followed by a back leg round-house kick, followed by a reverse punch moving forward

➤ Multiple kicks with the front leg, without putting it down, followed by hand techniques while moving forward or back, such as a front leg round-house kick and a side-thrust kick, both to the front and without putting the leg down, followed by a lunge punch

➤ Multidirectional kicks with one leg while balancing on the other, such as a front kick to the front, a side-snap kick to the side, a side-thrust kick to the side, and a round-house kick to the front, all with the same leg and without putting it down between kicks

Talk the Talk

Tokui kata means favorite kata.

Ouch!

If you don't learn the difference between pain that is irritating and pain that is dangerous, you might respond too dramatically if you get hit, and that will give the opponent a big advantage over you, whether you are sparring or in a self-defense situation.

Shodan kumite:

➤ Semi-free sparring, in which attacker and defender shift around freely, trying to apply their techniques realistically

➤ Advanced self-defense techniques against grabbing or holding

➤ Free sparring

Shodan kata:

➤ It is usually at the shodan level that the black belt candidate is required to perform his favorite kata, plus one or more kata randomly selected by the examiner.

It's important to understand, too, that different organizations have different views on what should constitute a black-belt ranking examination. Some schools believe that the examination should be physically demanding, but should emphasize technique more than physical fitness. Other schools believe that this examination should be a marathon test of both skills and endurance. In the former case, an exam might last only 30 minutes or so. In the latter case, it might last for hours—maybe even all day! Still other schools, as we mentioned earlier, don't believe in testing at all. They simply give you a black belt when they think you have earned it. No matter what the testing method is, though, the expertise of the first-degree black belt, as described previously, is more or less universal.

Psychologically, a first-degree black belt is a person who knows how to concentrate and who knows how to use the mind to increase awareness and decrease vulnerability to attack. This person has learned the difference between pain that is irritating and pain that is dangerous, and has learned to hide most vulnerabilities from opponents. A first-degree black belt usually can remain relatively calm when confronted with violence because he has learned to exercise some control over his emotions. In other words, psychologically, a first-degree black belt is a person who has mastered the basics of emotional stability, psychological strength, and awareness.

Not an Expert, but an Expert Beginner

Most styles of karate have between 5 and 10 degrees of black belt, with real experts holding the ranks of fifth degree and above. A first-degree black belt, though, is not an expert, but an expert beginner.

Progress in the black-belt rankings can be thought of in terms of learning to drive a car. Before you even get in the car to learn how to drive, you must study and know the rules of the road. The first time you get into a car to drive, you must have somebody with you who knows what's going on. That person must tell you every detail: "This is the ignition switch, where the key goes. This is the gas pedal that makes the car go; this is the brake pedal that makes it stop. Don't hit either one too hard." And on and on. Gradually, you learn how to start the car, how to make it move forward and backward, and how to make it stop. You learn where to keep your eyes on the road and how to use your mirrors. Just as when you first enter the dojo, no detail is too small, because every detail is ultimately important.

Following the same analogy, for a period of time, you must have somebody with you who can be responsible for your driving and help you gain experience. Somebody must critique your driving technique, just as your sensei critiques your karate technique. As you practice driving, each detail becomes more natural to you, until one day you get in the car, put the key in the ignition, start the engine, release the brake, step on the gas, and steer the car where you want it to go. And you do all this without thinking about it at all. You have practiced it so thoroughly that you have mastered it. That is, you have mastered the basics of driving a car, just as a first-degree black belt has mastered the basics of karate. But you—and the black belt—are far from being experts. Having mastered the basics of driving a car doesn't even begin to prepare you to hop into a million-dollar race car and compete in the Indy 500, nor does it mean that you are ready to haul gasoline cross-country in an 18-wheeler. Those things require years of experience and much more advanced training. In the same way, the first-degree black belt can perform the basic techniques of karate, can compete in tournaments, and can defend himself in most situations, but he is a long way from mastery of the art. Mastery is a gradual process that takes a lifetime of training, and the higher dan rankings are markers of your progress on that journey.

Play the Percentages: Who Stays, Who Goes

Before we take a look at what's involved in attaining advanced dan rankings, let's take a look at how easy or hard it is to get to the first-degree black belt level. Yeah, you guessed it: It's hard! Really hard! Most people just don't stick with it. Our experience is that only about 3 to 5 percent of all the people who try karate ever make it to first-degree black belt, and for every five who do make it, only one or two of them is likely to make it to the second degree. That doesn't leave very many people at all who will even be candidates for a third-degree black belt—much less the fourth, fifth, or sixth degree! One of the main reasons is that a lot of time must be spent between rankings before moving from one to another.

Karate Minute

When karate was introduced to the United States in the 1950s, most people believed that getting a black belt was almost impossible. Part of the reason for this misconception was that there were only a handful of real black belts in the whole country—Japanese instructors included!

While there is not a hard and fast universal rule about time in grade, some general guidelines were drawn up in the late 1960s by the Federation of All-Japan Karate-do Organizations, and these guidelines still generally reflect the minimum time in grade standards used by most Japanese karate organizations:

➤ First dan: More than two years total practice

➤ Second dan: More than two years after first dan

➤ Third dan: More than three years after second dan

➤ Fourth dan: More than four years after third dan

➤ Fifth dan: More than five years after fourth dan

➤ Sixth dan: More than six years after fifth dan

➤ Seventh dan: More than seven years after sixth dan, plus a minimum age requirement of 40 years

➤ Eighth dan: More than eight years after seventh dan, plus a minimum age requirement of 50 years

➤ Ninth dan: More than nine years after eighth dan, plus a minimum age requirement of 60 years

➤ Tenth dan: More than 10 years after ninth dan, plus a minimum age requirement of 70 years

Bear in mind that these are *bare minimum* time requirements. Remember that we said it was possible to attain first-degree black belt in two years, but most people take between three and five years. It's the same way with the advanced dan rankings: They almost always take longer than the minimum, which accounts for a lot of the attrition. As an example, let's assume that you start karate training at the age of 25 and, being generous, let's say that you make first dan in three years. So, now you're 28 years old and a first-degree black belt. Let's say, also, that you are a real wizard at karate, and you make every advanced ranking in the minimum amount of time. So, it takes you two more years to make second dan, at the age of 30. Third dan comes at age 33. Fourth dan comes at 37. Fifth dan makes you 42, and sixth dan makes you 48. At seventh dan, you're 55, and at eighth dan, you're 63. At that point, you've still got nine years to wait for ninth dan, which you would receive at 72. Usually only the chief instructor of a style receives tenth dan, so you probably don't have to worry about it. In some organizations, tenth dan is awarded only posthumously, but we personally think that standard is a bit too high!

Already it is easy to see why so few people make it to the higher dan levels, just because it takes so much time, if nothing else. But notice that the standards say "More than … years after …." Frankly, we don't know of anybody who has ever ascended the upper rank ladder in the minimum amount of time. A second-degree black belt realistically takes between 5 and 8 years of training, and a third-degree black belt rarely occurs with less than 10 to 12 years. Attaining a fourth-degree black belt rarely occurs without 15 to 20 years of experience, and it's hard to find a fifth-degree black belt who hasn't been around at least 25 years. So, let's say you turn out to be more average than extraordinary, and it takes you 25 years to make it to fifth-degree black belt. That makes you 50, with about eight years to wait for sixth degree. This makes it even easier to see why so few people make it to the top rankings. When we tell you about the actual requirements for the rankings, in addition to time considerations, you'll find it even easier to figure out why there are so few seventh, eighth, and ninth dans.

Grandmaster Who?

Now that you know how long it takes to reach the highest levels of karate ranking, you can pretty much be sure that most of the people who advertise themselves as "grandmasters" or tenth-degree black belts probably are not. In larger cities, advertising makes it seem like everybody's uncle is a tenth-degree black belt. No, they are not. The younger the person claiming those titles, the less likely this claim is valid. A 40-year-old person simply has not lived long enough to have the experience necessary for the highest rankings.

The Upside-Down Pyramid: Advanced Dans and Mastery

If you think of basic karate-do training as a pyramid with the first-degree black belt at the point of it, you should think of advanced karate-do training as an upside-down pyramid standing point to point with the basic one. The upside-down pyramid, though, has no ending point. This symbolizes several things:

➤ The first-degree black belt is the starting point for advanced training.

➤ Advanced karate training has no end; it is a lifelong search in ever-expanding directions.

➤ The first-degree black belt really is only mastery of basic techniques, not advanced mastery.

In another sense, the meeting point of the two pyramids is the point in your karate life when you need to decide whether you are willing to dedicate your energies toward the mastery of karate-do on a lifelong basis. This is not a decision to take lightly because mastery of karate-do requires more time and energy than almost anything else you will ever attempt. Of course, you could decide at the first-degree black-belt level to just keep chugging along like you have been, going to the dojo a couple times a week and keeping in shape. That's fine, but it won't ever turn you into a karate master. You will progress physically and mentally, but you won't ever reach the higher levels of mastery without a more exceptional dedication to the art. We're not saying that you should feel obligated to pursue the higher levels of karate-do, but if you do, we want you to know that it takes lots and lots of extra effort.

EEEE-YA!!!

Talk the Talk

Shihan means "a model for the rest," and is the word reserved for the very few people in a system who rise to the level of "teacher of teachers."

Advanced Karate-Do Is About Obligation

The oldest forms of Japanese martial arts were passed directly from teacher to student, usually in a one-on-one situation. Each teacher felt an obligation to his own teacher to pass along the art correctly and only to the most qualified students. This often resulted in a teacher teaching only one student the details of the art. This system of one teacher, one student is called *uchi-deshi*, which means "inside student." In the uchi-deshi system, the sensei (teacher) might consider applications from numerous potential students before deciding on the one he thought best qualified to learn and the most likely to pass his art on to the next generation.

Karate Minute

Almost all of Japan's old martial arts were transmitted from teachers to students by the *uchi-deshi* method, which meant that the student lived inside the house of the teacher and learned all about the art and life in general.

Once the student was accepted, though, it was nothing like being accepted into a karate dojo today. The accepted student was expected to move into the sensei's house and devote himself night and day to learning and mastering the sensei's art. The student was obligated to cook for the sensei, clean his house, do his laundry, handle repairs, and follow the sensei's orders, no matter what they might be. In return, the student was the only one to learn the deeper meanings and secrets of the sensei's art. The relationship went far beyond the dojo and the sensei's house, though. In fact, it was more like a father-son relationship in which the sensei took responsibility for the student's upbringing and imparted wisdom and guidance to him on every aspect of the student's life.

The sensei-student relationship in Japan grew partly out of Japan's long history of ancestor worship and strong respect for the past. The sensei, with his extreme dedication to preserving and passing along his art, was thought to embody this essential part of Japan's culture. Even today, it is hard to find a more profound respect than that shown by Japanese students of any art to the masters of that art. This is an important part of Japan's cultural heritage.

Today, of course, the uchi-deshi system is not much in evidence in martial arts such as karate-do, kendo, and judo. These have become popular arts, open to the public, with millions of practitioners. Still, the underlying feeling of profound respect for the sensei is strong. The sensei is expected to be a person who is completely dedicated to his art and one who studies much broader areas of life outside the dojo, to better relate his art to the everyday lives of the students. In return for the sensei's extreme dedication to teaching them properly, the students incur an obligation to listen to and follow the sensei without swerving off the path and without asking for anything except instruction and guidance.

Advanced karate students, even when they become teachers themselves, are taught that they still have an obligation to pass along their sensei's teachings and ideas. At the same time, they continue to seek advice from their sensei. As you discover what is required for advanced rankings, you'll see that advanced karate students need good advice and counsel because there's a lot they couldn't possibly figure out on their own.

251

What the Ranks Mean

We have already told you about the first-degree black belt and what it basically means—the mastery of the basic techniques along with the psychological and mental development necessary to make them effective. But what about the rest of the ranks?

➤ **Shodan—first dan.** This is very important to the sensei. When someone has achieved *shodan,* they have shown a dedication to the sensei's teachings and principles and have shown themselves to be worthy of the sensei's efforts.

➤ **Nidan—second dan.** This is the level at which the student has not only mastered the basics, but also has internalized them. This means that the student is now able to perform the techniques more spontaneously, and with more speed, power, and grace.

➤ **Sandan—third dan.** This is the "stepping out" ranking because it is much farther distant from nidan than nidan is from shodan. The sandan candidate is expected to have a clear understanding of all the underlying principles of all techniques and body movements.

➤ **Yondan—fourth dan.** This is generally considered the first teaching level of karate. That is, a person who attains yondan should be able to independently produce shodans, taking the students from white belt to black belt without any outside help.

➤ **Godan—fifth dan.** This is generally acknowledged as the "entry-level master" ranking. People attaining godan have probably been practicing steadily for at least 25 years and have a very deep understanding of their art and, based upon their training, of themselves.

➤ **Rokudan—sixth dan.** This level indicates that the person attaining it has performed advanced research that is of a universal benefit to all karate students.

➤ **Shichidan—seventh dan.** Sometimes "nanadan," this level indicates that the person attaining it has done extensive testing of his rokudan research and has applied it widely in actual application.

➤ **Hachidan—eighth dan.** This is reserved for people who have completed advanced research in a new and previously unknown area of karate technique, theory, or teaching.

➤ **Kudan—ninth dan.** This level is normally reserved for those very few individuals who have dedicated their entire lives to karate-do in an extraordinary way. A person attaining kudan is thought to be the living embodiment of the very best qualities a human being can develop through dedication to karate-do.

➤ **Judan—tenth dan.** This is usually reserved for the head of a style, although it is sometimes awarded to people who have achieved a level of respect accorded only to heads of styles. In many organizations, judan is awarded only in honor of the death of the person receiving it. Needless to say, there are very few legitimate judans in karate-do—neither past nor present.

Some organizations don't award higher than the fifth dan, so we will concentrate here on the first five dans in detail.

Shodan—First-Degree Black Belt

The sensei can't tell, of course, whether a particular shodan will be one of the chosen few who might carry the art forward into the next generation, but the sensei can see that the shodan has proved that he might be capable of doing that. So, in the sensei's eyes, the new shodan is pure clay, ready to be molded and formed into something truly beautiful.

Nidan—Second-Degree Black Belt

At nidan—as with shodan—application of the techniques is performed in accord with the student's own personal, unique physique. While at the shodan level, everybody is still trying to get their techniques to look like the model of the sensei or the seniors, at nidan everybody starts applying their techniques in ways that differ from everybody else's. A very tall, heavyset man, for example, will employ his techniques differently than a small, slim woman will. They will still use the same techniques, but they will employ them in different ways so that they can best utilize their own physique and body type. Nidan is a ranking closely related to shodan, so nidans are often thought of as very highly polished shodans.

In addition to the requirements for shodan, a typical nidan test might include the following:

Nidan kihon:

➤ Complex techniques that combine sliding and stepping movements with arm and leg techniques in a free style stance.

➤ Complex techniques that combine forward and backward movements with arm and leg techniques in a free style stance.

➤ Complex kicking techniques that require complete changes of body position and direction.

➤ Multiple kicks in different directions with the same leg without putting it down.

Sensei Says

Karate techniques do not vary from person to person, but the application of techniques varies widely, according to the person's size and physique.

Nidan kumite:

> ➤ There is usually a lot of free sparring in nidan tests, and the candidates must usually demonstrate their skills against one opponent after another. If the test includes self-defense, it is usually performed against a weapon such as a knife, a club, or a pole, or it may be performed from a chair- or floor-sitting position.

Nidan kata:

> ➤ Nidan candidates usually perform their favorite kata, followed by one or more advanced kata selected by the examiner.

Sandan—Third-Degree Black Belt

At the sandan level, students are required to demonstrate expert application of their karate techniques in varied circumstances and conditions. So, if the sandan candidates are required to demonstrate free sparring (and they usually are required to demonstrate a *lot* of it), they must show that they have not only fighting ability, but also strategy, superior timing, and control of both their techniques and their opponents.

A sandan candidate, therefore, fights completely differently against a brown belt opponent than a nidan or sandan opponent. By the time you reach sandan, you should be able to handle the techniques of a brown belt with very little difficulty; it should be an easy fight. You should also be able to handle the techniques of a nidan, but you would have to work harder at it. A sandan candidate should also be able to face much higher-level black belts and come out of it in one piece—something that is not expected of shodans or nidans.

Sandan is frequently referred to as the "application" stage of karate development. So, while you might have had some idea of what kind of self-defense you would be required to demonstrate at the nidan test, you'll find that anything goes in the sandan test. Examiners usually select a self-defense situation on the spot, and you must defend yourself without any preparation or even a clue as to what the attack might be. You might even have to defend against multiple attackers, all attacking at once!

Also at the sandan level, you might be asked to perform one or more kata randomly selected from 15 or 20—or more—kata.

Ouch!

A sandan (third-degree black belt) examination is often referred to as the "dangerous" examination because candidates, in their eagerness to show their advanced fighting ability, sometimes lose control and end up hurting each other. When this happens, the offender is sometimes required to face an advanced member of the examining board to learn more about control.

Considering how difficult the sandan test is and how much a sandan has to know, it's pretty easy to see why sandans are almost universally acknowledged as truly advanced representatives of their style of karate.

Yondan—Fourth-Degree Black Belt

Yondan is generally considered the first teaching level of karate. That is, a person who attains yondan should be able to independently produce shodans, taking the students from white belt to black belt without any outside help. The testing requirements for yondan vary widely, but they frequently include kata performance followed by an oral exam about areas of technique in the kata. Sometimes free sparring is required, and sometimes yondan candidates are required to demonstrate their teaching skills. Also, it is not unusual for them to be required to submit a thesis in advance, which they are required to present and defend before the board of examiners. The thesis usually is on some aspect of the candidate's research in free sparring or self-defense, and sometimes it is a thesis about a particular teaching method developed by the candidate.

People attaining yondan sometimes are referred to as "apprentice masters," just as brown belts are sometimes referred to as "apprentice black belts." Another common phrase applied to yondan is that it is the level of "learning without teachers." That doesn't mean that the yondan doesn't need a teacher anymore (*everybody* needs a teacher!). It simply means that yondans must make a commitment to go outside of themselves and study very deeply, personally researching karate techniques and trying to gain a deeper understanding from their own point of view. To be good teachers, they must bring their own insights, education, and general background to bear upon their teaching methods.

Godan—Fifth-Degree Black Belt

People who have attained godan have persevered to the extent that they can teach advanced black belts, and they have completed advanced research in some specific area of karate-do, either technical or philosophical. It is common for godan candidates to be required to submit a detailed thesis describing their research and then to present it and defend it in front of a board of examiners. While thoughts on the subject of even using the term *master* vary widely, godan is the first rank that most karate people think of as a level of mastery. Some organizations have no rankings at all beyond the level of godan.

Sensei Says

Master is a term not used very much in karate–do because every time we move up the rank ladder, we gain new insights into our art. This is what we call "new eyes," and we must go back to the beginning to examine everything about our art with our new eyes, just like a beginner does.

Recommended Ranking

Many organizations make ranking allowances for people who dedicate themselves to karate, but who are physically limited or handicapped. These people often cannot be realistically expected to perform karate techniques as proficiently as those who are not limited, so provisions are made for them to measure their progress and enable them to move up the rank ladder.

Some criteria for recommended ranking include the following:

➤ Continuous practice and spiritual development.

➤ Distinguished service to karate-do through practice and teaching.

➤ Distinguished service to karate-do through research and development of teaching methods.

Karate Minute

Because karate-do ranking represents the development of the whole person, and not just physically, many disabled people have been able to attain high ranking because of their dedication and personal development.

Honorary Ranking

Many organizations confer honorary black belt rankings on people who don't practice karate, but who contribute in a significant way to the promotion of the art. Typical standards for honorary rankings are these:

➤ **Shodan.** Indirect support of karate at the local community level.

➤ **Nidan.** Direct support of karate at the local community level.

➤ **Sandan.** Indirect support of karate at the national level.

➤ **Yondan.** Direct support of karate at the national level, or a local dignitary or community leader who has provided indirect support of karate.

➤ **Godan.** Indirect support of karate by a national dignitary in social, financial, or educational areas; or direct support of karate by a local dignitary.

➤ **Rokudan.** Direct support of karate by a national dignitary.

➤ **Shichidan.** Indirect support of karate by a national sovereign or high official.

➤ **Hachidan.** Direct support of karate by a national sovereign or high official.

➤ **Kudan.** Indirect support of karate by an international leader or internationally respected figure.

➤ **Judan.** Direct support of karate by an international leader or internationally respected figure.

School to School and Style to Style

The ranking standards we have described here are very general and might vary widely from school to school and style to style. Some schools might have their own unique set of standards for rankings, and some styles might have detailed standards for weapons expertise. In general, though, the standards we have presented here are more or less universal among the major Japanese styles of karate-do in terms of skill level at each level of ranking. Whether a school requires weaponry skills at the shodan level is not important. What is important is that the overall level of physical skills required at the shodan level is comparable to the general levels outlined by the major organizations.

The Least You Need to Know

➤ A first-degree black belt is not an expert, but an expert beginner.

➤ Earning a black belt usually takes between two and five years of study.

➤ You can gain a lot of expertise by practicing regularly, but you must make an extraordinary commitment to become a master.

➤ Each level of black belt has a distinctly different meaning and examination.

Chapter 20

Duel in the Sun

> ### In This Chapter
>
> ➤ How today's tournaments differ from the first competitions
>
> ➤ An overview of what karate competition is about
>
> ➤ The difference between individual and team competition
>
> ➤ How competition divisions are determined
>
> ➤ Bottom line—the pros and cons of competition

At one point or another, almost everyone involved in karate will have some experience with karate tournaments and competition. After the very first time you compete, you may decide, "This is it!" and never want to stop. Or, you may compete a few times and decide that competition just isn't right for you.

But even if you don't compete, you will surely end up watching tournaments, either as a way to learn more about your art or to support your dojo, your friends, or family members who train. Most tournaments also depend on volunteers to function, so there is always the opportunity to help, by either timing matches, scoring results, organizing athletes, or running concessions. Lots of people become involved in tournaments as coaches as well, especially if you have kids or students who are competing. Finally, as you become more experienced, you will have the opportunity to arbitrate, judge, and referee the matches themselves.

As you will see in this and the next two chapters, there is a lot to know about the karate tournaments you are likely to be involved in. There are different types of competition, different rules, and different expectations. Some things, however, are pretty standard. Generally, when you compete, your divisions will be divided by gender, by age, by experience, and often by weight. (This means that you aren't going to have to fight somebody twice your size, who has three times your experience.) You will be able to compete in kumite (sparring), in kata (forms), or in both. Also, although you will certainly compete as an individual, frequently you also will have the opportunity to compete as part of a team representing your dojo, your style, your organization, or your country.

Sensei Says

Practice karate, not just tournament karate! There's plenty of time to specialize when you start competing internationally. If you just like to spar, you still need to do your kata—it will make your karate better. And if you just like to do kata, you still need to spar.

Types of Tournaments

Tournaments come in all sizes. Some—national and international championships, for instance—are very big, with thousands of contestants competing in literally hundreds of different divisions. Some tournaments are small, perhaps just containing the students of a few nearby clubs. Others are invitational tournaments, inviting only participants from a particular style or organization. Still others are open, where anyone who walks in the door, has a gi, and pays the fee can compete. Regardless of their size, traditional karate tournaments all emphasize discipline, a correct way of acting, good sportsmanship, and the ability to control your techniques and your emotions.

Tournaments are exciting for competitors and spectators.

Realize that although you don't have to compete in lots of tournaments to get good at karate, competition is something you will probably need to experience as part of your training. To this end, your instructor likely will encourage you to take part in some competitions and will recommend which events you should attend and which you should avoid. If you find that you enjoy competing, as many do, you will probably be able to get extra competition training from your instructor and your club's senior students.

Karate Tournaments Are Really Pretty New

Initially, karate was not developed to be a sport; it was designed as a form of combat. This is not to say, however, that no competition took place. Human nature being what it is, karate-ka in the past were always finding ways to compete with each other. Usually, the method they chose was called fighting—and, as you can imagine, people got hurt. As karate gained in popularity, and as karate-ka developed strong loyalties to specific teachers, styles, and associations, it became clear that an organized method of competing was needed before chaos broke out.

The First Tournaments

The first karate tournaments were organized and developed at the university level in Japan in the early 1950s. Various karate leaders experimented with many different kinds of competitions including these:

➤ Full contact without pads—too many injuries

➤ Full contact with pads and protective gear—too cumbersome

➤ Absolutely no contact at all—too boring

By exchanging ideas and experimenting, they finally came up with the idea of controlled techniques to limited target areas (the eyes, for example, were off-limits) and limited impact (the face could not be hit, and power could not penetrate into the body). Still, early tournaments in Japan were rough-and-tumble affairs, and it was not until 1956 that the Japan Karate Association (JKA) developed a uniform set of rules. In 1957, the JKA staged the first All-Japan Karate Championship Tournament in Tokyo. By 1960, most of the other schools of karate in Japan had adopted the JKA rules, often with some modifications, as their own.

Some major differences exist between the first tournaments and today's competitions. First, as in the dojo, competition sparring in karate is controlled, or noncontact. It seems, however, that the concept of control has changed over the years. In general, early tournaments allowed more contact than is allowed now, and many more injuries occurred in the past.

Another difference between then and now is that previously nobody used protective equipment. There were no hand protectors, no mouth guards, no groin protectors, and no headgear (which is now used for youth competitors). It was just you and your gi.

Finally, and most critically, there were fewer divisions in a typical tournament than there are now. Originally, a tournament had just two divisions: kata and sparring. If you wanted to compete, that's what you entered. There also was no separation according to rank, weight, sex, or experience. Only gradually, as more women, children, and families started becoming involved in karate, did the tournaments change.

Karate Minute

In early karate tournaments, the typical sparring division was made up of a bunch of black belts, some brown belts, and a few crazy green or white belts. There were no divisions for women or for kids.

From Club to Club ...

Tournaments and competitions don't have to be big to be a positive and exciting format in which to test your skills. On any given weekend, hundreds and perhaps thousands of karate tournaments take place in high school and college gymnasiums throughout the country. These events typically draw anywhere from 50 to 200 contestants from the surrounding area, or from a group of like-minded dojos. Although they don't train together regularly, most of the contestants and instructors know each other from similar events held throughout the year. The officials will be the local instructors and black belts from the participating clubs. Frequently, everyone will converge on the local pizza parlor to socialize afterward.

Talk the Talk

The Japanese term for competition is **shiai,** and tournament sparring is called **shiai-kumite.**

Often these types of tournaments will be held with a specific focus. Maybe the day's competition will be just for kata, or for kids, or for lower-ranking students. Sometimes the competition will be held specifically to give local officials a chance to improve their skills as judges and referees.

For most students, these small tournaments usually are considered an end in themselves. They allow you the opportunity to test your karate skills under new, relatively safe, and yet (productively) stressful circumstances. They are an exciting addition to your regular training schedule, and if your dojo has a requirement that you compete or participate in a certain number of competitions a year, these usually meet that requirement.

Additionally, these tournaments are a good starting point if you want to go on to bigger competitions.

... To the Big Time

Most of the major karate styles and the bigger karate organizations host their own national and international championships. Frequently, these groups hold local and regional competitions that serve as selection tournaments for these events.

National championship tournaments are big events that fall into one of two categories. The first is divided by style, which means that each style, or organization within a given style, will have a national championship. Yes, that also means that in any given year, there will be lots and lots of national champions running around out there. The second type is a multistyle championship that brings athletes together from all styles to select national champions in several different divisions, which are divided by experience, gender, and age. These division champions frequently form a pool from which national teams are selected for international competition.

The large, multistyle, national championships typically run for four to five days. Aside from the competition, there are seminars for officials, coaches, and athletes, along with training classes by famous karate masters for whoever wants to participate in them.

National Pride

The speed, power, and skill level of world-championship, international karate is inspiring to see. Although karate is not as popular in North America as other sports, internationally it has a very strong following. The competition is intense, the athletes are well trained, the stakes are high, and the competition almost always involves national pride and honor—the countries come to win.

If you are interested, and with enough training, one day you may be selected to represent your country in an international competition. Clearly, this is a great honor, and, of course, the competition will be exciting. More importantly, though, you will learn from every aspect of the experience. You will meet new coaches and teammates, you probably will train harder then you ever have before, you will get to travel to new places, and you will develop camaraderie and friendships with your team members that will last far longer then the competition itself.

International karate is intense. Here, Germany and Sweden face off at the 1995 World Shotokan Karate Association championships in Sunderland, England.

You become a team in international competition. The USA/AAU National Shotokan Karate team traveled to Calgary, Canada, in 1993.

It's Not a Free-for-All

As we continue, you will see that the regulations for modern karate competition are very specific as to what is allowed and what is not allowed. You (or your coach) will need to know lots of rules, you can enter many different divisions, and you can play many different roles.

Most traditional karate tournaments try very hard to hold onto the philosophical underpinnings of the art as it was initially intended to be practiced. As we talked about earlier in the book, however, there is a big difference among sport, art, and self-defense. Sometimes tournaments are successful in being an extension of the art, but sometimes they are not.

Remember, as in other sports, you will be rewarded for doing good things, such as performing a strong kata or scoring on your opponent with clean techniques, but you will be penalized for doing bad things, such as forgetting your kata or violating the rules and making contact with your opponent.

Withhold Your Hand or Withhold Your Anger

The most important principle of a karate competition—and, in many ways, karate itself—is control. Most of us tend to think of control as being able to do fast, strong techniques and still not injure our partner or opponent. In part, that's true, but control goes much further than that. Control also means being able to control your emotions and, despite how you may feel at the moment, to display good sportsmanship at all times.

As you compete, at times you won't like a decision, or a judge's call, or the score you receive on a kata. This happens to everyone, but this is not the time to say something you'll be sorry for later, or to storm off the floor. Look around, and you'll see that most people feel that way. In fact, the only people who are ever really happy with the decisions or the judges are the people who actually end up winning their divisions or the tournament at the end of the day.

Also, as you compete, your opponent may do something that makes you want to really hit him in anger. Don't! This is a sport, not a brawl. You will need to control those emotions and play by the rules. If you don't, you won't be allowed to play at all. Also remember that your actions represent your dojo and your instructor, as well as you. Acting in a way that embarrasses them doesn't do anyone any good.

Razor Rings and Slashing Bracelets

The second factor that is important to all karate competition is safety. As in the dojo, you won't be allowed to compete if you are wearing any earrings, bracelets, watches, necklaces, rings, or other jewelry that might hurt you or someone else. Also be sure to keep your fingernails and toenails trimmed, and your gi clean for each competition.

Bulletheads and Bullies

Occasionally (but really not very often) people show up at a tournament and just don't know how to act (this is a sign of very poor training). They come in with a poor attitude, thinking that they are going to bully everyone around or that they don't need to follow the same rules as everyone else. Dealing with these people is not your job! Let the tournament officials handle this. As in any other sport, a good tournament will have zero tolerance for poor sportsmanship, rule violations, and bad attitudes.

If Your Body Goes Where a Foot or Fist Is

As much as everyone tries to be safe, karate is a combative sport, and accidents happen. Every tournament should have an emergency medical person on hand to deal with minor injuries and assess more serious ones. If you are injured, the medical person should determine whether you are able to continue—not you (because your spirit is strong, you willingly will fight to the death), not your sensei (because his spirit is strong, and he knows you will willingly fight to the death), and not your coach (because his spirit is strong and—well, you get the idea).

Fight Hard but Play Safe: Gear Up!

With some slight variation, almost all traditional karate tournaments require the use of safety equipment for adults and children. The United States Amateur Athletic Union's National Karate Program is the country's largest multistyle karate organization. Its safety equipment requirements are representative of most national and international organizations.

The AAU National Karate Program requires that competitors aged 5 to 18 wear the following safety equipment when sparring:

1. White foam headgear with chin strap

2. White cloth or naugahyde fist pads

3. Mouth guard

4. Groin protector for males

Ouch!

There should be no contact when kids spar. The head gear is to keep them from hitting their heads on the floor in case they fall down.

The AAU National Karate Program requires that competitors aged 19 and above wear the following safety equipment when sparring:

1. White cloth or naugahyde fist pads

2. Mouth guard

3. Groin protector for men

Karate kids get protected from top to bottom—they need headgear, hand pads, and a mouth guard.

In addition, some optional equipment is also allowed. For example, women can wear a plastic chest protector under their gis, all competitors are allowed to wear soft shin pads, and competitors in the junior divisions may wear cloth shin/instep protectors.

When Can I Compete?

When you start to compete pretty much depends on you and your instructor. Different dojos have different philosophies concerning competition. Also, people are different, and you may be ready to compete at a different time than somebody else who started training at the same time as you.

Back when the authors of this book started training, it was very uncommon for anyone below the rank of brown belt to compete because you didn't start learning to free spar until then. So, most competitors had a minimum of two years of training before they started entering tournaments.

Now, most tournaments have beginner divisions for both youth and adults. In theory, this means that you can compete as soon as you learn how to tie your belt. However, we don't recommend it! Give yourself some time to get comfortable with doing karate. See what karate competition looks like, and get involved in your dojo's sparring classes before you go charging out there.

Who Fights Whom?

You'll be happy to know that they don't just throw everyone into a small room, lock the door, blow a whistle, and yell "Begin!" to start a tournament. Divisions are divided by gender, age, and experience. Everyone does not fight everyone, or do their kata against everyone else.

The most traditional method of creating divisions is to use belt rankings. This means that white belts go against white belts, green belts go against green belts, and on up. The trouble with this method is that different schools award belts at different times. So, sometimes you end up with a brown belt with two years of experience fighting a brown belt with seven years of experience.

To make the divisions more standard and fair, the larger national and international multistyle organizations are now creating divisions based on amount of time training. This means that divisions are starting to be divided in the following way:

➤ **Beginner division.** Less than one year of training

➤ **Novice division.** One to two years of training

➤ **Intermediate division.** Two to four years of training

➤ **Advanced division.** Four or more years of training

Ladies and Gentlemen of All Ages ...

Don't forget, though, that aside from experience and gender, divisions also are divided by age. Smaller tournaments with fewer contestants usually don't make as many divisions as the larger ones—there just aren't enough contestants to go around, and you would end up with one or two people in each division.

At the larger tournaments and national championships, to be as fair as possible, there is a division for almost every age and level of ability. This makes for very large competitions.

For example, in the AAU National Karate Championships, there are separate male and female kata and sparring divisions for beginner, novice, intermediate, and advanced competitors for every year between the ages of 5 and 18. That's 224 youth divisions alone.

In addition, there are adult male and female beginner, novice, and intermediate kata and kumite divisions. There are senior kata and kumite divisions for beginner, novice, intermediate, and advanced competitors between the ages 35 to 39, 40 to 44, 45 to 49, 50 to 54, and 55 and up. Add to this weapons divisions and adult and junior kata and kumite team competition, and you can see why these tournaments run for four to five days.

Watch Your Weight

One final distinction is made for the tournament elite, the male and female, 19- to 34-year-old advanced divisions. These are the tournament hot shots, the ones most likely to represent their countries in international competition. If you get to this level, you will compete against all other advanced men or other women in kata, but you will be divided into the following weight categories for sparring:

Males:

➤ 132 lb. limit

➤ 143 lb. limit

➤ 154 lb. limit

➤ 165 lb. limit

➤ 176 lb. limit

➤ 187 lb. limit

➤ 198 lb. limit

➤ 198.1 lb. and up

Females:

➤ 110 lb. limit

➤ 121 lb. limit

➤ 132 lb. limit

➤ 143 lb. limit

➤ 154 lb. limit

➤ 154 lb. and up

Karate Tots

Karate is a wonderful activity for children. As we've discussed earlier, if presented well, it allows children to develop good physical and personal strengths and lots of positive characteristics and abilities. As you can see from the previous section, kids are able to compete in karate from the age of 5, and for most kids, competition is a positive activity. It's fun, it's exciting, it's a little scary, and it teaches you to deal with success and failure on a very immediate level.

However, we offer some cautions. As with some adults, competition isn't for everyone. At the age of five and six, or even 11 and 12, some kids will be ready to get out there and mix it up or do their kata in front of a gym full of people, but some will not be. Make sure to talk to your karate kids and their instructor about what is best for them and when they should start competing.

With the right attitude and support from parents, instructors, and coaches, kids can have a great time at a karate tournament— win or lose.

Also, as with any other sports program, such as Little League, swimming, basketball, or gymnastics, make sure that you recognize that kids' competition is for the kids— not the adults. Win or lose, there is a positive lesson to be learned; help your karate kid learn it. More then most sports, karate is meant to be about individual effort and the willingness to try your best, regardless of the outcome. Don't make it just about wins and losses.

Going Solo—or One of the Pack

There are two ways for you to enter a tournament. First, you can enter as an individual. This means that even though you may be at a tournament with lots of other people from your dojo, you enter individual elimination events. Basically, this puts you against everyone else in that division, regardless of where they're from.

For example, the score you get on your kata—we'll talk about scoring in the next chapter—in individual kata competition is compared against everyone else's kata score. The highest score wins, the next score gets second place, the next gets third, and on down the line.

Or, if your individual kumite division starts with 32 people, after the first round of matches, there will be 16 competitors left. After the next round, there will be eight, and then four, then two, and, finally, it's just you (hopefully) standing there with a smile on your face, a medal around your neck, and a trophy in your hand.

The second type of competition is team competition. In this, your kata team competes against other kata teams, and your kumite team (usually three or five people) competes against other kumite teams.

Team kata is a three-person synchronized event: You and two others do the same kata at the same time. Aside from all the other kata criteria, your team is judged by how well they stay together during the kata.

In team kumite, your team fights another team, one at a time. At the end of the matches, the team with the most victories wins.

Don't Burn Out: A Tournament a Week?

When you start competing, you may feel that karate competition is the greatest, most exciting thing you have ever done. You may become a serious competitor and devote all your training to developing the skills you need to be successful. In fact, many of today's best instructors did just that. During one 5- or 10-year period in their karate careers, win or lose, they were on teams, they trained like maniacs, and they competed a lot.

Be aware, though, as you've seen so far in this book, that there is much more to karate then just competition. Even though there might be a tournament a week, you don't need to go to all of them! From what we've seen, the most successful competitors and best karate-ka approach karate competition as a sport—with a season. Although they train in the martial art of karate all year long because they like it and because it has become a positive part of their lives, they compete in karate during their karate season.

Family Feuds: Karate Politics 101

You'll find lots of good karate instructors, styles, and organizations out there (and, of course, some that aren't so good). At some point in your training, you will realize that all the groups feel that their particular group or style is the best. This is natural, in part, because the more energy we invest in something, the more we come to value it. In general, though, organizations are just that—organizations. Like families—which is what the original styles and ryus essentially were—each has positive and negative aspects. When trying to figure it out for yourself, look a little deeper than the hype you might run into at the tournaments.

270

Try to remember that the important thing about karate is what happens inside you and on the dojo floor, not what happens in the offices. Do you have instructors whom you can respect, and who respect you? Do they value the karate itself? Do you feel at home in your dojo? Are you learning something of value? Although challenging and difficult at times, is it a positive experience? And, if you compete, are the competitions fair?

Think about why you started training in the first place. If you're like most people, you want karate to bring out the best of you as an individual. You want to learn an effective and serious form of self-defense that is also a demanding and exacting traditional art. And, if you compete, you want to be exposed to fair, intense, and challenging competition at the local, regional, national, and international levels.

If you feel that you have that, you're home. If not, you can always marry into another family.

The Bottom Line on Competition

The generation of karate instructors who first developed competition karate in the 1950s, always verbalized the belief that while tournaments were exciting, they were not what karate was supposed to be all about. Tournaments were supposed to be a training method (one of many) for improving your technique and your spirit—not an end in themselves.

To be perfectly honest, karate competition offers many pros and cons. We conclude this chapter with some of the major considerations.

Cons:

➤ **Limitations.** For safety reasons, what you can do in a karate competition is fairly limited in the techniques you can use and the targets you can attack. So, if you practice only for competition, you end up practicing a very small percentage of what karate offers you. Because of this, some people end up thinking that they are more effective then they really are, while others end up thinking that they are less effective then they really are.

➤ **Confusing reward system.** Rewards in karate dojos are based on effort, intensity, and dedication. Sometimes the results of a competition don't reflect that. Winners may be rewarded for good athletic ability but indifferent training habits, while the losers may not be rewarded for the effort they put in.

➤ **Potentially dangerous illusions.** Without good, intense training, competition may give you the impression that fighting is safe and painless. It's not!

➤ **Ranking impermanence.** Tournament results are never permanent. Today's winner may be tomorrow's loser, and vice versa. (Hmmm, maybe this should go in the pro column as well.)

➤ **Subjective decisions.** By far the biggest frustration that most people have with competition relates to the fact that the decisions and results are almost entirely subjective. As in gymnastics, all decisions are a matter of the judges' opinions. Therefore, it is extremely important for judges and referees to be well-trained and as objective as possible. Now, sometimes it's true that the best person may not win due to an error on the part of the judges, and that's certainly reason for disappointment. More often, though, the subjectivity gives poor losers a chance to blame someone else (usually the referee) for the fact that they didn't do as well as they wanted to, or thought they did.

Pros:

➤ **Great opportunities.** Karate competition is exciting and fun, and it's a great chance to do something special with the people from your dojo.

➤ **Goal-oriented.** Karate competition gives you a special goal to train for and gives you an intense, but safe, karate experience.

➤ **Tests for your training.** Karate competition gives you the opportunity to test your techniques, your training, your courage, and your spirit in strange settings against people you don't normally train with. This will make your karate better.

➤ **Opportunities to see new styles.** Karate competition exposes you to other styles of karate and other competitors. (As a beginner, it is always a good idea to stay and watch the advanced divisions. There is a lot to be learned by watching more experienced people do karate.)

➤ **Humility.** Karate competition keeps you humble and honest. Usually, the more you train, the better you do.

➤ **Travel.** Karate competition gives you the opportunity to travel and meet new people.

➤ **Great life lessons.** Karate competition lets you experience the thrill of victory and the agony of defeat.

The Least You Need to Know

➤ Karate competition is fun and exciting.

➤ You don't need to compete to get good at karate.

➤ Self-control and safety are the most important considerations in karate competition.

➤ There are competition divisions for almost everybody.

Chapter 21

Know the Score—There Are Many Ways to Compete

In This Chapter

➤ How points are scored in sparring competition

➤ How to execute the perfect technique

➤ The different types of penalties you can earn when sparring

➤ The criteria judges use in choosing kata and weapons winners

In this chapter, we discuss the nuts and bolts of sparring, kata, and kobudo competition. Specifically, we discuss what you need to do as a competitor, what scores, what fails, what you should be trying to achieve, and what will get you into trouble. We also take a look at what the judges and referees are looking for when they are officiating.

As in the last chapter, we will continue to use the AAU National Karate Program rules as our reference point. These rules are representative of those used by most national and international karate organizations.

Sparring: The Basics

The kumite competition area is a smooth, flat, square surface that usually measures eight meters on each side.

There is a center referee, the *shushin* (who has absolute control over the ring—the referee's word is law); an arbitrator, the *kansa;* and either two or four corner judges, the *fukushin,* who award points to the fighters.

Karate Minute

Don't mess around. The referee's word is law. Competitors never talk to the referee. If you have a complaint, your coach should handle it.

Sparring ring positions for sanbon kumite match.

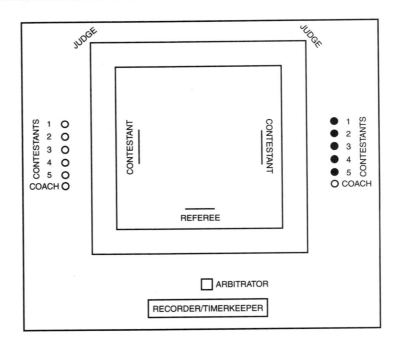

Sparring: Scoring Points

In principle, winning a karate match is pretty simple: You just need to score more points on your opponents than they score on you. Points to specific target areas are scored with kicks, punches, or strikes, and earn a value of either one full point (*ippon*) or a half-point (*waza-ari*). Depending on the type of tournament you are fighting in, you will either need three points (*shobu sanbon*) or one point (*shobu ippon*) to win the match. As we've discussed earlier, your techniques need to be delivered with speed, power, and control. Depending on the tournament rules and what division you are fighting in, the matches are generally either two or three minutes in length.

274

Karate Minute

Traditional kumite competition takes two forms: three-point (*sanbon*) matches and the less popular one-point (*ippon*) matches. Although they are very similar, there are some important differences between the two. First, because losing in just one point is a different game then losing in three points, the fighting strategy is usually different. Second, because fewer points are given in ippon competition, the judges make those points harder to get. The criteria of what constitutes a point is more exacting, and greater emphasis is generally placed on generating power with the technique.

You might be saying, "Come on, I get it! Let's cut to the chase. Simple question: What kind of techniques should I do in order to score points?"

Okay, simple answer: perfect ones.

How to Win: Make It Perfect

For you to score and be awarded an ippon (full point) on your opponent, your technique will have to meet all of the following criteria:

1. **Have good form.** Now, this is pretty obvious. Whatever you do needs to actually look like karate.

2. **Demonstrate a strong attitude.** This means you have to be serious and intense about what you are doing. It also means that you have to show respect to your opponent and the officials. For example, it is not good to jab your finger into your opponent's chest, yelling, "In your face!" after you have scored with a round-house kick to the head.

3. **Apply your technique vigorously.** This means that your technique must be delivered with enough speed and power to have actually hurt someone, if it hadn't been controlled.

Talk the Talk

The **shushin** is the referee. The **fukushin** are the judges. The **kansa** is the arbitrator.

Talk the Talk

Waza-ari is a half-point. **Ippon** is a full point. **Shobu sanbon** refers to a three-point match. **Shobu ippon** refers to a one-point match.

275

4. **Have good timing.** It's not enough for your technique to show up at the right place; it needs to get there at the right time. The best is if you can score on your opponent just as he starts moving toward you.

5. **Maintain good distance.** Your body and technique must be at the exact distance you need to make the technique effective. Remember, you're not pulling the technique, you're controlling it. This means that the technique must have the potential to penetrate the target if you wanted it to.

6. **Have *zanshin* (a perfect finish).** This means that you must keep your attitude even after you have scored the technique. No running around in victory circles ripping your gi top off, no spiking your mouth guard, and no jumping up into the stands to kiss your honey. Keep it together before, during, and after the technique scores.

EEEE-YA!!!

Talk the Talk

Zanshin means "perfect finish."

Sensei Says

Good karate is good karate. The best way to train for a tournament is to train a lot. Whether you are doing karate at the dojo or at a competition, always do the best karate you can.

Now, let's say that your technique isn't perfect, and a little something is missing from one of the six criteria. Your technique can still get a full point for the following reasons:

➤ It's a technically difficult (fancy) technique, such as a kick to the head.

➤ It happens right after you have deflected (blocked) a strong attack from your opponent and counterattacked an area of your opponent's body that he had no chance of protecting.

➤ It happens right after you have swept or thrown your opponent.

➤ It is a combination of half-point techniques.

➤ It has perfect timing. It gets to your opponent at the precise moment that he starts to attack.

A final thing on scoring points: If it turns out that your technique is good—not perfect, but really good—you can still get a half-point (waza-ari). This isn't bad, because two half-points make a full point. You just need to start adding them up. Whoever has the most points at the end of the match wins.

Be on Target

You need to be accurate. You can't just go out there and start whomping anywhere you want on your opponent's body and score a point. You can score only on these specific targets:

➤ The head

➤ The face

➤ The neck

➤ The abdomen

➤ The chest

➤ The back, but not the top of the shoulders

➤ The sides of the body

The shaded areas are your targets.

Be Careful: There Are Lots of Ways You Can Lose

If you're not careful, you can lose a match with absolutely no help from your opponent. Yep, your opponent doesn't even need to score on you. You can do it all by yourself, simply because you aren't paying attention or because you lose control of yourself in some way.

Let's look at the four major categories in which you can do something that causes you to lose the match.

Contact!

The most dramatic rule violations are what are known as contact violations. In this situation, one fighter does something, usually hitting or kicking the other fighter, in a way that physically injures the opponent. Even though most tournaments take contact pretty seriously, it is not always based on black-and-white criteria. For example, although contact is prohibited in all divisions, what is considered contact for 6-year-old female beginners is not considered contact for the 19- to 34-year-old male open weight fighters. With experience, you will learn what is appropriate for each level. It usually comes down to this: If what you do in any way reduces your opponent's ability to fight and win the match, you will be penalized.

> EEEE-YA!!!

Talk the Talk

Jogai means *"out of bounds."* **Mubobi** means *"loss of spirit."* **Atenai-ayoni** is a verbal warning. **Keikoku** is a half-point penalty. **Hansoku chui** is a full-point penalty. **Hansoku** is given if you lose the match because of a penalty. **Shikkaku** is a total disqualification.

You also can earn contact violations, whether your opponent is injured or not, when you do …

➤ Make any contact with the throat.

➤ Attack the groin, the joints of the arms and legs, or the instep.

➤ Deliver attacks to the face and the eyes with open-hand techniques.

➤ Use dangerous throws that you can't control.

➤ Purposefully attack your opponent's arms or legs.

Noncontact—but Off-Limits!

As the name implies, nobody actually gets hit with noncontact violations. These are usually violations of etiquette, attitude, manner, and intent, and can cover a pretty broad range of things.

For example, you can earn noncontact penalties for the following:

➤ Swinging wildly or using techniques that are out of your control, and that you couldn't stop even if you wanted to

➤ Talking to your opponent (especially if you are angry and you say bad things)

➤ Talking to the referee (especially if you are angry and say bad things)

➤ Showing poor sportsmanship

➤ Not stopping when the referee says to stop

➤ Running around the ring and waiting for time to run out (you might be ahead on points, so you just try to avoid your opponent until time is up)

Jogai! You Need to Watch Where You Are Going

The third type of violation involves whether you can stay inside the ring. We'll talk about the different levels of penalty severity later in the chapter, but with the *jogai* violation, it really is pretty cut and dried:

➤ You will get a verbal warning from the referee the first time you step outside the ring.

➤ The second time you step out, you get a half-point penalty (keikoku) and your opponent receives a half-point.

➤ The third time you go out, you get a full-point penalty (hansoku-chui), and your opponent gets a full point (by now you can see where this is going).

➤ On the forth time you step out, you lose the match (hansoku). Yep, no punches, no kicks, but you're outta' there, just the same!

So stay in the ring! Even better, try to get your opponent to go out (there are lots of ways to do this—ask your coach). As you can see, how well you manage your ring position can have a dramatic effect on the outcome of the match.

Hey! This Is Supposed to Be About Self-Defense

The fourth and final category of violation is called mubobi. Basically this is used when you put yourself in danger, cause your own injury, or in some way lose your fighting spirit. The big question with mubobi is "Why would I do that?" Well, we don't know, but a lot of people do.

Some of the ways you can earn a mubobi include these:

➤ Attacking without thinking about your own safety. This means that you are in such a hurry to dash in and score on your opponent that you run your head, face, or stomach into your opponent's hand or foot, causing your own injury.

➤ You are so sure your attack scored that you stop fighting before the referee tells you to, and you go running back to your starting position.

➤ You pretend that you are injured when you aren't (so that your opponent gets a contact violation). Please, don't ever do this! It's humiliating to you and everyone who knows you.

➤ You don't protect yourself. You stop fighting and just drop your hands or turn your back on your opponent.

Ouch!

Mubobi has got to be the worst. Not only can you get hurt, but you can end up getting a penalty. Talk about missing the point!

279

Don't Do That Again!

If you do violate one of rules we've just discussed, you probably will not be immediately disqualified (unless the violation is very serious, in which case you can lose right there and then). The referee and judges will decide how severe a violation was and then penalize you accordingly. Most likely you will first be warned—and if you do it again, you will be penalized more severely.

As you've seen when we discussed the jogai penalties, there are five levels of penalty that you can receive:

➤ **Atenai-ayoni.** The first is the verbal warning. Basically the referee tells you what you did, and not to do it again.

➤ **Keikoku.** Second is the half-point penalty. If you get this in three-point sparring, your opponent gets a half-point.

➤ **Hansoku-chui.** Third is the full-point penalty. If you get this in three-point sparring, your opponent gets a full point.

➤ **Hansoku.** Fourth, you lose the match outright. If you get this in three-point sparring, your opponent wins.

➤ **Shikkaku.** The fifth and most serious penalty that can be imposed is a complete disqualification from the tournament. This results in disqualification from every event in the entire tournament—and, in some cases, a ban on competition for one year. This happens very rarely, but when it does, it is very serious. The AAU rules manual describes the circumstances for imposing a shikkaku in these words: "when a contestant commits an act which harms the prestige and honor of karate-do and when other actions are considered to violate the rules of the tournament." Usually, this involves a conscious and intentional disregard for the rules.

Final Point

Matches can be decided by any combination of earned points and penalty points. Whoever has the most points at the end of the match wins.

Pick Your Game: Reading Between the Lines

Now for some confusing and sometimes conflicting truths. Even though most karate tournaments follow the same basic rules and are equally concerned about the overall safety of the competitors, there are different opinions as to what actually constitutes contact. Remember, the rules try to take into account a variety of factors: your ability to control your technique, the actual injuries to the opponent, and how much that injury inhibits your opponent's ability to win the match.

From "Touch, You Lose" to "Hey, Get Up and Fight!"

Some tournaments and karate organizations take the view that "no contact" literally means no touching at all. If you touch in any way, you lose. On the other hand, some groups let their fighters hit with full force to the body and take a pretty good whack to the head before they penalize a contestant.

Most groups, however, including the major national and international associations, fall somewhere in the middle. They take a strict interpretation of the "no contact" rule with children and lower-level adult divisions, while at the same time allowing more leeway in their interpretation for the advanced divisions.

Play by the Rules

Regardless of what side of the argument you eventually come down on, and regardless of what training philosophy you and your dojo follow, be aware that when you enter a tournament, you are agreeing to follow the rules of that tournament. You, your instructors, and your coaches should know the rules and the interpretations of those rules before you decide to compete. Then, when you do decide to enter, don't grumble and complain. Do your best, and be prepared to play by the rules of the day.

Parental Discretion Advised

For parents, however, the authors of this book strongly urge you not to allow your children to enter any competitions where *any* amount of contact is tolerated or encouraged for kids. It's not safe, and it gives children the wrong message about the value of martial arts. Additionally, it is never reasonable for any adult to say that it is okay for one kid to hit another kid in a sporting event.

It's Not All Fighting: Competing with Kata

Kata competition takes place in the same ring in which you spar. A chief referee and four judges score a kata performance, in much the same way that a gymnastics or figure skating routine is scored.

The most common way to compete in kata requires that you stand in front of a panel of judges and perform your kata for a score, which is compared to everyone else's score. The person with the highest points wins.

At most competitions, you will be allowed to pick the kata you are to perform. In these cases, it is usually best to pick a kata that you know well, and have practiced the most rather than the fancy one you learned just last week. Some tournaments, however, require that you do only a form that is associated with your rank. For example, if you are a beginner, you will need to pick a beginner's level kata.

At some national and international championship events, the advanced competitors will have to do one round of beginner kata (to select the top 16 semifinalists), then one round of intermediate kata (to select the top 8 finalists), and finally one round of advanced kata, to select the champions.

Kata and kobudo judges sit on the outside of the ring as contestants compete in the middle of the ring.

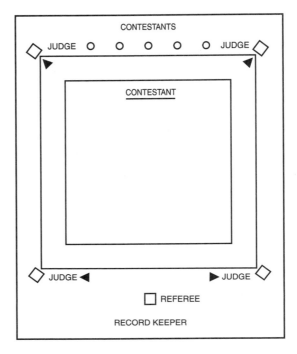

More Than Just a Pretty Face

When judges evaluate a kata performance, they aren't simply looking for somebody who looks good. They are evaluating you on the basis of a very specific set of criteria. As you read this next section, realize that you should try to meet these criteria whenever you practice your kata—whether you are competing or doing the kata in your garage on an early Saturday morning.

Cover These Bases

Most importantly, the techniques in your kata should be performed in a serious and realistic fashion. Remember, kata isn't a dance or a tumbling routine; kata is a means of demonstrating your technique, your spirit, and your concentration.

The following are what national and international judges are trained to look for when evaluating your kata in competition:

➤ Competency and a clear understanding of the principles of the kata. This means that you need to look like you know what you are doing, and the kata's techniques need to look like karate. For example, you can sit down at a piano and

282

pick out all the notes of a song, but unless you play them with the right tempo, rhythm, and feeling, it will not sound like music.

➤ Correct breathing.

➤ Good use of power, speed, timing, balance, and *kime* (focus).

➤ Consistency and correctness of stances.

➤ Correct weight distribution according to the kihon (basic techniques) being demonstrated.

➤ Smooth and even transition (*hara*, the center of the body, remaining weighted down) between stances.

➤ Correct tension in stances.

➤ Feet edges planted firmly on the floor.

Quite a lot, huh? Basically, this means that all the important aspects of your basic karate techniques must be present in your kata.

In addition (yes, there's more), the techniques need to demonstrate the following:

➤ Accuracy.

➤ Correct and consistent basic techniques with the style being demonstrated.

➤ Correct tension and focus.

➤ Proper understanding of the kata bunkai (technique applications). This means that you need to show that you understand what the applications of your kata techniques mean. What move is a block? Which move is an attack? What is a hold and throw? Do you know where the punches and kicks are supposed to go? Or are you just out there flailing around, doing movements?

Finally, your kata should clearly demonstrate the following:

➤ Unwavering concentration

➤ Contrast in tension, breathing, and movement

➤ An understanding of those techniques being demonstrated

➤ A realistic, rather than theatrical, demonstration of kata meaning

This means that the entire kata should be an expression of your spirit and concentration.

It's a lot of stuff, isn't it? But you have to figure that it's not really anything new. It's all the stuff that you are supposed to be working on every time you do a kata anyway. So relax, and go for it! If you practice well, you'll perform well.

283

What's the Score?

At the end of your kata performance, the referee and four judges will hold up cards with your score on it. Generally, the top and bottom scores are dropped, and the remaining three are added for your final score.

Karate Minute

Kata scores generally reflect the ability of the athletes. Beginners often score in the 5.0 to 7.0 point range, novices in the 5.5 to 7.5 range, intermediates in the 6.0 to 8.0, and advanced competitors in the 6.5 to 8.5 range.

Get It Together

Another form of kata competition is team kata. In this type of event, three people do the same kata at the same time. All of the previous judging and evaluation criteria apply, but in addition, the team must be precisely and exactly synchronized—the team members must stay together throughout the kata. This becomes quite a challenge when doing a kata that features a lot of turns, jumps, kicks, and changes in rhythm.

Kobudo Competition

Kobudo (weapons) competition works very much like kata competition. You can do weapons katas using the following weapons: bo (the staff), tonfa (the rice grinder—must be used in pairs), eku (the oar), nunchaku (the wooden flail), and the sai (the short trident—must be used in pairs).

In general, the same scoring criteria that apply to empty-hand kata also apply to weapons events, with some additional considerations:

➤ You can be disqualified if you lose control of or drop your weapon.

➤ You can be disqualified if the way you handle your weapon is dangerous to others.

Whether you compete in kumite, kata or both, enjoy their experience. Use the competition to test yourself, and see if you can do your best when you need to.

The Least You Need to Know

➤ You can compete in both kata and sparring.

➤ You can lose a match just by earning penalties.

➤ A perfect technique has good form, a strong attitude, speed and power, timing, distance, and zanshin, a perfect ending.

➤ "Too much contact" may mean different things at different tournaments.

➤ The best kata isn't necessarily the fanciest kata.

Okay, Just Point Me in the Right Direction

In This Chapter

➤ What it costs to go to a tournament

➤ What to expect on tournament day

➤ Tournament etiquette

➤ The hardest job

Successful karate tournaments involve a lot of different people doing a lot of different things. It isn't simply show up, fight your fights, do your kata, get your trophies, and go home. There are numerous logistics and considerations to take into account, and there are costs and schedules to plan for.

Additionally, it takes a lot of people to put on a tournament—probably more than you think. That's why, depending on the size, it usually takes the effort of an entire dojo, association, or organization to host one. And the truth is, if not for the volunteer workers, including the referees (who are frequently volunteers), it would be impossible to have tournaments at all. So, even if you aren't a competitor, there is plenty to do: taking tickets, selling supplies, timing and scoring the matches, and organizing the competitors and the events. If you are a karate-ka, you also can referee and judge (with training) and act as a coach for the competitors from your dojo. Everyone can get involved in the competitions your dojo puts on or goes to.

How Much Is This Going to Cost?

First things first. It costs money to compete. Almost all (probably 98 out of 100) tournaments charge competitors an entry fee, and most charge spectator fees as well. As we discussed earlier in the book when we talked about training costs, it's hard to say what the fees will be because they vary from event to event. Some fees, perhaps those for small, interclub competitions, might be as low as $10 or $15. Bigger tournaments in large, urban areas might go as high as $50. Generally, fees come in at about $35. Note, though, that although some tournaments charge one fee that covers any and all events you participate in, others charge you separately for each event.

EEEE-YA!!!

Talk the Talk

Dojo-moms or **dojo-dads** are parents who volunteer and help at events and tournaments. **Ring-moms** are parents (male and female) who keep the little kids organized from before their divisions right up to the moment they fight their matches.

Depending on your division, you probably will spend either the entire morning or the entire afternoon at a tournament. As you become more advanced and compete in more events, or if you stay to watch your friends and teammates compete after you are done, you may end up spending the whole day there. Well, you've gotta eat. Lots of people—especially families and groups that attend a tournament together—frequently bring food and drinks to save themselves time and money, and to avoid having to eat burgers and fries three times in a single day.

As we talked about in the last chapter, large tournaments and the major national championships may have hundreds of divisions and thousands of contestants. These tournaments usually include one or two days of seminars for contestants, officials, and coaches, plus three or four days of competition. This is where the costs can mount up. There will be transportation, hotel accommodations, and other expenses. Fortunately, the sponsors of these events usually realize that this type of participation requires a substantial investment of the participants' time and money. So, as best they can, they try to choose enjoyable vacation destinations to make the trip worthwhile for the participants. In recent years, national championships have been held at Disney World and in southern California, Las Vegas, and Hawaii.

As you attend these events, you'll notice that many karate families schedule their vacations to coincide with the major tournaments so that they can kill two birds with one stone.

It's Fun to Go with a Group

Very few people go to a tournament by themselves. After all, who wants to march into battle alone? You want to have people there to give you support and to back you up. Think of *The Dirty Dozen, The Seven Samurai, The Fantastic Four,* or *The Three*

Musketeers. Even Don Quixote had Sancho Panza there to pick him up, dust him off, slap him on the butt, and tell him what a great job he did.

Tournaments are just more fun as group activities. Dojos and clubs, large and small, usually sit together, cheer for each other, give each other support, and provide encouragement. Also, going with people you know gives you someone to talk to while you wait between events, someone you can stretch out with, and someone you can safely spar with to warm up.

Aagghh! It's Tournament Day

Regardless of how much experience someone has, it's not likely that he considers tournament day to be just another day. Everyone is nervous. Hey, this is Game Day, and you're going to feel it. Being nervous is par for the course—in fact, it's normal. People respond to pressure and the anxiety associated with performance in different ways. Some people feel exhilarated by the feeling, while others get so nervous on the day of competition that they throw up (fortunately, however, this is the exception).

We know several former and current national champions who talk about hating competition right up to the moment that they win their first match, and then they feel great and never want to do anything else. As with every other aspect of karate, experience will help. As you become more experienced, you will learn to control these emotions and actually use them to give you the extra energy you need to do your best.

Can't Sleep

Even though you may not feel like it, try to get a normal night's sleep before the tournament. Just because you're excited, don't stay up all night running around and talking to your family, friends, and teammates. Try to stay close to your regular schedule. If you can't sleep, relax, lie there, and mentally rehearse what you are going to do on the day of the tournament. Be positive. Visualize yourself doing your best. Eventually you'll doze off and probably sleep until morning.

Can't Eat

A lot of people lose their appetite before a big or exciting event. Almost nobody eats on the morning of their wedding. The trouble is that because tournaments can last all day, if you don't eat when you can, you might not get the opportunity to eat at all. Second, most tournaments are held in a high school or college gymnasium—not exactly a health food mecca. So, at least make an effort to eat something reasonably healthy early in the day. Then you're pretty much on your own.

Where's the Bathroom?

Try to get to the tournament a little early so that you know your way around the site. You need to know where you register, where you change into your gi, where you can leave your stuff (most people leave it in the stands with friends), and where you go to line up for your divisions. Also, you need to know where the bathrooms are—if you're like most of us, with all the nerves and excitement, you'll probably be going there a lot.

Karate Minute

Trust us on this: Nothing is worse than being barefoot and following 150 nervous little boys into the bathroom so that you can go potty, too. If you are competing, or judging, or helping as a timer or score keeper, be sure to bring some cheap beach sandals with you. Don't go in there barefoot if you can possibly avoid it!

Hurry Up and Wait!

There are other reasons to get to the tournament on time. Most importantly, you need to be there before the registration for your event closes, or you might not get to compete at all.

Now for the dark but well-known secret of karate tournaments. Every tournament, no matter how big or small it is and no matter how many or few contestants there are, will last all day and occasionally into the night. We're not really sure why this happens, but it's true. Most tournaments seem to go on forever. Prepare yourself for extended periods of waiting. This is a good time to watch the other divisions compete because you can learn a lot, both from people's mistakes and from their moments of brilliance. This is also a good time to talk to your friends, write to people you haven't seen in years, and do your homework—yes, come prepared.

Opponents Are Easy—It's the Butterflies That Get You!

We think that the most useful aspect of karate competition is that it helps you be the master of yourself. Being in a tournament teaches you to deal with nerves, strong emotions (such as fear), and face-to-face competition in a controlled and organized environment. If you can be your best here, you can be your best anywhere. This is good practice run for life.

Suggestion number 1: Regardless of how you feel, try to burn off your excess energy by thoroughly warming up before you compete. It's funny, but sometimes when you're nervous (and especially if you've been lying awake all night, staring at the ceiling), you don't feel like you have the energy to really warm up. Even though you're in great shape, it just seems difficult to get moving. Fight that! Get up and break a sweat. You'll do much better.

Suggestion number 1B: Don't warm up too much—you'll just burn yourself out! Try to figure out how long you have before your event, and warm up accordingly. Loosening up for five hours to fight for two minutes is not good sports science. Experience plays a big part here. It's kind of like a surfer standing on the beach reading the waves: At some point, you just know. If your instructor isn't a referee, or if your dojo has some coaches on the floor, he will be in a good position to help you out and tell you when to warm up and when your division will start.

Sensei Says

You shouldn't just train for a tournament; you should train all the time. If you're going to compete, however, be ready. Nothing provides as much confidence as preparation.

Nothing to Fear but Fear Itself

Remember, tournaments are controlled competitive events. For the amount of energy and the number of kicks and punches that get thrown around, very few injuries occur. Of course, your best insurance is being well trained and physically and emotionally prepared, but that goes without saying. Usually, the biggest obstacle in doing well in competition is yourself. You're there to see if you can do your best when you need to, not just when you want to.

Also, in all likelihood, your dojo training will (hopefully) be harder than what you face in competition, so you'll be ready. The excitement comes from the opportunity to see how your techniques work against people you don't know—and who don't know you.

Ouch!

Warming up before an intense physical event is important to peak performance and in avoiding injuries. No one just walks into a class and starts hard, fast sparring. The day of competition shouldn't be any different.

Keep Cool: This Is No Place for Hotheads

We've already talked about how competitors are expected to act at a competition. Now, here are a couple things to keep in mind for people who come and watch you compete, or if you go to watch someone else.

First, in theory, a karate tournament is—or should be—an extension of the dojo. Yet, sometimes when perfectly nice people come to a tournament to watch their sons and daughters or husbands and wives compete, they go crazy and start acting like they were raised in a cave. It must be all that adrenaline and energy that starts moving around the room, but a lot of people seem to lose perspective. They start acting in a way in which they would never act if they were seeing the same kata or sparring match when visiting a dojo.

Talk the Talk

"Jerks" are people who yell stupid and insulting things from the stands.

Here's some basic karate spectator etiquette: Clapping, cheering, yelling encouragement, and offering congratulations is all good. Booing (either a decision, another competitor, or the referee) is bad. So is yelling threats at your son's opponent or insulting the girl that beat your daughter in overtime. Don't do it.

Officials—the Toughest Job

Of all the jobs out there, undoubtedly one of the hardest is being the referee or judge of a karate tournament. The pay is terrible, because—except for rare occasions, there is no pay. The hours are long, the clothes are uncomfortable, the food is bad, and, worst of all, at the end of a 12-hour day, the only person in the tournament who thinks you did a decent job is the person who won. Everyone else goes home thinking that you're either blind or a cheater.

As with other aspects of karate, referees and officials continually undergo training to improve their skills and abilities. Most national organizations offer seminars and require officials to hold local, regional, national, and international licenses, depending on their level of ability and experience. This is where a lot of competitors go when their competition days are behind them.

Senior referees who have the knowledge and ability to officiate at national and international competitions are well trained and usually must meet the following criteria:

➤ Minimum rank of sandan (third-degree black belt)

➤ Minimum age of 30

➤ Several years of refereeing experience at local and regional levels

➤ Proficiency and understanding of national and international rules, as demonstrated in previous tournaments

➤ Proficiency and understanding of rules, as demonstrated before a national board of examiners, and by passing an extensive written examination

A Short Conclusion

As we've tried to show throughout this book, karate is a complex and multifaceted activity. There is history, tradition, and philosophy to learn about, principles to understand and apply, techniques to master, and a lifetime of challenges to confront and overcome. What ever your attraction to karate—curiosity, an abstract interest, or whether you are a student or an instructor—we hope that you have found something useful in this book.

Study well! Train hard! Have fun!

The Least You Need to Know

➤ Competition costs money.

➤ You'll find it more fun to go to competitions with a group.

➤ You're going to be nervous the first 100 or more times that you compete.

➤ Karate officials are required to be well trained.

Associations and Federations

In the United States, you'll find hundreds of karate associations and federations, along with hundreds more independent clubs and instructors who do not belong to any larger group.

It would be impossible for us to list the many different organizations accurately, so we have decided to list the largest nonprofit, multistyle organizations in the United States and internationally. We offer no endorsement of any of these organizations, but if you contact all of them, we think that you are bound to find something to suit you in your area.

U.S. National Multistyle Karate Organizations

Amateur Athletic Union (AAU) National Headquarters
Attention: AAU Karate Program
The Walt Disney World Resort
P.O. Box 10,000
Lake Buena Vista, FL 32830-1000
USA
Phone: 407-934-7200
Fax: 407-934-7242
Web site: www.aaukarate.org

USA National Karate-do Federation (USANKF)
P.O. Box 77083
Seattle, WA 98177-7083
USA
Phone: 206-440-8386
Fax: 206-367-7557
Web site: www.usankf.org

International Multistyle Karate Organizations

International Traditional Karate Federation (ITKF)
1930 Wilshire Blvd., Suite 1208
Los Angeles, CA 90057
USA
Phone: 213-483-8262
Fax: 213-483-4060
Web site: www.itkf.org

World Karate Federation (WKF)
Secretariat
George Yerolympos
c/o Hellenic Amateur Karate Federation
149 Vizantion St.
14235 Athens
Greece
Phone: 30-1-2717564
Web site: www.wkf.net

Publications and Resources

Following are some of the most popular and enduring publications of interest to aspiring karate students.

Publications

Black Belt magazine
(Also publishes *Karate Illustrated, MA Training,* and others)
Box 918
Santa Clarita, CA 91380-9018
805-257-4066

CFW Enterprises
(Publishes *Martial Arts Illustrated, Inside Kung Fu,* and others)
4201 West Vanowen Place
Burbank, CA 91505
818-845-2656

Journal of Asian Martial Arts
821 West 24th St.
Erie, PA 16502
1-800-455-9517

Ryukyu B&P, Inc.
(Largest distributor of martial arts books and magazines)
P.O. Box 535
Olathe, KS 66203
913-384-3345

Resources

Academy of Karate Martial Arts Supplies
118 North Black Horse Pike
Bellmawr, NJ 08031
609-547-5445

Asian World of Martial Arts
11601 Caroline Road
Philadelphia, PA 19154
1-800-345-2962

Century Martial Arts Supply
1705 National Blvd.
Midwest City, OK 73110
1-800-626-2787

East Coast Martial Arts Supplies
1646 East Colonial Dr.
Orlando, FL 32803
407-896-2487

Kim Pacific Trading Company
4141 Business Center
Fremont, CA 94538
1-800-227-0500

KI International
10938 West Pico Blvd.
Los Angeles, CA 90064
310-475-4691

Kinji San Martial Arts
3010 Ave. M
Brooklyn, NY 11210
718-338-0529

The Kiyota Company
2326 North Charles St.
Baltimore, MD 21218
410-366-8275

Panther Video
1010 Calle Negocio
San Clemente, CA 92673
1-800-332-4442

Macho Products
10045 102nd Terrace
Sebastian, FL 32958
1-800-327-6812

The Martial Artist
9 Franklin Blvd.
Philadelphia, PA 19154
1-800-726-0438

Pacific Rim Products
3500 Thomas Road, Building G
Santa Clara, CA 95054
1-800-824-2433

Glossary

This glossary has been divided up into a few parts to help you become familiar with the terms. The first section is from Japanese to English, and defines terms or commands that you may hear during training and tournament competition. The second section is from English to Japanese, and gives the terms for parts of the body as well as different techniques within the art of Karate.

Japanese to English—Terms and Commands from the Dojo to Competition

Basic sparring *kihon kumite*

Bow *rei*

Budo (boo-doh) "Martial way."

Distance *ma-ai*

Do (doh) Literally means *way* or *path*. *Do* is the way for the ultimate perfection of human character.

Dojo (doh-joh) Training hall. Literally, "the place of the way."

Five-step sparring *gohon kumite*

Focus *kime*

Formal exercise *kata*

Free style sparring *jiyu-kumite*

Gi (gee) A karate uniform.

Hai (hah-ee) Used for affirmation, as in "yes" or "okay." It is also used to give commands, as in "Okay, let's go!" or "Okay, line up!"

Hajime (HAH-jee-meh) "Begin!" "Start!" "Go!"

Hayaku (hah-ya-koo) "Move with speed."

Kamaete (kah-MAH-eh-teh) A command to move into a stance, ready for action.

Karategi (kah-rah-teh-gee) A karate uniform.

Karuku (kah-roo-koo) A command to move lightly, but with correct motion.

Kata (kah-tah) Form or formal exercise. There are two major classifications of kata in training: 1) **Godo-kata:** Group form in which a group of students perform the same kata in unison; 2) **Kojin-kata:** A form performed alone by an individual student.

Kata-no-keiko (kah-tah-noh-keh-ee-koh)   Practice in formal exercise.

Ki (kee)   "Vital force" or "mental energy."

Kiai (kee-ah-ee)   A sharp sound made at the moment of *kime* to aid in the tensing of body muscles and focusing of the mind for a more effective *kime*.

Kicking techniques   *keri-waza*

Kihon-no-keiko (KEE-hon-noh-keh-ee-koh)   Practice in basic techniques.

Kime (KEE-meh)   Focus. The pinpoint concentration of mind and body to achieve maximum effectiveness.

Kiotsuke (kee-oht-soo-kay)   "Come to attention."

Kogeki (koh-geh-kee)   To attack.

Kohai (KOH-hah-ee)   A junior member of the dojo.

Kumite-no-keiko (koo-mee-teh-noh-keh-ee-koh)   Practice in sparring.

Maai (mah-ah-ee)   Distancing. The correct distance between two opponents.

Mae ni (mah-eh-nee)   "Move forward."

Makiwara (mah-kee-wah-rah)   A punching board that is padded and struck forcefully to develop focusing of body strength.

Mawatte (mah-waht-teh)   "Turn around."

"Mind like the moon"   *tsuki-no-kokoro*

"Mind like water"   *mizu-no-kokoro*

Modotte (MOH-doht-te)   "Return to the original position."

Mokuso (moh-ku-SOH)   Quiet contemplation. The purpose of *mokuso* is to achieve mental and physical tranquility.

Mukai atte (moo-kah-ee-aht-teh)   "Face each other."

Naotte (nah-oht-teh)   "At ease" or "Relax."

Narande (NAH-rahn-deh)   "Line up."

Obi (OH-bee)   Belt.

One-step sparring   *kihon-ippon kumite*

Opening   *suki*

Osu (ohss)   Traditional karate greeting. A contraction of **Osae shinobu**, which means to press, or to keep patience.

Otagai-ni-rei (oh-tah-GAH-ee-nee-REH-ee)   "Bow to each other."

Punching techniques   *tsuki-waza*

Rei (REH-ee)   Bow. Other terms used with rei are: 1) **Shomen ni rei:** Bow to the front; 2) **Sensei ni rei:** Bow to the teacher; 3) **Otagai ni rei:** Bow to each other.

Ryu (ree-yoo)   School or "style."

Seiretsu (SEH-ee-reht-soo) "Line up in an orderly fashion."

Seiza (SEH-ee-zah) The Japanese formal method of sitting on the floor with the knees bent and the legs under the body.

Semi-free sparring *jiyu-ippon-kumite*

Sempai (SEHM-pah-ee) A senior person in a school or organization.

Sensei (sehn-seh-ee) Teacher. The term may be applied to anyone who guides or instructs another, such as a doctor or lawyer. Literally, *sensei* means "one who has gone before."

Shomen (SHO-mehn) Front. In the dojo, the *shomen* is the front wall where a photograph of the founder of the school is placed.

Sparring *kumite*

Stamping techniques *fumikomi-waza*

Striking techniques *uchi-waza*

Tatte (TAHT-teh) "Stand up."

Techniques *waza*

Three-step sparring *sanbon kumite*

Throwing techniques *nage-waza*

Tsuyoku (t'soo-yoh-koo) "Execute strong, fast techniques."

Undo (oo'n-doh) Exercises or calisthenics.

Ushiro ni (OO-shee-roh-nee) "Move backward."

Yame (yah-meh) "Stop."

Yasume (yah-soo-meh) "Relax."

Yoi (YOH-ee) "Be ready."

Yowaku (YOH-wah-koo) "Move lightly."

Yukkuri (yoo-koo-ree) "Move more slowly."

Zanshin "Remaining mind."

English to Japanese—Terms for Techniques

Blocking (Uke)

Blocking techniques *uke-waza*

Circular block *mawashi uke*

Downward block *gedan barai*

Forearm block *ude-uke*

Inside forearm block *uchi-uke*

Knife-hand block *shuto-uke*

Outside forearm block   *soto-uke*

Rising block   *age-uke*

Sweeping block   *nagashi-uke*

Hands, Feet, and Fists

Back fist   *uraken*

Ball of foot   *koshi*

Bottom fist   *tettsui*

Elbow   *empi*

Foot edge   *sokuto*

Forearm   *ude*

Fore-fist   *seiken*

Heel   *kakato*

Instep   *haisoku*

Knee   *hittsui*

Knife hand   *shuto*

Middle-finger one-knuckle fist   *nakadate-ippon-ken*

One-knuckle fist   *ippon ken*

Palm heel   *teisho*

Ridge hand   *haito*

Sole of foot   *teisoku*

Spear hand   *yonhon-nukite*

Kicks (Keri)

Back kick   *ushiro-geri*

Back thrust kick   *ushiro-geri-kekomi*

Front kick   *mae-geri*

Front snap kick   *mae-geri-keage*

Front thrust kick   *mae-geri-kekomi*

Round-house kick   *mawashi-geri*

Side kick   *yoko-geri*

Side-snap kick   *yoko-geri-keage*

Side-thrust kick   *yoko-geri-kekomi*

Punches (Tsuki)

Close punch   *ura-zuki*

Fore-fist straight punch   *seiken-choku-zuki*

Lunge punch   *oi-zuki*

One-knuckle fist punch   *ippon-ken-zuki*

Reverse punch   *gyaku-zuki*

Round punch   *mawashi-zuki*

Short punch   *kizami-zuki*

Spear-hand thrust   *nukite-zuki*

Straight punch   *choku-zuki*

Stances (Dachi)

Attention stance   *musubi-dachi*

Back stance   *kokutsu-dachi*

Cat stance   *neko-ashi-dachi*

Front stance   *zenkutsu-dachi*

Half-front facing posture   *hanmi*

Horse stance   *kiba-dachi*

Hourglass stance   *sanchin-dachi*

Natural stance   *shizen taii*

Open-leg stance   *hachiji-dachi*

Ready position   *kamae*

Rooted stance   *fudo-dachi*

Square stance   *shiko-dachi*

Strikes (Uchi)

Back-fist strike   *uraken-uchi*

Elbow strike   *empi-uchi*

Hammer-fist strike   *tettsui-uchi*

Knife-hand strike   *shuto-uchi*

Ridge-hand strike   *haito-uchi*

Elements of Technique Evaluation

This appendix will help give you an idea of how different schools may evaluate your skill level.

Specific Examination Points

If you were being examined on the basic techniques presented in this book, specific examination points the examiner would look at might include these:

Front stance:

➤ Distance between the legs

➤ Direction of both knees

➤ Abdomen perpendicular to ground

➤ Weight distribution (60 percent front; 40 percent back)

Back stance:

➤ Weight distribution (30 percent front; 70 percent back)

➤ Front leg stretched and pushing down

➤ Back leg bent strongly, toes turned in, knee pushing out

➤ Hip tucked

Side stance:

➤ Even weight distribution (50 percent each leg)

➤ Knees strongly bent, pushing outward

➤ Toes turned in

➤ Hips pushing forward toward the knees

Punching:

➤ Accuracy to the target

➤ Punch goes in straight line for maximum speed

➤ Concentration of power at impact

Lunge punch:

- ➤ Hips forward over supporting leg when advancing
- ➤ Strong push with back leg
- ➤ Hips low and level throughout

Rising block:

- ➤ Elbow stays inside body line
- ➤ Proper distance from arm to forehead
- ➤ Elbow snaps over fully
- ➤ Wrist higher than the elbow

Forearm blocks:

- ➤ Angle of blocking arm
- ➤ Distance between blocking arm and body
- ➤ Height of the fist
- ➤ Posture (upper body) 45 degrees to the target

Knife-hand block:

- ➤ Timed rotation of torso with blocking action
- ➤ Withdrawing hand in front of abdomen
- ➤ Hip tucked

Front kick:

- ➤ Knee up high before and after kicking
- ➤ Tight ankle of support leg
- ➤ Degree of knee (up before kick starts)
- ➤ Good snap (out and back)
- ➤ Pendulum motion of torso

Side kick:

- ➤ Snap (pivot) in the knee joint
- ➤ Pendulum motion of torso in snap kick
- ➤ Full extension of hip in thrust kick
- ➤ Proper chamber and recovery
- ➤ Proper angle of foot at impact

Point Systems

If a point system were being used, the examiner might assign 10 points each to kihon, kata, and kumite as follows:

1. Kihon

   ➤ Lunge punch sequence, 3 points

   ➤ Rising block sequence, 1 point

   ➤ Forearm block sequence, 1 point

   ➤ Knife-hand block sequence, 1 point

   ➤ Front kick sequence, 1 point

   ➤ Side kick sequence, 1 point

   ➤ Spirit and eye projection, 2 points

2. Kata

   ➤ Correct sequence of movements, 4 points

   ➤ Application of strength (strong vs. mild), efficient contraction and expansion of the body, and proper speed, 2 points

   ➤ Attitude, 2 points

   ➤ Embusen (correct demonstration line), 0.5 points

   ➤ Spirit, kiai, and eye projection, 1.5 points

3. Kumite

   ➤ Fast, spirited attack on offense, 2 points

   ➤ Focus of attack on offense, 2 points

   ➤ Effective block, 2 points

   ➤ Accurate and effective counterattack, 2 points

   ➤ Smooth transition from block to counterattack, 2 points

Novice and Middle-Level Rank Examinations

Seventh Kyu Kihon

These are the different elements involved in the rank examination for the Seventh Kyu Kihon:

➤ Punching at different levels (face instead of stomach) or punching in combination with other techniques

➤ Performing techniques such as rising blocks and forearm blocks in combination with counter-punching

➤ Kicking at higher targets

➤ More difficult kicking techniques, such as the round-house kick

Seventh Kyu Kumite

These are the different elements involved in the rank examination for the Seventh Kyu Kumite:

➤ Performance of three-step or five-step sparring without prompts from the examiner

➤ Closer and more effective distancing in offense and defense

Sixth Kyu Kihon

These are the different elements involved in the rank examination for the Sixth Kyu Kihon:

➤ More complex punching combinations.

➤ More complex block-counter combinations that require you to change stances and techniques between them. An example is an outside block in front stance followed by a sideways elbow strike counterattack in side stance. Another example would be a knife-hand block in front stance, followed by a spear-hand thrust counterattack in front stance.

> ➤ Multilevel kicking, such as two front kicks, one aimed at the stomach and the other at the face.

> ➤ Multilevel attacking techniques while changing stances, such as a front kick to the stomach followed by a lunge punch to the face with the opposite side of the body.

Sixth Kyu Kumite

These are the different elements involved in the rank examination for the Sixth Kyu Kumite:

> ➤ Block and counterattack against single punching attacks to the face

> ➤ Block and counterattack against single punching attacks to the body

Fifth Kyu Kihon

These are the different elements involved in the rank examination for the Fifth Kyu Kihon:

> ➤ Multilevel kicking using more difficult techniques, such as a round-house kick

> ➤ More complex attacking techniques, such as a front kick, a round-house kick, and a reverse punch while moving forward

Fifth Kyu Kumite

These are the different elements involved in the rank examination for the Fifth Kyu Kumite:

> ➤ Block and counterattack against single kicking techniques, such as a front kick

> ➤ More complex body shifting

Fourth Kyu Kihon

These are the different elements involved in the rank examination for the Fourth Kyu Kihon:

> ➤ Combination techniques that include striking techniques, such as outside block in front stance followed by a side-elbow strike and a back-fist strike in side stance

> ➤ More complex attacking techniques, such as a front kick, side-thrust kick, and reverse punch while moving forward

Fourth Kyu Kumite:

These are the different elements involved in the rank examination for the Fourth Kyu Kumite:

➤ Block and counterattack against more difficult kicks, such as a side-thrust kick and a round-house kick

➤ More complex body shifting while moving into and away from the attacker

Self-Defense Safety Tips

Play It Smart

This appendix outlines the common self-defense safety tips that will make all the difference in staying safe, no matter what the situation is.

On the Street

Keep these tips in mind whenever you are on foot:

➤ If you know you will have to walk a long distance, wear long hair up. Long hair worn down can be grabbed easily and can interfere with running.

➤ If you are planning a walk, wear comfortable pants and good running shoes.

➤ Do not walk close to bushes or dense shrubbery. If you have any doubts, especially at night, walk down the middle of the street.

➤ Pay attention to your route home from school, work, friends' houses, and other places you might frequent. Take note of stores that stay open late, buildings with doormen, and police and fire stations. Also take note of and avoid bushes, alleys, and unlighted areas.

➤ If cars pull up slowly, cross the street and walk in the other direction.

➤ If you feel that someone is following you, do not hesitate to turn around and check. Try changing your pace or crossing the street. Again, if necessary, walk down the middle of the street, and use car mirrors and windows to check your surroundings.

➤ If you are sure that someone is following you, be aware of the distance between you and him, and keep a steady pace to maintain the distance. When you see a safe place or a lighted house, run all of a sudden, screaming all the way.

➤ If you are in trouble, never yell "Help!" or "Rape!" Always yell "Fire!" People who don't want to get involved almost always will respond if they think their house is on fire.

➤ If you run to a house and are still being pursued, bang on the door, ring the bell, and keep screaming "Your house is on fire!" If you don't get a response, smash a window if you can, and keep screaming. Windows can be repaired and replaced; your life cannot.

Special Tips for Joggers and Exercisers

If you're out for a little exercise, try to keep these special tips in mind:

➤ Try to walk or jog with a friend.

➤ Stay in populated areas.

➤ Don't follow the same route every day.

➤ Don't exercise to the point of exhaustion. Try to keep some energy in reserve for emergencies.

At Home

Although most people feel their safest when they are in their own home, it's still important to make sure that you've done everything that you can to really make your home safe.

➤ Install strong deadbolt locks on all doors. Most doors have spring latch locks that can be opened easily by sliding a credit card or a thin sheet of metal between the door and the frame. If you try it, you probably will find that you can pick your own door locks with a little practice.

➤ Be sure that all entrances are well lit.

➤ Never leave a key under your doormat, in the mailbox, or any other place where it might be found by the wrong person.

➤ Check with your local hardware store for window latches that can't be opened from the outside. It's also a good idea to put heavy objects such as flower-pots, decorative bottles, or rocks on all your windowsills. These will cause noise when someone tries to enter through the window. Small decorative bells attached to the window, top and bottom, are also a good idea.

➤ If you have sliding doors, install channel locks that act as a sliding door deadbolt. Of all the locks in your house, those on sliding doors are the least safe.

➤ Don't sleep with the windows wide open. Open them enough to let in air, but not enough so that a person can climb through them. A stick can be placed between the top of the bottom window and the top of the frame to prevent the window from being opened farther.

➤ Secure window air conditioning units and window fans so that they can't be removed and so that the windows can't be raised above them.

➤ Don't allow shrubbery to grow around your windows. Far from discouraging an intruder, shrubbery actually acts as an ideal concealment for him.

➤ If you are a female living alone, don't advertise the fact by using your first name or Mrs., Miss, or Ms. on your mailbox, credit cards, return address mail, magazine subscriptions, mail orders, or in the phone book. If it's necessary to display your name on your mailbox, display it in a way that indicates that more than one person lives in your home, like "The Smiths" or "The Johnson Family."

➤ If you live in a secure apartment building or condominium, be sure that your intercom system is in good working order and that you don't open the security door for anyone unless you have confirmed who is trying to get in. Check all stairwells, hallways, elevators, entrances, and fire exits to be sure that they are well lit and protected by the security system. Familiarize yourself with the people who live on your floor, and report any suspicious people you don't recognize. If you find deficiencies in the security system, bring them to the attention of other tenants, and discuss them with the landlord or owner. Demand that changes be made, and keep demanding until something is done.

➤ If you live in an apartment building or condominium with a laundry room, try to arrange a buddy system with a neighbor so that you never have to go into the laundry room alone.

➤ Install chain locks and peep-hole devices on your doors. If you are at home alone, never open the door unless you are sure who is there. Even then, be reluctant to open the door to people who have come by unexpectedly. Always ask for identification from meter readers, repairmen, and salesmen. If you have any doubts about their sincerity, have them wait outside while you call their company to confirm their credentials. If they are reputable, they won't mind waiting. Also be wary of people taking surveys.

➤ Don't invite trouble by putting a box for a new purchase by the curb with the trash—it will only advertise that you may have something in your house that someone else could want. Always cut the box into small pieces and place it inside the trash receptacle or in plastic bags.

➤ Keeping a dog as a pet is a good self-defense idea because they make a lot of noise when somebody tries to come into the house. If you don't have a dog, buy the largest dog bowl you can find, scuff it up a bit with a kitchen knife, fill it with water, and keep it outside in plain view. Putting a dog's name on the bowl is also a good idea. For self-defense purposes, "Butch," "Thor," and "Black Thunder" are good choices.

➤ Especially if you are female, never let a stranger know that you are alone. If you're at home alone and somebody unexpectedly knocks on the door, go close to the door and yell out in a loud, clear voice, "I'll get it, Bill!"

➤ If you are alone and are awakened in the night by what sounds like someone in your house, yell out in a loud, clear voice "Bill, there's someone in the house! Get the gun, and be sure it's loaded!"

➤ A separate telephone line or a cell phone in your bedroom are good ideas, in case an intruder gets into your house at night and removes the receiver from the phones in other parts of the house. With the bedroom telephone, you might be able to call for help.

➤ If you are at home and want to leave the door unlocked for some reason (your children playing outside, for example), attach a bell to the door so that you can hear it when the door is being opened. This will keep you from being taken by surprise.

➤ When you leave the house, leave some lights and a radio on to give the impression that the house is occupied. Preferably, the radio should be tuned to a talk station. Don't always leave the same lights and the same radio on every time you leave. Alternate rooms and radios with televisions. If you use an automatic timer to turn on lights, move it to a different light every few days.

➤ Never leave objects such as knives lying around, and never keep a loaded gun handy. If these things are handy for you, they will be just as handy for an intruder.

➤ Never make appointments over the phone with a stranger who calls and requests an appointment to demonstrate a product or sell insurance. Always take the phone number, check it against the phone directory listing, and call the company's supervisor to verify the person's credentials. If you can't find the number in the phone book, call the Better Business Bureau for a reference.

➤ Most police departments will come to your house and inspect it for safety against intruders. Check with your local police department about this free service.

In Your Car

You can be your most vulnerable in your car, so use these tips to help keep aware of your surroundings:

➤ Always have your key in your hand when you are going toward your car so that you will not have to fumble in your purse or pocket for it.

➤ Always check the back seat of the car before you get in. If you get in without checking and then remember, turn around and check immediately. If someone is there, get out and run!

➤ Always lock your car doors, both when parked and while you are driving.

➤ Keep a cell phone in your car so that help can always be at hand.

➤ Try to park in well-lighted areas at night, and avoid deserted areas. But don't park directly under bright overhead lights. Bright lights directly above tend to create shadows inside the car, which makes it more difficult to see in. Try to park near rather than directly under overhead lights.

➤ If you think that you are being followed by another car, change directions, make a U-turn, speed, and pull into a lighted area where other people are visible. Don't get out of your car, though. Stay inside until help comes.

➤ If you determine that you definitely are being followed, keep your hand on the horn, speed up, and do anything you can to attract attention. If you are in a deserted area, drive to the nearest lighted house and keep blowing the horn. If possible, drive to a police station or fire station, but don't get out of the car. Just keep blowing the horn until help comes to you.

➤ Never pick up hitchhikers under any circumstances.

➤ If you are stopped by an unmarked police car and approached by a policeman in civilian clothes, stay in your locked car with the window down no more than an inch, and request identification. If you are still uncertain, ask him to radio for another patrol car for backup.

➤ Avoid valet parking, if possible. If you must give your keys to a parking attendant, give only the keys needed to operate your vehicle. Never give your house keys or anything with your address on it.

➤ If a car runs into you and causes minor damage, do not get out of your car to check. Immediately try to note the license number of the other car, and stay in your car until the police arrive.

If Your Car Breaks Down

This is one of those situations when you have less of an ability to control your surroundings, so these tips are very important for keeping yourself safe:

➤ If you have a cellular phone, call for help.

➤ If you do not have a phone, raise the hood as a distress signal.

➤ Until help arrives, stay in your locked car.

➤ If strangers approach you to help, keep your windows rolled up and the doors locked, and ask them to call the police. Do not get out of the car.

Index

I

325

Essential Shotokan

Featuring:

Edmond Otis—6th Dan

In two formats: VHS-video or an exciting and easy-to-use interactive CD-ROM series.

Essential Shotokan is the instructive and dynamic series that clearly illustrates the relationship between karate's techniques, principles, and applications in a fresh and eye-opening way. Not theory for theory's sake, but what every karate-ka needs to make their kata, bunkai, kumite, and self-defense more natural and effective.

Essential Shotokan is surprising in its depth, quality, clarity, and detail and is unlike anything else on the market today.

Volume I—Principles and Applications is designed for use by beginning through advanced practitioners and for any instructor who wants access to a useful teaching and class planning tool.

By combining the interactive capabilities of cutting-edge CD-ROM technology, and a crystal clear digitally recorded three-camera perspective, *Volume I* ...

➤ Clearly demonstrates and explains how the essential principles of Shotokan Karate relate to the application of each and every basic karate technique.

➤ Teaches the relationship of timing and distance to the application of each and every basic technique.

➤ Shows the key points and common mistakes associated with each and every basic technique.

And most important ...

➤ Demonstrates numerous, separate, beginner, intermediate, and advanced level applications and training methods—for each and every basic technique.

The *Essential Shotokan* interactive CD-ROM series is unique. No martial arts library would be complete without it! To order a copy of Essential Shotokan Volume 1 or for more information visit:

www.essential-shotokan.com

E-mail: info@essential-shotokan.com

Phone: 706-769-4670

Recognition (A Novel), **by Stan Schmidt with Randall G. Hassell** $9.95

Promising young athlete, Jonathan Walker, is felled by serious injury and thrust into a strange environment fraught with conflict and loneliness. While painfully struggling to come to terms with his solitude, self-worth, emerging sexuality, and physical limitations, Jonathan unexpectedly falls under the guidance of a mysterious karate master from another land. By secretly observing this enigmatic man, Jonathan begins to see deeper into his own nature and the true nature of those around him.

Be sure to visit Randall G. Hassell's Web site:
www.damashi.com

YES, send me my copies of Randall's karate books:

Shotokan Karate: Its History and Evolution—Revised & Illustrated Edition	$15.95
Conversations with the Master: Masatoshi Nakayama	$12.95
Samurai Journey	$17.95
The Karate Spirit	$12.95
Zen, Pen, and Sword: The Karate Experience	$15.95
Karate Ideals	$12.95
Karate Training Guide Volume 1: Foundations of Training	$12.95
Karate Training Guide Volume 2: Kata—Heain, Tekki, Bassai Dai	$12.95
Recognition (A Novel), by Stan Schmidt with Randall G. Hassell	$9.95

Subtotal　　　　　　　　　　　　　　　　　　　　　　　　　　　　　_____

FREE SHIPPING! (U.S. addresses only)
ALL OTHERS, please add $5 shipping charge (under $40):　　　　　_____
Add an additional $5 if total is over $40:　　　　　　　　　　　　_____
Missouri residents add 7.225 percent sales tax:　　　　　　　　　_____

TOTAL　　　　　　　　　　　　　　　　　　　　　　　　　　　　　　_____

Payment must be made in U.S. funds. Prices and availability subject to change at any time without notice.

_____ Check or money order enclosed.
_____ Please charge my MasterCard, Visa, American Express, Discover card.

Acct #: _____

Exp. Date: _____

Signature: _____

Send this order form with your check, money order, or charge information to:

Damashi
800 First Capitol Drive, Suite 310
St. Charles, MO 63301
Phone: 1-800-563-6287
Fax: 636-896-9494

Please allow three to five weeks for delivery.

Ship to:
Name: _____
Address: _____
City: _____ State: _____ Zip: _____
Country: _____
Daytime telephone (required): _____
E-mail: _____